The American
Revolution in New Jersey

Rivergate Regionals

Rivergate Regionals is a collection of books published by Rutgers University Press focusing on New Jersey and the surrounding area. Since its founding in 1936, Rutgers University Press has been devoted to serving the people of New Jersey and this collection solidifies that tradition. The books in the Rivergate Regionals Collection explore history, politics, nature and the environment, recreation, sports, health and medicine, and the arts. By incorporating the collection within the larger Rutgers University Press editorial program, the Rivergate Regionals Collection enhances our commitment to publishing the best books about our great state and the surrounding region.

The American Revolution in New Jersey

Where the Battlefront Meets the Home Front

EDITED BY

JAMES J. GIGANTINO II

RUTGERS UNIVERSITY PRESS

NEW BRUNSWICK, NEW JERSEY, AND LONDON

LIBRARY OF CONGRESS CATALOGING-IN-PUBLICATION DATA

The American Revolution in New Jersey : where the battlefront meets the home front / edited by James J. Gigantino II.

pages cm. — (Rivergate regionals)

Includes bibliographical references and index.

ISBN 978–0–8135–7192–8 (hardcover : alk. paper) — ISBN 978–0–8135–7191–1 (pbk. : alk. paper) — ISBN 978–0–8135–7193–5 (e-book (web pdf)) — ISBN 978–0–8135–7273–4 (e-book (epub))

1. New Jersey—History—Revolution, 1775–1783.   2. United States—History—Revolution, 1775–1783.   I. Gigantino, James J., II, 1983– editor, author.

E263.N5A45   2014

974.9'03—dc23

2014027526

A British Cataloging-in-Publication record for this book is available from the British Library.

Visit our website: http://rutgerspress.rutgers.edu

Manufactured in the United States of America

For Diane

CONTENTS

ACKNOWLEDGMENTS

Like many edited projects, this one grew over time into its present form with help from many people along the way. It was originally conceived by the staff at the Museum of Early Trades and Crafts in Madison, New Jersey, to complement their exhibit on the American Revolution in New Jersey. Former museum curator Siobhan Fitzpatrick deserves many thanks for her initial efforts to organize the authors. Marlie Wasserman showed an active interest in bringing the book to Rutgers and helped to shape these collected essays as well as assisted a first-time editor in navigating some difficult waters. However, without financial support from the University of Arkansas, this book would not be in readers' hands today. Generous subventions from the Office of the Provost and the Department of History made publication possible. My special thanks to the provost, Sharon Gaber, and Kathryn Sloan, chair of the history department, for their support. Finally, as in all things in life, none of the authors in this collection would be where they are today without support from their families. From putting up with our fascination with what most would consider mundane materials to suffering our absences as we travel to archives around the world, their friendly smiles, kind words, and love on our return help make us better historians. For me, my sister has been with me every step of the way on my journey through life, providing advice, support, and love. I dedicate this volume to her.

The American
Revolution in New Jersey

Introduction

JAMES J. GIGANTINO II

Generations of scholars have echoed historian Leonard Lundin's 1940 argument that New Jersey was the "cockpit" of the American Revolution, a central site in the struggle over the fate of a continent. More recently, Mark Lender confirmed that assessment: New Jersey was a crossroads where opposing armies battled on an almost daily basis. However, to Lender, the cockpit description means more than just the most engagements recorded in any colony. To him, the "military experience of New Jersey became a microcosm of the wider war," and to understand the military interactions in New Jersey would be to "understand the military history of the revolution generally." The chapters in this volume continue to explore New Jersey's central role in the American Revolution by examining not just military affairs but also the intertwined relationship between the front lines of the Revolution and the home front. In the Garden State, those lines were frequently blurred: civilians lived with the war on a daily basis. The Revolution therefore had a dramatic effect on New Jerseyans' economic well-being, the relationships they formed with their neighbors, as well as their very lives and freedom. Those who lived in New Jersey from 1775 to 1783 truly believed they were caught up in the cockpit of the Revolution.[1]

In the past three decades, historians of the Revolutionary era have taken a more expansive view of the conflict, showing how the first half of the eighteenth century primed the colonies for the Revolution and how the Revolutionary experience affected succeeding generations of

Americans. Like the prevailing historiography, this volume examines New Jersey's revolutionary experience in a wider context, paying close attention to how the war changed, or frequently did not change, the state after the guns fell silent.

New Jersey is perhaps one of the best places to measure the relationship between the colonial population and the Revolution because the colony and its people participated in almost every major eighteenth-century social and political movement. On the eve of the Revolution, New Jerseyans had been influenced by ideas, events, and issues from around the globe that would affect the progress of the Revolution. Most of these connections came about because of the state's position between two major ports: Philadelphia and New York. Commerce flowed from New Jersey into these urban gateways and, as the historian Gary B. Nash has argued, helped enrich them and make them central players in the eighteenth-century Atlantic World.[2]

New Jersey, as an agricultural powerhouse, had intense economic relationships with Europe, Africa, and the Caribbean. From almost the very beginning, Jersey farmers had worked to develop an export-based economy. Wheat became the state's cash crop, and its export to Philadelphia and New York brought expanding connections with merchants and traders who crisscrossed the British Atlantic World. Smaller agricultural operations near the Hudson River and along the southern Delaware became key exporters of milk, cheese, and vegetables to these urban centers as well. New Jersey's exports to the Caribbean were even more telling of the state's Atlantic connection. Jersey foodstuffs, especially pork, regularly supplied the Caribbean sugar islands in exchange for sugar, coffee, slaves, and manufactured goods. In 1789, geographer Jedediah Morse even mentioned that "New Jersey hams are celebrated as being the best in the world" and a favorite in the West Indies.[3]

This strong economic connection with the Atlantic on both its northeastern and southwestern borders brought new goods, new people, and new ideas to the colony throughout the eighteenth century. New Jerseyans became fully immersed in what T. H. Breen calls "an empire of goods." As Breen argues, by mid-century, Americans were fully engaged in a consumer revolution that bonded the disparate and seemingly divergent colonial populations based on a common relationship with the booming

Atlantic economy. This consumer culture, however, spread indebtedness across New Jersey's culturally, ethnically, religiously, and economically diverse population, allowing the market and market forces to take on special meaning as the eighteenth century progressed. Against the backdrop of this debt-ridden economy, protests over the Stamp Act and the boycott movements of the 1770s helped form intercolonial bonds that united colonists with diverse backgrounds in what would eventually become the American Revolution.[4]

The constant interaction between New Jerseyans and the Atlantic also ensured that Enlightenment ideas about self-improvement and reason would penetrate colonial discourse and challenge New Jerseyans to question their notions of themselves and the world around them. Intellectuals on both sides of the Atlantic began to think critically about uniting disparate peoples under the banner of progress. Many in the colonies began to apply this enlightened thought not as an abstract concept but as a way to explain and deal with social inequities and perceived violations of newly delineated natural rights.[5] For example, the land riots that erupted across rural New Jersey in the 1730s and 1740s represented a failure of the royal government to sort out conflicting land claims from the colony's earliest days. Disaffected yeoman farmers rebelled against royal authority by applying John Locke's labor theory of property to argue that settlers who had improved vacant land deserved ownership of it. Likewise, they attempted to use natural law to create a new social contract, one that "threatened the foundations of monarchial authority" and certainly made New Jersey a hotbed of Enlightenment thought in the years before the Revolution actually began.[6]

New Jerseyans had begun to think deeply not only about natural law but also about the very foundations of what freedom meant in the colony. Beginning in the 1750s, Quakers in West Jersey joined with their brethren in Philadelphia to spread abolitionism. New Jersey Quaker leader John Woolman had come to the conclusion that slavery was inconsistent with Quaker theology and, along with Anthony Benezet, encouraged the Religious Society of Friends to outlaw the practice among its members. By the beginning of the American Revolution, abolitionism was a dominant ideology among Quakers. Both inside and outside Quaker meetings, observers took note that while Quakers had been advocating freedom for

Jersey blacks, white colonists were debating their own freedom from Great Britain. Many in the state began to see a symmetry between these two causes and fused them together, using ideology from the Enlightenment to argue for greater freedom for all Americans.[7]

On the eve of the American Revolution, New Jerseyans already had decades of experience with Atlantic connections, Enlightenment ideologies, and anti-authoritarian actions. The central role that New Jersey played in the economic and ideological debates over the beginning of the American Revolution was repeated in the actual fighting of the war. Although the first shots of the Revolution were fired at Lexington and Concord, New Jersey quickly became the focal point of the struggle for independence. After the fall of New York to the British in late 1776, American forces under General George Washington retreated across New Jersey and into Pennsylvania. General Sir William Howe recognized that the agricultural bounty just across the river from his stronghold in New York could keep his army supplied with firewood, food, and other provisions. For his part, Washington began discussions with Governor William Livingston about destroying supplies before the British invaded, quickly identifying that what happened in New Jersey could tip the balance of the war in either direction.[8]

After Howe's successful invasion of New Jersey, a large swath of the state came under British occupation in late 1776 and forced many of the state's citizens to decide whether to remain neutral, support the retreating Patriot forces, or swear allegiance to the king. As British troops marched into their hometowns, some joined Loyalist units to oppose the Patriot insurgency. The question of allegiance became even more important as New Jerseyans understood that their land and supplies were critical to both armies and could be seized at any time for military purposes with little or no compensation. Although this early occupation was largely removed by Washington's victories in January 1777 at Trenton and Princeton, the constant warfare shattered unity among state residents. By the Revolution's midpoint, more New Jerseyans chose to serve in the king's army than in Washington's. As Maya Jasanoff contends, questions of loyalty "cut right across the social, geographical, racial, and ethnic spectrum of early America," with each Loyalist exhibiting "a range of reasons, ideological and otherwise," for continuing to support the king. In what those on both sides described as a civil war, this early occupation of New Jersey, felt by some to be of the most savage kind, splintered New Jerseyans, forced neighbor against neighbor for seven years, and defined how they understood the conflict unfolding before them, both on the home front and on the front lines.[9]

Even though largely liberated by Patriot forces, New Jersey remained a constantly contested battleground where Loyalist and Patriot militias fought for supplies, land, and influence. British-occupied New York served as a base of operations for foraging parties throughout the war. The varying levels of combat—daily skirmishes were sometimes punctuated by major battles—and the different types of participants ensured that military affairs frequently affected the home lives of thousands of New Jerseyans. The real Revolutionary experience in New Jersey was the hard-fought daily struggle for survival. New Jersey had become "a ragged borderline between the two Americas, Loyalist and Patriot," where, especially in the eastern part of the state, "the violence was most brutal." In the end, this constant raiding helped solidify the choice of loyalty. By 1780, war-weary Patriot New Jerseyans turned up in droves to fight at Springfield to defeat the foe that had threatened their livelihoods since the initial invasion in 1776.[10]

Historical analysis of the contest for control of New Jersey allows for a fuller understanding of the personal impact of the American Revolution on the lives of colonists. This volume's focus on the connections between the actual fighting and the domestic front is therefore especially important. In nine essays that rely on extensive archival research and the newest historical approaches to the study of Revolutionary America, this volume's authors break new historiographical ground in showing the powerful and long-lasting impact of the Revolution on New Jersey's diverse population.[11]

The American Revolution in New Jersey is divided into two parts, the first of which explores the interconnections between the battlefront and the home front during the war years. The five essays in this section detail how ordinary New Jerseyans dealt with Patriot, Loyalist, British, Hessian, and French soldiers in their own backyards and vividly show how civilians frequently became wrapped up in the larger global conflict. In the first essay, William L. Kidder examines how the state's civilian population reacted to militia service during the war years. The frequency with which the militia needed to be called out and the distance its men needed to travel from their home counties to defend against slave insurrections, marauding bands of Loyalists, or a British onslaught wreaked havoc on agricultural production, especially in counties where a substitute labor force was in short supply.

Similar to Kidder's interest in how militia service altered everyday life for New Jerseyans, Gregory F. Walsh's research details how wartime shortages of food and supplies gave rise to an illegal trade network that smuggled essential items across enemy lines and into the homes of Essex County residents. Those on the margins of society—the average, the poor, and the otherwise unconnected—were drawn to the illegal trade out of necessity, because it provided economic stability amid intense disruption.

Likewise, Eleanor H. McConnell measures how the war affected the daily lives of New Jerseyans by opening up opportunities for economic growth while at the same time imposing limitations on the realization of that potential. In examining the changes in iron and salt production during the Revolution, McConnell shows how the war intensified longstanding problems of tenancy, squatters, slave labor, and absentee landlords and exacerbated persistent logistical problems of managing a business and bringing a product to market during wartime. The consistent demand for economic productivity in the midst of war made these interconnections especially important throughout the colonies.

Todd W. Braisted and Robert A. Selig explore the connection between the battlefront and the home front by examining the military history of the Revolution in New Jersey. Building upon Adrian Leiby's classic work, Braisted revisits the strategically important and hotly contested Hackensack River Valley to illustrate how loyalties were determined, how economic destruction spread, and how the civilian population dealt with military incursions.[12] He specifically examines the role of Loyalist refugee units, which, along with their British counterparts, waged a series of battles in and around Fort Lee, a strategically important outpost in Bergen County near British-occupied New York. Selig is interested in the experience of New Jerseyans with the French army. The most important American ally during the Revolution, France provided money, weapons, supplies, and, most important, men and ships to the cause against its rival great power. The presence of large numbers of French troops in the colonies less than a generation after Americans helped Britain to defeat them in the Seven Years' War brought back painful memories for many. But Selig concludes that New Jerseyans greeted the French kindly as allies and as the solution to one of the most damaging problems of the war: currency depreciation due to the constant printing of paper money. The hard specie currency with which the French paid for supplies and services erased any lingering ill will toward their former foes.[13]

The second part of this volume goes beyond the war years in four essays that ask larger questions about how the American Revolution made a tangible impact on American society. Michael S. Adelberg starts by raising perhaps the most important historiographical question for scholars of Revolutionary America: Was the Revolution revolutionary? Adelberg builds on the work of others who have studied this issue in New Jersey, most notably David J. Fowler and Maxine N. Lurie, by using deep archival research to determine how the war affected Revolutionary society economically.[14] Taking Monmouth County as a case study, Adelberg determines that there was a surprising level of economic stability throughout the war, even though Monmouth saw some of the most savage skirmishes. He confirms that residents found a way to survive the Revolution relatively intact, without much realignment of property or social status.

Bruce A. Bendler's essay and my own seek to expand on Giles R. Wright's work on the important issue of how the Revolution influenced the northern abolition movement. Bendler argues that the war became a "Quaker Revolution" of freedom, that Quakers throughout West Jersey freed their slaves in large numbers and dramatically affected the future of African American freedom in New Jersey. For Bendler, the Revolutionary era advanced Quaker antislavery efforts and eventually led to the demise of slavery in the Mid-Atlantic states. My essay uses this Quaker antislavery activity as a starting point to examine the effectiveness of Quaker and Enlightenment rhetoric in convincing the non-Quaker population to support abolition. I argue that pro-slavery forces in New Jersey successfully opposed any move to make the American Revolution a beacon of hope for enslaved New Jerseyans by playing on fears of race war. Instead, Jersey slaves took it upon themselves to strike out for freedom and joined the

British army to achieve it. It would take until 1804 even to begin gradual abolition in the state and until 1865 to complete it.[15]

Finally, Donald Sherblom uses the Vought family and their Loyalist connections as a case study to delve into some of the most important and enduring questions of the American Revolution. Sherblom follows the Voughts from their initial pledge of allegiance to the king through the postwar dispossession that spread New Jersey's Loyalist population around the world. The status of Loyalists after the Revolution was constantly debated, and New Jerseyans struggled to make their state whole again after many of their neighbors had, in their eyes, betrayed them.

In the end, *The American Revolution in New Jersey* brings new voices to the historical debate about the importance of the Revolution and shows how in New Jersey there existed tangible and important connections between the front lines and the home front. These connections tell us much about how average Americans experienced the Revolution and allow us to provide a more complete picture of the impact and importance of the American Revolution.

NOTES

1. Leonard Lundin, *Cockpit of the Revolution: The War for Independence in New Jersey* (Princeton, NJ: Princeton University Press, 1940); Mark Lender, "The 'Cockpit' Reconsidered: Revolutionary New Jersey as a Military Theater," in *New Jersey in the American Revolution*, ed. Barbara J. Mitnick (New Brunswick, NJ: Rutgers University Press, 2005), 45–46.

2. Gary B. Nash, *Urban Crucible: The Northern Seaports and the Origins of the American Revolution* (Cambridge, MA: Harvard University Press, 1986), esp. 99–146.

3. Peter O. Wacker and Paul G. E. Clemens, *Land Use in Early New Jersey: A Historical Geography* (Newark: New Jersey Historical Society, 1995), 139–145, 175–188, quotation at 185.

4. T. H. Breen, *The Marketplace of Revolution: How Consumer Politics Shaped American Independence* (New York: Oxford University Press, 2004), xiii–xvii; David J. Fowler, "These Were Troublesome Times Indeed: Social and Economic Conditions in Revolutionary New Jersey," in Mitnick, ed., *New Jersey in the American Revolution*, 17–20.

5. John Fea, *The Way of Improvement Leads Home: Philip Vickers Fithian and the Rural Enlightenment in Early America* (Philadelphia: University of Pennsylvania Press, 2008), esp. 1–7.

6. Brendan McConville, *These Daring Disturbers of the Public Peace: The Struggle for Property and Power in Early New Jersey* (Ithaca: Cornell University Press, 1999), esp. 167–174.

7. Thomas P. Slaughter, *The Beautiful Soul of John Woolman, Apostle of Abolition* (New York: Hill and Wang, 2008), 132–136; Maurice Jackson, *Let This Voice Be Heard: Anthony Benezet, Father of Atlantic Abolitionism* (Philadelphia: University of Pennsylvania Press, 2009), 35–37; Jean R. Soderlund, *Quakers and Slaves: A Divided Spirit* (Princeton, NJ: Princeton University Press, 1985), 8–14, 169–172.

8. Robert Middlekauff, *The Glorious Cause: The American Revolution, 1763–1789* (New York: Oxford University Press, 2005), 360–369; Adrian Leiby, *The Revolutionary War in the Hackensack Valley: The Jersey Dutch and the Neutral Ground, 1775–1783* (New Brunswick, NJ: Rutgers University Press, 1962), 55–57; Lender, "The 'Cockpit' Reconsidered," 45–46; Fowler, "These Were Troublesome Times Indeed," 24.

9. Middlekauff, *Glorious Cause*, 360–369; Maya Jasanoff, *Liberty's Exiles: American Loyalists in the Revolutionary World* (New York: Vintage, 2011), 8–9; Fowler, "These Were Troublesome Times Indeed," 23; Thomas Fleming, "Crossroads of the Revolution" in Mitnick, ed., *New Jersey in the American Revolution*, 7.

10. Simon Schama, *Rough Crossings: Britain, the Slaves, and the American Revolution* (New York: HarperCollins, 2006), 113–114; Lender, "The 'Cockpit' Reconsidered," 45–46.

11. Lender, "The 'Cockpit' Reconsidered," 45–46.

12. Leiby, *Revolutionary War in the Hackensack Valley*.

13. Fowler, "These Were Troublesome Times Indeed," 25–26.

14. Ibid., and Maxine N. Lurie, "New Jersey: Radical or Conservative in the Crisis Summer of 1776?" in Mitnick, ed., *New Jersey in the American Revolution*, 15–44.

15. Giles R. Wright, *Afro-Americans in New Jersey: A Short History* (Trenton: New Jersey Historical Commission, 1988), esp. 22–30; Giles R. Wright, "Moving Toward Breaking the Chains: Black New Jerseyans and the American Revolution," in Mitnick, ed., *New Jersey in the American Revolution*, 113–137.

PART ONE

A Revolutionary Experience

1

A Disproportionate
Burden on the Willing

WILLIAM L. KIDDER

The militia system in effect during the American Revolution ensured that the battlefront met the home front of virtually every New Jersey family that did not actively oppose the Patriot cause. The dramatic impact on daily life was most notably seen in the experiences of families of the militiamen of the First Hunterdon County Regiment, who lived in what is today part of Mercer County in the city of Trenton, north of the Assunpink Creek, and the adjoining townships of Ewing, Lawrence, and Hopewell. These militiamen were expected to keep the economy going strong by farming, producing goods as craftsmen, and engaging in other economic activity while at the same time turning out for militia duty so frequently that they began to feel like full-time soldiers. Not surprisingly, they could perform neither task very well and were roundly criticized for their failures.

Each of the English colonies, from their earliest days of settlement, set up militia systems for local defense based on the ancient concept that all free residents of a community had a moral obligation to defend it from invaders. However, the variety of cultures and geographical situations throughout the thirteen colonies produced variations in militia preparedness. In the absence of significant outside threats to local communities during New Jersey's colonial period, the militia laws were not taken seriously by the residents and not strictly enforced by the legislature. On the eve of the Revolution, New Jersey would have been hard pressed to assemble a militia army such as the one that confronted the British in Massachusetts in the spring and summer of 1775.[1]

Like Massachusetts, though, New Jersey had experience forming extralegal militias to seek redress of grievances, especially the property rights of local farmers. When conflicting claims over land ownership in the 1730s and 1740s led to violent confrontations between proprietors and farmers, the colonial government found itself unable to call out the established militia because it was composed of the same farmers who were protesting and "rioting." Later, during the early protest phase of the Revolutionary era, ad hoc militia companies similar to those of the 1740s formed again to stand up for colonists' rights. Between the hostilities at Lexington and Concord in April 1775 and the adoption of the Declaration of Independence in July 1776, Patriot committees in New Jersey gradually took over the functions of government, including control of the militia, from royal authority. Patriot leaders expected that standing together as militiamen in protest against British government actions would bring about reconciliation and that militia duty would be a minimal obligation and not interfere with economic pursuits. The realities of the Revolution proved to be vastly different.[2]

Revolutionary New Jersey's first militia law was enacted by the Provincial Congress a year before independence was declared. Like early regulations passed in all the new states, this June 1775 law was a watered-down version of the colonial law and was the first in a series of statutes enacted throughout the war in an attempt to create a "well-regulated" militia. However, just as in the other states, the New Jersey militia law was never considered satisfactory by those responsible for the state's defense. After full-scale war broke out, the more professional and full-time Continental army was created to engage the British army. The thirteen state militias still existed, however, and military leaders continually debated how to use these men to assist and supplement the professionals most effectively. The evolving militia laws kept families in constant uncertainty as to how they could satisfy the requirements of the current law and also keep life and household together. Militia service was not voluntary, and men between the ages of sixteen and fifty who did not enlist in the Continental army or obtain an exemption due to physical or mental health, religious conviction, or some form of designated public service were automatically assigned to their local militia company. However, being on the militia rolls and actually turning out for active service when called were two different things. The laws established legal ways for men to avoid active service by paying fines or providing substitutes, and some men simply tried to ignore the laws because they were not strictly and uniformly enforced. Consequently, one of the major complaints about the militia was that not enough men turned out when needed. The reasons a man might choose to stay home varied from half-hearted support for the cause to the need to keep his farm or business from failing. All of the states saw their laws evolve in reaction to similar problems and outcomes.[3]

The adoption of the Declaration of Independence forced each family in the thirteen new states to reevaluate its support for the cause. Some men, including officers, who were actively serving in the militia to redress grievances could not abide fighting for independence. For example, Captain Robert Harrison of the First Hunterdon resigned his commission on July 8, 1776, and joined a Loyalist regiment. Families opposing independence had to decide whether to keep a low profile and support, as passively as they dared, the state government that now ruled them or to abandon their homes and seek refuge with the British army.[4]

The militia laws in all the new states, with local variations, required individual ownership of military equipment that was expensive and represented a sizeable chunk of most family budgets. In New Jersey, each man had to own a flintlock smooth-bore musket equivalent to those used by the professional armies of the time, along with a bayonet, powder, lead balls, flints, a cartridge box to hold ammunition, and a wire brush and pick to clean the firing mechanism. A few men owned a more expensive hunting rifle instead of a musket. Although slower to load, it was more accurate than a musket and was soon allowed as a substitute, along with its different set of accoutrements. Each man was also supposed to provide his own haversack and canteen, often homemade items. No uniform was mandated, and most men simply wore their civilian clothing, though some chose to use a fringed linen hunting shirt as an informal uniform when out on militia duty. Militiaman Elijah Moore recalled getting five bullet holes in his hunting shirt at the Battle of Monmouth. Keeping a militiaman outfitted with the required equipment was a monetary, time, and labor drain on families.[5]

Each man of a family required his own set of weapons and accoutrements, but in times of short supply it was not always possible for a militiaman to purchase everything, even if he had enough money. Failure to own a particular item could result in a fine each time a man turned out for drill or active duty, although captains could waive a fine when convinced that the individual had done his best to comply. As the war dragged on, wear and damage to firearms and accoutrements often required additional costs for repair or replacement, expenses again borne by the militiaman and his family. On many occasions men turned out with borrowed equipment or even without a firearm or other required item.

Passage of a law did not mean that it could be fully implemented. For example, when the British were preparing to leave Philadelphia in June 1778, General Philemon Dickinson commanded several militia regiments at Trenton, including the First Hunterdon. Because Trenton was considered a potential British target, Dickinson on June 9 ordered defensive earthwork redoubts constructed at the lower Trenton ferry under the direction of Colonel Joseph Phillips of the First Hunterdon. Regimental adjutants were told to "bring on, all their unarmed Men daily, to compleat the Work already begun at the lower Ferry." At first these workers supplemented soldiers who did have weapons, but on June 12 Dickinson directed that "the Fatigue party at the lower Ferry will only consist of the unarmed men, belonging to each Regiment, who are to be brought on daily, until the work is finished." These orders reveal that a considerable number of men were without arms and were available for construction work while the armed men performed guard duty and patrols. Fortunately, Trenton was not attacked, and the militiamen stationed there became part of the force that harassed the British army on its march east across New Jersey and participated in the Battle of Monmouth, actions for which they received high-level commendation.[6]

Militia companies were extensions of local family and community social structures. This close proximity made it difficult for officers in command of brothers, sons, nephews, cousins, in-laws, and neighbors to be disciplinarians and order family and friends into combat. Conflicts could arise at any time, because a captain could choose when to levy a fine on a militiaman for not attending drill, not turning out when called, not having a musket or other required equipment, or any other failure to abide by the militia law. He could excuse a man when he knew of extenuating circumstances, but these decisions could create tensions and hard feelings. Because all the officers and privates lived with each other in their civilian lives, it was difficult not to carry personal conflicts from one aspect of life into the other. Although the First Hunterdon seems to have been cohesive, the neighboring Third Hunterdon in Amwell Township experienced almost continual dissension among its officers, resulting in court-martial proceedings in the spring of 1781 in which the lieutenant colonel, a major, and several captains exchanged charges and counter-charges alleging various acts of fraud, neglect of duty, and undermining authority. Colonel Phillips and other officers of the First Hunterdon were assigned to the court that sorted things out and severely punished some of the parties.[7]

Militia duty hit the home front particularly hard as the war dragged on and the men were called out virtually every other month during the British occupation of New York City and vicinity from 1776 through 1783. The First Hunterdon companies spent the majority of their active duty time opposite Staten Island—clear across the state from their home communities on the Delaware River. This posting added a week or so of travel time to their absences from home and was an extra burden on their families. In addition to providing large contingents for outposts near enemy-held territory and joining the Continental army in major battles, militiamen were called on quite frequently to arrest Loyalists, guard prisoners, protect the legislature or the governor, gather intelligence, provide and drive supply wagons, and other sundry duties. Historian Don Higginbotham has pointed out that, if we consider the "all-encompassing role" the militias of all the states "were asked to play, then we can better understand their limitations and their failures."[8]

The requirements of militia duty increased the already heavy labor demands on families. Most militiamen were farmers accustomed to allocating workers among various jobs during the course of the agricultural year. How much a farmer could produce on whatever amount of land he owned was determined to a great extent by how much labor he could employ at critical times. Labor sources began with family members, including wives and children, and exchanges of labor with neighbors. This "free" labor could be supplemented, to the degree a man could afford, with hired labor, apprentices, and purchased indentured or enslaved servants. From his workforce, a farmer was faced with supplying men periodically for militia duty as just one of the many jobs needing to be done. New Jersey's entire militia was rarely called out at the same time, and companies were divided into groups of men, called classes, which could be summoned in alternate months to form composite companies with classes from several companies. As in other states, men from the same family usually were assigned to different classes so that the call-up of one class would not remove too many men from one family.[9]

What many military leaders considered to be a major flaw in the militia legislation of New Jersey and other states was a provision that allowed men to pay a fine or provide a substitute to avoid personal service when called out. Wealthier men could often afford to pay a fine during the critical months they needed to work at home, or even every month they were called. Some men could hire a substitute for some or all of the months they were called out, or they could routinely send a family member as a "free" substitute. For example, a son might serve one month for himself, the next for his father, the next for himself, and so on for some period of time. Militiaman Oliver Hunt was apprenticed to shoemaker Richard Hunt and served alternate months for himself and his master. For all practical purposes, Oliver Hunt was a full-time militiaman, while Richard Hunt was left to pursue his trade without interruption. For a farmer, finding someone to perform his militia duty was similar to finding additional labor for seasonal farm work he could not complete by himself.[10]

Militiamen held the full range of attitudes toward the war; while many were ardent Patriots, others were neutral or even opposed to the war and might passively obey the law to keep their land and not become refugees. Legally avoiding militia duty left a man open to criticism for staying out of harm's way while others served for him. Because of the impassioned feelings of many Patriots, a man who might be a true supporter of the cause but chose to focus more on his farm and avoid active militia service could find himself subject to community suspicion that he was a closet Loyalist, which in fact some men were. He also had to deal with personal guilt for sending someone else, sometimes a son or apprentice, into harm's way. Militiaman Jonathan Smith served every other month in the First Hunterdon as substitute for someone who had paid his captain, but only the captain knew who was serving for whom.[11]

As a result of the mixed feelings about the war and the loopholes in the militia law, the most frequent complaint about the militia was the poor turnout. General Washington himself commented frequently on the ineffectiveness of the militia in general and New Jersey's in particular. The oft-debated question of effectiveness is complex because the militia was asked to do so much more than just assist in major battles and skirmishes. Particularly in New Jersey, the battlefield effectiveness of the part-time militia compared with the full-time soldiers of the Continental Line was very uneven due to the militia structure, the intensity of the war in New Jersey, the variable commitment to the cause of individual militiamen, and the ways in which militia service impacted the home front. The mere fact that militiamen were part-time soldiers with full-time jobs in the civilian sector effectively limited their ability to fulfill the many and varied demands on the militia. In fairness to the militiamen, historians must look beyond purely combat duties and consider their success in meeting many other expectations while keeping the civilian economy going and providing food and material to the army from those enterprises.[12]

Had the militia been employed solely as a local defense force to repel enemy attacks on the immediate community, the men could have carried on their civilian occupations most of the time. But the reality in New Jersey was that some portion of each militia regiment like the First Hunterdon was almost always out on duty in areas within the state but not necessarily close to home. And even if the men of one family were not out with the militia in a given month, the families of relatives and neighbors might have men out on duty and need help. The constantly "harassed and exhausted" militiamen and their families became increasingly reluctant to answer militia call-ups. The failure to close the loopholes in the militia law created the unintended consequence described by Governor William Livingston as placing "a disproportionate burden on the willing."[13]

The families of First Hunterdon militiamen usually experienced the war through the frequent one-month absences of their men. But the war came right to their front doors and into their homes during the British occupation of New Jersey in December 1776. Between June and November 1776 a number of First Hunterdon men served with a state militia regiment that was raised to serve for five months to augment the Continental army resisting the British and Hessian soldiers invading New York. These men

were in the thick of the fighting from Brooklyn on Long Island in late
August through the Battle of White Plains in late October, and several were
killed or captured. The subsequent losses in November of Fort Washington
on Manhattan and Fort Lee across the Hudson in New Jersey initiated the
long Continental army retreat through New Jersey with the British forces
in pursuit. Those First Hunterdon militiamen who did not join the five-
month regiment served alternate month-long tours at posts opposite
Staten Island; the men on duty there in late November joined with the
main army in retreat along a road leading directly to their hometowns.
The enlistments of the five-month men ended on November 30, and they
were part of the large contingent of troops Washington unsuccessfully
implored to stay with the army. But the First Hunterdon men could not
escape the war by going home. They left the army for a week or so to travel
ahead of it and secure their families, then rejoined their local militia
companies to help fight the British around Trenton.[14]

In spite of a chaotic breakdown in the regimental structure, men of
the First Hunterdon found ways to participate with the army in the events
leading up to the Christmas crossing of the Delaware and the Battle of
Trenton.[15] For example, militiaman Ben Titus from Hopewell received his
verbal discharge at New Brunswick and later said, "I went home to my
grandfather's who lived on the road from N. York to Philada. I moved my
mother & younger brothers out of the way of the British as I thought, to
Stoney brook. The British were spreading over the country & as soon as
I got my clothes & myself cleaned I shouldered my knapsack and repaired
to Yardley's ferry in Buck's County Pennsylvania, in Capt. John Mott's
Company. . . . I volunteered till we could get the British checked."[16]

Patriots from the area fled in advance of the British. Gunsmith John
Fitch escaped from Trenton with as many of his tools as he could fit in
"only one small Wagon Load."[17] In Princeton, Margaret Sergeant, wife of
Continental Congress delegate Jonathan Dickinson Sergeant and daughter
of Trenton Presbyterian minister Elihu Spencer, was warned to leave town
by her neighbor Dr. Absalom Bainbridge in the middle of the night, just
ahead of the British arrival. Although related to several First Hunterdon
militiamen, Bainbridge was a Loyalist and stayed behind to welcome
General Howe and join with the British army, serving the Loyalist New
Jersey Volunteers as a surgeon. Margaret Sergeant and her family,

including her father and her siblings, all went to Johnson's Ferry on the Delaware opposite McConkey's Ferry on the Pennsylvania shore and managed to cross to Bucks County. Her younger sister recalled the event as resembling "the day of judgment: so many frightened people were assembled, with sick and wounded soldiers, all flying for their lives, and with hardly any means of crossing the river." Most of the boats had been taken to Trenton to transport the American army across to Pennsylvania ahead of the British.[18]

In an effort to end the war without additional bloodshed, General Howe in late November made a genuine offer of amnesty and protection to those who signed an oath of allegiance to the king. Each family had to make the difficult decision whether or not to accept this offer, knowing that the British forces had been victorious in their encounters with the disintegrating American army. Although as many as five thousand people accepted Howe's offer, the British forces did not recognize the protection papers and plundered the residents indiscriminately.[19]

Historian William Stryker summed up the damage inflicted on New Jerseyans during the 1776 retreat. In addition to the physical damage to farms, houses, crops, livestock, and public buildings, "society was thoroughly disorganized, quarrels were engendered, families were subject to every indignity or else were obliged to flee for their lives." Howe had moved his army slowly in pursuit of the Americans to avoid a pitched battle, but instead of preventing destruction of private property, he unintentionally increased it. His soldiers had more need, time, and opportunity to inflict damage on the civilian population than if they had been kept moving at a faster pace.[20]

When the British arrived in Princeton on the evening of December 7, they learned "that the first farm beyond Stony Brook belonged to a rebel." A foraging party brutally mistreated the father of First Hunterdon militiaman Enoch Armitage and the family's slave, broke glassware and pottery, smashed and burned furniture, and carried off items from the house. Chickens, pigs, and cattle were summarily butchered or herded away to help feed their army. Armitage's father, who was essentially blind, was left to wander in his woods by British soldiers who took him there demanding to know where he had buried family valuables. His daughters found him after the soldiers left.[21]

From Princeton, the British army marched through Maidenhead (Lawrence Township) toward Trenton. One house they burned along the way belonged to the widow of militia private Aaron Mershon, who had been killed at the Battle of Brooklyn in August. Widow Mershon and her two young boys lost much personal property as well in the fire.[22] The wife of militia Captain George Green, with four children, fled their farm in Maidenhead ahead of the British and took refuge across the river in Bucks County. Local tradition says that the Hessian soldiers who occupied the place used bureau drawers from the ransacked house as feed troughs for their horses.[23]

After December 8, central New Jersey was essentially under British occupation. Although many inhabitants had fled to Pennsylvania, some militiamen remained at or near home to protect their families and land. Many men had to decide whether it was better to see their life's work destroyed or sign Howe's loyalty oath and risk censure by their neighbors. They had seen firsthand the shrinking and disheveled American army, and some had served in it and experienced its defeats. Many must have believed the whole enterprise was over—even Washington expressed thoughts along those lines in his personal correspondence.[24]

Despite Howe's campaign to win back the loyalty of the rebels, British soldiers continued to plunder indiscriminately. After the American army crossed the Delaware to Pennsylvania on December 7, the British army was cantoned between Princeton and Trenton. At midnight on December 8 a large force marched through Pennington and on to Coryell's Ferry (Lambertville) to seize boats the British army could use to cross the river and follow Washington. (None were found because American militiamen had secured every boat within many miles of the ferry.) During this foray, British soldiers raided the homes of Samuel Stout and John Phillips, both of whom lived just south of Coryell's Ferry and had sons in the First Hunterdon militia. They destroyed Stout's "deeds, papers, furniture and effects, of every kind, except what they plundered. They took every horse away, left his house and farm in ruins, injuring him to the value of two thousand pounds, in less than three hours. Old Mr. Phillips, his neighbour, they pillaged in the same manner, and then cruelly beat him."[25]

James Hunt's family had no intention of signing a loyalty oath. When warned that a British patrol would be on their road on a given night, they refrained from lighting their home in the hope it was located far enough back from the road to avoid notice. The ruse failed, and Hunt heard soldiers outside the house order the door to be opened or they would break it down. Once inside, an officer informed Hunt that he was a prisoner and would be taken to General Cornwallis at Pennington, who would administer the loyalty oath. Hunt's daughters did not understand why their father was being taken away and followed after him, carrying on hysterically. Not wanting to rouse enough people to confront them, the officer released Hunt, telling him he was "too old to be good for anything and he could go home and take care of his babies."[26]

News reports on the British depredations around Maidenhead and Hopewell indicated that those areas had been "entirely broke up" and "no age nor sex have been spared." The newspapers claimed that homes had been "stripped of every article of furniture." and that soldiers "drove off" all the cattle and sheep in the area. By the end, "scarce a soldier" among the British forces did not have "a horse loaded with plunder." As a result, "Hundreds of families are reduced from comfort and affluence, to poverty and ruin, left at this inclement season, to wander through woods without house or cloathing." The somewhat exaggerated reports concluded with a calculated message to Patriots: "If those scenes of desolation, ruin and distress, do not rouse and animate every man of spirit, to revenge their much injured countrymen and countrywomen; all virtue, honour, and courage must have left this country, and we deserve all that we shall meet with."[27]

The British and Hessian soldiers made little distinction between Patriot and Loyalist families, but they did make special efforts to punish high-profile Patriots. Members of the Hart family of Hopewell were constant targets. John Hart, a signer of the Declaration of Independence, had to be constantly on the alert and often simply hid out. His cousin Ralph Hart was also a target because he could possibly lead the British to John. Ralph's wife, Penelope, became a local heroine by bringing food and water to Ralph and John while protecting their hiding place. The British were looking for her, too, so she dressed in man's clothing, avoided walking on public roads, and never stayed in the same house two consecutive nights.[28] The British also tried to find John Hart's neighbor, the active militiaman Captain Joab Houghton, who was known to have organized ambushes of British patrols. Local tradition claims that he once evaded capture by climbing up into the wide chimney of his fireplace and sitting "securely perched" on the lug pole while the British soldiers searched in vain.[29]

Loyalists also harassed the Patriots during the occupation. Three Loyalists from Amwell came to Pennington during the British occupation and took up residence "at & near John Hunts, about two miles up the Amwell Road, when they killed sd Hunts hogs desired for his own use & also geese Fowls & and destroyd & took up much of his furniture." One of the Loyalists, Cornelius Williamson, also rounded up several local people, including Jacob Stout of Hopewell, and forced them to go to Pennington to sign loyalty oaths and obtain protection papers. Another one of these Loyalists, Joseph Thatcher, was a former captain in the Third Hunterdon militia from Amwell and had recently served alongside First Hunterdon men stationed near Woodbridge.[30]

While twenty-four-year-old Nathaniel Cain was serving with his militia company, his property and the property of his father, Thomas Cain, were destroyed by the British. Nathaniel's wife fled ahead of the British with their child and did not return until after the Battle of Princeton.[31] However, two of Nathaniel's sisters, Sarah and Elizabeth, became victims of British atrocities at the home of a neighbor, Edmund Palmer, who had a son and two grandsons in the First Hunterdon militia.[32] Thirteen-year-old Abigail Palmer was at her grandfather Palmer's house with Elizabeth and Sarah Cain when some British soldiers arrived. Abigail and Elizabeth were physically abused, threatened with death, and raped repeatedly "for three days successively." On the evening of the third day, soldiers came to the house again and abused the girls before carrying them off to their camp; they were again raped before two soldiers were convinced to take them to a neighbor's house, where Thomas Cain retrieved them the next day.[33] In another incident at Edmund Palmer's, Mary Phillips, his daughter and the widowed mother of First Hunterdon militiaman Palmer Phillips, was staying with him when four British soldiers came to the house one morning. She ran to some nearby woods to hide but was caught by a soldier who "damned her, and told her she was going to the damned rebels" and "forced her to go to the barn, and then and there had carnal knowledge of her body." In another instance, Mary Campbell, wife of militiaman Daniel Campbell, testified that a number of British soldiers came to her father's house and, although her mother pleaded with them, three of them "successively had knowledge of [her] body . . . she being five months and upwards advanced in her pregnancy at that time."[34]

For the men of the First Hunterdon, the war had become very personal, and revenge had become a motivating factor. In the two weeks leading up to the Battle of Trenton on December 26, 1776, militiamen of the First Hunterdon made a number of forays across the Delaware River both to harass the British and Hessian soldiers and to check on their homes and the family members who had not escaped to Pennsylvania. When Washington made his famous crossing of the Delaware at McConkey's Ferry and marched his army to Trenton, militiamen from the First Hunterdon were recruited to serve as guides on the stormy night march.[35] The writer of a letter in the December 28 edition of the *Pennsylvania Evening Post* declared that British behavior "has so exasperated the people of the country, that they are flying to arms, and forming themselves into parties to waylay them and cut them off wherever they can meet with them." The writer hoped that the British and Hessians would "soon find their situation very disagreeable in New-Jersey."[36]

Even after the British departed Hunterdon County and the militia resumed its month-long tours in other parts of the state, the war continued to affect daily life. When a man went off with the militia, his family never knew whether he would return or be able to take up his regular work again. Militia duty was inherently dangerous, and even noncombat injuries could devastate a family. On September 2, 1776, Sergeant John Dougherty of Captain William Tucker's company from Trenton was posted opposite Staten Island at the New Blazing Star Ferry and accidentally discharged his musket, sending the ball through his right hand. Dougherty was a tailor, and the wound rendered him unable to work at his trade. At the time there was no system to assist wounded militiamen; all his captain could do was write to the state legislature on his behalf.[37]

In January 1779, militiaman Nathaniel Cain, who had served a number of one-month tours and whose family had been brutalized during the British occupation in 1776, went out on duty under Captain John Hunt to Elizabethtown. One day when routinely leaving the house where his company was quartered, another soldier accidentally discharged his musket; the bullet struck a doorsill and ricocheted, entering Nathaniel's foot at the heel. He was able to return home by riding a horse provided by a neighbor who was fortuitously visiting his brother in Cain's company at the time, but he was crippled for life.[38]

The impact of militia duty on the home front was always present, even between tours of active service. An occasion as domestic as a wedding could be complicated and shaped by militia service. Edward Hart of Hopewell was called out in October 1777 and served until December 1. During October he was given a six-day furlough to get married. His wife recalled he was home for only two days before and three days after the wedding. There is no evidence that wives accompanied their husbands as camp followers when the men went out on militia duty, as sometimes happened with the regular army, but Nancy Hart claimed she visited Edward when he was stationed close to home at Trenton for three months in the spring of 1778, just before the Battle of Monmouth.[39]

Active and willing service in the Patriot militia should have prevented unpleasant encounters with other Patriot militiamen. But because they usually wore civilian clothing, militiamen were frequently suspect in areas where they were not known. They were often given written passes to use when returning home from active duty across the state, but otherwise had no real identification papers. Even a commonplace act such as courting could be problematic under these conditions. Trenton tavern keeper and militiaman Henry Drake was married to a woman from Monmouth County who had a friend he thought would be a good match for his friend Absalom Hart. He invited Absalom to visit him in Monmouth while he and his wife were visiting her relatives. Monmouth County had a large number of Loyalists, and the local Patriot militiamen were always on guard for Loyalist sympathizers. Absalom was intercepted by some local militiamen who thought him a possible Loyalist because he did not have a pass from a Patriot authority; his excuse that he had "come a courting" did not convince them. Fortunately, Henry Drake was known in the county and was able to convince the skeptical militiamen that Absalom was a "good Whig" and served enthusiastically in the militia.[40]

By 1780 the war had been raging for almost four years in New Jersey, and the people were suffering. On March 13, 1780, the legislature drafted a message to the Continental Congress, noting that from the time the British took control of New York City and Staten Island, "a very considerable

Proportion of the Labour and Time of the Inhabitants of New-Jersey has been employed in Militia Service, and in transporting the Supplies of the Army." Moreover, "for the last two Years, almost the whole Surplus of the Produce and Manufactures of the State, beyond a bare Subsistence for the Inhabitants, has been necessarily purchased or taken for the Use of the United States."[41] Men were constantly torn between meeting their militia obligations and keeping their families fed and safe. It is ironic that when Washington became very frustrated with the poor turnout of militiamen because many paid a fine instead, he complained that he needed men, not money. However, earlier in the war he had offered extra pay to militiamen to compensate them for turning out during harvest season. Still, the men did not turn out in large numbers because, just like Washington, they needed their labor more than they needed money. Throughout the war, labor was in short supply for both the army and the civilian economy, with the result that everyone suffered on the home front when trying to meet the conflicting demands. Those who continued to meet their full militia obligation at the sacrifice of their civilian economic pursuits exemplified those who suffered the disproportionate burden of the willing.[42]

It is said that all history is local, and this is especially true when trying to understand the experiences of militiamen in New Jersey and the other states. Thirteen different militia systems existed in thirteen different settings. This meant that, among the states and even within each state, there was great variety in the number and types of encounters between militia units and the British army, Native Americans, or Loyalist forces. In spite of some notable battlefield successes, militiamen never received as much recognition for their sacrifices as Continentals did. When militiamen were finally given the chance to apply for small federal government pensions in 1832, fourteen years later than Continentals, they had to prove a minimum of six months of active service in order to qualify. The varieties of militia laws and realities in the various states, combined with the scant official records of individual militia service, meant militiamen often had difficulty "proving" their specific tours of active service. John Fidler of the First Hunterdon was initially rejected for a pension because he claimed three consecutive months of active service. The pension official ruled that his statement of service could not be accurate because New Jersey militia law only required him to serve every other month.

The official's mistake was to look at the written law rather than the reality. In fact, Fidler had been one of the men willing to take on a disproportionate burden by sometimes serving as a substitute in addition to completing his own required tours. Intervention at a high level eventually gained recognition of his service and approval of his pension.[43]

The men of the First Hunterdon served in a state that required militiamen to endure higher levels of activity than did other states, which taxed their ability to carry on any semblance of a normal life. They lived in a part of the state that had low levels of Loyalist activity but experienced some heavy engagements with the British. In other states and other areas of New Jersey, militiamen were more involved with protecting themselves and their neighbors from Loyalist or Native American attacks and making counterattacks. The specific ways the home front was affected by the battlefront in the other twelve states, and in other parts of New Jersey, were variations on the common themes seen for the First Hunterdon. Detailed research on other states' and regiments' experiences needs to continue so we can develop more than a very general understanding of the experiences of the militiamen who supplemented the Continental army in various local ways throughout the war.

NOTES

1. For the colonial-era militia laws, see Bernard Bush, *Laws of the Royal Colony of New Jersey*, New Jersey Archives, 3rd ser., 4 vols. (Trenton: New Jersey State Library, 1977–1986).

2. For more on the land disputes and extralegal militias, see Brendan McConville, *These Daring Disturbers of the Public Peace: The Struggle for Property and Power in Early New Jersey* (1999; Philadelphia: University of Pennsylvania Press, 2003).

3. For the June 3, 1775, initial militia law, see *Minutes of the Provincial Congress and the Council of Safety of the State of New Jersey* (Trenton: Naar, Day & Naar, 1879), 179–181. See also *Pennsylvania Packet* (Philadelphia), July 3, 1775, 2, for a summary of the militia law. The many additions and modifications to the basic militia law can be traced in the *Minutes of the Provincial Congress and the Council of Safety of the State of New Jersey* and the annual *Votes and Proceedings of the General Assembly of the State of New-Jersey* (Trenton: Isaac Collins, 1777–1784). For a discussion of the nature of the militia laws in the new states, see Don Higginbotham, "The American Militia: A Traditional Institution with Revolutionary Responsibilities," in *Reconsiderations on the Revolutionary War: Selected Essays*, ed. Don Higginbotham (Westport, CT: Greenwood Press, 1978), 83–103. Two excellent studies of the specific militia issues in other states are Richard Buel Jr.,

Dear Liberty: Connecticut's Mobilization for the Revolutionary War (Middletown, CT: Wesleyan University Press, 1980), and Steven Rosswurm, *Arms, Country, and Class: The Philadelphia Militia and the "Lower Sort" during the American Revolution, 1775–1783* (New Brunswick, NJ: Rutgers University Press, 1987).

4. *Minutes of the Provincial Congress and the Council of Safety of the State of New Jersey*, 496. For more on Harrison's career with the Loyalist forces and his settlement in New Brunswick, Canada, after the war, see Trenton Historical Society, *A History of Trenton, 1679–1929*, 2 vols. (Princeton, NJ: Princeton University Press, 1929), 1:145; William S. Stryker, *"The New Jersey Volunteers" (Loyalists) in the Revolutionary War* (Trenton: Printed for private distribution, 1887), 49; and E. Alfred Jones, The *Loyalists of New Jersey: Their Memorials, Petitions, Claims, etc. from English Records* (Boston: Gregg Press, 1972), 88.

5. The many additions and modifications to the basic militia law concerning required weapons and equipment can be traced in the *Minutes of the Provincial Congress and the Council of Safety of the State of New Jersey* and *Votes and Proceedings of the General Assembly of the State of New Jersey*. Elijah Moore Pension File S2852 in National Archives and Records Administration (NARA) microfilm publication M804, *Revolutionary War Pension and Bounty-Land-Warrant Application Files* (Washington, DC: National Archives and Records Service, General Services Administration, 1974), hereafter cited as NARA M804.

6. Philemon Dickinson, *Order Book Major General Philemon Dickinson Commanding the New Jersey Militia 1777–1778* (Trenton: Public Record Office, 1929), 23–24, 32, 34, 39–42.

7. The letters to Governor Livingston from accusing officers are found in *The Papers of William Livingston* (Ann Arbor, MI: University Microfilms, 1986), reel 14, items 447, 524, 544, 577, 638, 937, 1068, and 1117. Other items relating to the court-martial are found in *The Papers of William Livingston*, ed. Carl E. Prince et al., 5 vols. (Trenton: New Jersey Historical Commission; New Brunswick, NJ: Rutgers University Press, 1979–1988), 4:144–145, 193–194. Newspaper articles about the trial were printed in the *New Jersey Gazette* (Burlington), February 21, 1781, 4, and May 16, 1781, 3.

8. For examples of comments on travel time, see: Gershom Herin Pension File S22299 and widow of William R. Green Pension File W7560 in NARA M804. For details on the extensive requirements of the militia, see Larry Kidder, *A People Harassed and Exhausted: The Story of a New Jersey Militia Regiment in the American Revolution* (CreateSpace Independent Publishing Platform, 2013). Higginbotham, "American Militia."

9. Comments on the class system are frequent in pension application files. See, for example, David Golden Pension File W7553, Andrew Reeder Pension File W4059, and Joshua Furman Pension File W543 in NARA M804. For another example of a classing system, see Buel, *Dear Liberty*, 95–96.

10. Oliver Hunt Pension File S2638 in NARA 804.

11. Jonathan Smith Pension File S31380 in NARA M804.

12. For a good discussion of the debate on the effectiveness of the militia in general, see Higginbotham, "American Militia." Because the militia was "expected to perform virtually every military function imaginable," he concludes that "the overall impression of the militia should be one of admiration, not derision" (95).

13. William Livingston to the Assembly, August 3, 1777, *Papers of William Livingston*, 2:51–54.

14. George Washington to Provincial Congress, June 10, 1776, George Washington Papers at the Library of Congress, 1741–1799. *Minutes of the Provincial Congress and the Council of Safety of the State of New Jersey*, 548–551.

15. Kidder, *A People Harassed and Exhausted*, chap. 11.

16. Benjamin Titus Pension File W6287 in NARA M804.

17. Thompson Westcott, *The Life of John Fitch, the Inventor of the Steam-boat* (Philadelphia: J. B. Lippincott, 1857), 60–61; Thomas Boyd, *Poor John Fitch, Inventor of the Steamboat* (New York: Putnam, 1935), 50–51.

18. Samuel Miller, *The Life of Samuel Miller, D.D., LL.D., Second Professor in the Theological Seminary of the Presbyterian Church, at Princeton, New Jersey* (Philadelphia: Claxton, Remsen and Haffelfinger, 1869), 147–148.

19. David Hackett Fischer, *Washington's Crossing* (Oxford: Oxford University Press, 2004), 173, 175.

20. William S. Stryker, *The Battles of Trenton and Princeton* (Boston: Houghton, Mifflin, 1898), 22.

21. Alice Blackwell Lewis, *Hopewell Valley Heritage* (Hopewell, NJ: Hopewell Museum, 1973), 32–33, 36. John VanKirk Pension File S841 in NARA M804.

22. Apparent draft, undated and unsigned, of a petition from Aaron Mershon's son to the US Senate and House of Representatives, in Mershon Family Archives, Lawrence Township Historical Society Archives, Lawrence Branch of the Mercer County Library, Lawrence Township, New Jersey. He states that the family never received any compensation from the US government for these British depredations, but does not say whether a claim was made to the state during the Revolution; those records have not survived.

23. William Kelly Prentice, "Cherry Grove," *Princeton Herald*, June 28, 1946, 5.

24. For example, see George Washington to Lund Washington, December 10–17, 1776, *The Papers of George Washington, Revolutionary War Series*, vol. 7, *21 October 1776–5 January 1777*, ed. Philander D. Chase (Charlottesville: University Press of Virginia, 1997), 289–292.

25. *Massachusetts Spy* (Boston), January 2, 1777, 3; *Connecticut Currant* (Hartford), December 30, 1776, 3. Also in Peter Force, *American Archives*, 5th ser., 3 vols. (Washington, DC: M. St. Clair Clarke and P. Force, 1848–1853), 3:1188. *Archibald Robertson, Lieutenant-General Royal Engineers, His Diaries and Sketches in America, 1762–1780*, ed. Harry Miller Lydenberg (New York: New York Public Library, 1930), 115.

26. Ralph Ege, *Pioneers of Old Hopewell: With Sketches of Her Revolutionary Heroes* (Hopewell: Race & Savidge, 1908), 97–98.

27. *Massachusetts Spy* (Boston), January 2, 1777, 3; *Connecticut Currant* (Hartford), December 30, 1776, 3.Also in Force, *American Archives*, 3:1188.

28. Lewis, *Hopewell Valley Heritage*, 39.

29. Ibid., 14; Ege, *Pioneers of Old Hopewell*, 21. Ege refers to him as "Col. Houghton" although he was a captain at the time and later became lieutenant colonel of the First Hunterdon and then in the state troops. The lug pole, as well as the wooden box that held his tricorn hat, are in the Hopewell Museum as mementos of Hopewell's history in the Revolution.

30. *Papers of William Livingston*, microfilm edition, reel 4, folio 614. There were at least three John Hunts in Hopewell connected with the First Hunterdon. John Hunt senior and junior both appear in a muster for the company of Captain Henry Phillips, and there was also a Captain John Hunt.

31. Nathaniel Cain Pension file W843 in NARA M804.

32. Abstract of Edmund Palmer's will, June 28, 1780, in *Documents Relating to the Colonial, Revolutionary, and Post-Revolutionary History of the State of New Jersey*, 1st ser., vol. 35, *Calendar of Wills, Administrations, Etc.*, ed. Elmer T. Hutchinson (Trenton: MacCrellish & Quigley Co., 1939), 297. Palmer died in 1784.

33. The rape affidavits are in *Papers of the Continental Congress, 1774–1789* [microform] (Washington, DC: National Archives and Records Service, General Services Administration, 1971).

34. Ibid.

35. Fischer, *Washington's Crossing*, 192–205, 225n515.

36. *Pennsylvania Evening Post* (Philadelphia), December 28, 1776, 613.

37. Manuscript #676 in New Jersey Department of Defense, Adjutant General's Office (Revolutionary War), Numbered Manuscripts [microform], New Jersey State Archives.

38. Nathaniel Cain Pension File W843 in NARA M804.

39. Edward Hart Pension File W7628 in NARA M804.

40. Absalom Hart Pension File W425 in NARA M804.

41. *Votes and Proceedings of the General Assembly of the State of New-Jersey*, Fourth Assembly, 153.

42. George Washington to Governor William Livingston from Morristown, January 24, 1777, *The Writings of George Washington from the Original Manuscript Sources, 1745–1799*, ed. John C. Fitzpatrick, 39 vols. (Washington, DC: Government Printing Office, 1931–1944), 7:56–57.

43. John Fidler Pension File S2552 in NARA M804.

2

"Most Boundless Avarice"

Illegal Trade in Revolutionary Essex

GREGORY F. WALSH

More than a thousand men from Essex County, New Jersey, rendered some form of military service in the Revolutionary War, but few served the war effort as readily or in as many different capacities as Baker Hendricks of Elizabethtown. In 1777, Hendricks worked as a spy on Staten Island and successfully gathered information concerning the island's inhabitants and defenses for George Washington. In addition, Hendricks served in the Essex militia, where he was elected captain of his regiment, and he was later wounded in June 1780 while fighting to repel a large-scale British invasion of Essex County at the Battle of Connecticut Farms. His injuries, however, did not prevent him from continuing to serve, and in May 1781 he was once again wounded, this time on Staten Island while retaliating against a recent Loyalist raid that stole fifty cattle from Elizabethtown residents. Finally, Hendricks was also a privateer who attacked British vessels around New York City and often returned from his voyages with provisions, weapons, and prisoners captured from the enemy.[1]

Baker Hendricks's lengthy and diverse military career reflected the sacrifice that Whig authors believed was necessary to secure independence. Despite his career as a successful spy, militia officer, and privateer, Hendricks's legacy as a brave Patriot twice wounded by enemy forces was forever tarnished by his willingness to conduct illegal trade with those same foes. Continental spies on Staten Island often sold goods to their enemies as a means to gain trust and maintain their cover, but Hendricks "carried to the Enemy greater Quantities of Provisions than necessary to disguise [his] design in going to the Island," according to Governor William Livingston.[2] His smuggling operation in 1777 stirred a "popular clamour" against Hendricks and his colleagues, but he managed to avoid prosecution through the intervention of George Washington, who probably requested his release from state custody.[3] Hendricks later exploited his privateer license as an opportunity to smuggle goods to and from enemy lines, and Livingston revoked his commission by 1782.[4] Hendricks's frequent smuggling activities ruined his reputation among many of his neighbors long after the war's conclusion. In 1848, one surviving member of the Revolutionary generation compiled a "List of Tories in Elizabethtown" to help a local minister who was writing a book on Elizabethtown's Revolutionary hero James Caldwell. Baker Hendricks was included on this list, along with notorious Loyalists who fled behind enemy lines and guided British raiding parties into Essex communities.[5]

Hendricks was merely one of countless Americans who traded illegally with British forces during the War for Independence. The problem was ubiquitous throughout the fledgling republic. While the Continental army suffered at Valley Forge during the winter of 1778, Pennsylvania farmers sold their produce to the British occupation force at Philadelphia. Residents of southwestern Connecticut had an ongoing trade with the British garrison at New York City because it was profitable and effectively reduced the frequency of British raids into their communities.[6] After the British military shifted its attention to the southern states in 1778, numerous southerners were eager to sell their goods to the invading soldiers. Illegal trade was so widespread by 1781 that George Washington complained, "men of all descriptions are now indiscriminately engaging in it," including those who "two or three years ago, would have shuddered at the idea of such connexions."[7]

Americans had a long history of trading with their enemies throughout Britain's eighteenth-century wars for empire, but political and military leaders such as George Washington and William Livingston expected their countrymen to cease this practice during the Revolutionary War. According to Whig leaders, the War for Independence was more than a contest for control of North America; it was a struggle between the forces of tyranny and the defenders of liberty. Washington and Livingston believed there was no sacrifice too costly in such a noble contest, and they repeatedly called on Americans to offer no aid to their enemies and behave in a more virtuous manner than they had during the French and Indian War, when illegal commerce reached unprecedented levels.[8] They consistently demanded stronger measures to eliminate illegal trade in New Jersey and throughout America. According to them and other Whig leaders, few crimes were as despicable or as treasonous as conducting trade with a hostile invading force while simultaneously denying those goods to the soldiers charged with America's defense.

Essex residents shared Washington and Livingston's dream of American independence, but they clearly did not adopt their leaders' attitude toward commerce with British forces or embrace Whig arguments concerning the nature of the war. Many Essex residents not only ignored repeated demands by political and military leaders to cease all trade with the enemy but also extended leniency and forgiveness to those guilty of this crime. Few of the convicted smugglers in Essex County suffered the significant or lasting damage to their reputations that Baker Hendricks eventually did. Rather than waste away in prison or face social and legal pressure to emigrate behind British lines, known smugglers remained politically and socially active members of their communities for the remainder of the war, despite the public's knowledge of their guilt. The flourishing trade between the inhabitants of Essex and their wartime enemies demonstrates the ideological gulf that often separated America's Whig leaders from the general public throughout the Revolution.

THE BRITISH ARMY played a prominent role in the day-to-day lives of the inhabitants of Essex County throughout the Revolution because British soldiers and their Loyalist allies resided in nearby New York City and on Staten Island for almost the entire duration of the war. Between 1776 and 1783, Essex's inhabitants endured several full-scale military invasions, frequent incursions by British or Loyalist raiding parties, and the persistent fear that these attacks could occur at any time. The close proximity of British forces, however, also allowed these wartime adversaries to engage in mutually beneficial commerce. Despite their irreconcilable political differences, many Essex residents saw the British as a convenient means to satisfy their material wants and needs. Inhabitants of northern Essex communities like Aquackanonk or Newark could easily trade with British

merchants or their envoys in nearby Bergen County. Likewise, residents of
Elizabethtown who lived near the coastline could cross the narrow channel to Staten Island, conduct trade, and return in only a few hours without
being seen because their knowledge of local geography helped them evade
the American military units monitoring the coast.[9] Continental army
and militia regiments were regularly stationed in Essex throughout
the war, but they lacked the manpower necessary to patrol the region's
coastline effectively. Soldiers repeatedly failed to detect enemy raiding
parties that numbered between one dozen and several hundred soldiers;
a single man or woman familiar with the region would have even less difficulty traveling unnoticed between enemy lines.

The ongoing commerce between the revolutionary population and
British soldiers—the London Trade, as it was often called—provided a
means for Essex residents to acquire highly sought-after European goods
such as tea, which had not been readily available in the region since the
boycotts of the early 1770s. The Hessian mercenaries employed by the
British throughout the Revolution marveled at Americans' unquenchable
thirst for tea. Philipp Waldeck, a Hessian chaplain stationed on Staten
Island following the British evacuation of New Jersey, observed in 1778, "it
is impossible in traveling through North America to find a single house,
from that of the fanciest gentleman to that of the oyster digger, where
people do not drink a cup of tea at midday. The men could sooner get their
wives to give up their finery than to do without tea." Americans' love of
tea was so great that Waldeck believed, "if a law were passed making tea-
drinking illegal, I do not doubt for a moment that the entire population
would take up arms and begin a rebellion such as now exists."[10] Tea drinking was not illegal in America during the Revolution, but loyal Americans
were expected to procure their tea from sources other than British suppli-
ers. This proved difficult at times. The British blockade of America's coasts
remained porous throughout the war, but traditional supply lines were
nonetheless disrupted throughout the nation. Items that colonists had
normally enjoyed, such as Dutch tea, became more difficult to secure, and
many Essex residents could not resist the allure of the tea available behind
British lines. In the summer of 1777, for example, Elizabethtown resident
Benjamin Hetfield was arrested for transporting rum, tea, and sugar from
Staten Island into Essex. In December 1780, Newark resident Jonathan

Wade captured Jasper Tenbrook as he entered Essex carrying an array of British commodities, including several pounds of tea.[11] Likewise, in June 1781, Abner Price was apprehended as he returned from British-occupied territory carrying tea, lemons, sugar, and various other items.[12] Tea had been a politicized good since Parliament's Tea Act of 1773, and ardent Whigs regarded Americans' boycott of British tea as a sign of patriotism. Demand for tea within Essex, however, remained so strong that many residents were willing to purchase it from their enemies when conventional supply lines failed.

Such behavior seemed inexplicable to Governor Livingston, an Essex resident himself. He had seen these communities successfully boycott British goods to achieve their political objectives in the past, and the local population had demonstrated its ability not only to make sacrifices during these boycotts but also to hold accountable community members who failed to do so. Moreover, by the summer of 1777, Livingston expected all Essex residents wholeheartedly to support his government and the laws it passed in its effort to secure independence. The governor had been steadfast in his efforts to remove any lingering Loyalist influence throughout the state. All New Jersey citizens were required to disavow their allegiance to the British crown and swear an oath to the new state government by August 1777; those who did not forfeited their political and property rights within the state. Officials seized and auctioned off Loyalists' personal property and real estate between 1777 and 1780 to raise money for the war effort, bringing financial ruin to those who refused to denounce British authority and dissolving all economic ties these Loyalists had in their former communities.[13] Livingston's government was so thorough in its quest to remove Loyalists from Essex that it ordered militiamen to apprehend the wives and children of two dozen departed Loyalists and escort them to enemy lines.[14] In the wake of such measures, Livingston fully expected all Essex residents to be loyal citizens of the new government and to demonstrate their allegiance by doing nothing that would bring aid or comfort to their enemies.

Livingston's shock over the ongoing tea trade within Essex was compounded by inhabitants' willingness to journey to British lines to acquire the fabrics they had grown accustomed to wearing. Despite the abundance of natural resources available throughout the colonies, domestic manufacture of goods such as ceramics and cloth remained extremely limited throughout the eighteenth century. Most colonists, regardless of where they lived, had migrated to America because they were attracted to its plentiful and inexpensive land; they therefore focused nearly all their energy on cultivating that land rather than pursuing other economic opportunities. Furthermore, eighteenth-century Americans felt little need to produce homespun cloth because it could never match the color, texture, price, and quality of the fabrics sold by British merchants.[15] Americans' rampant consumption of British fashions in the colonial era made fabrics a politicized good during the Revolution. Whig leaders like Livingston regarded homespun garments as a reflection of patriotism, and he encouraged citizens to maintain sheep for wool production rather than as a source of food.[16] His encouragement of domestic industry and appeals to patriotism, however, could not quench the Essex population's desire for European fashion, and fabrics remained one of the most popular items within the London Trade. For example, in June 1781, Anna Bruen of Newark wished to make a coat for one of her sons. Rather than produce or purchase homespun cloth, she convinced Continental army spy Jonas Crane to secure a higher-quality British fabric for her the next time he went behind enemy lines.[17] Bruen was interested in cloth for only one particular item, but other Essex residents smuggled enough fabric and accessories from enemy territory to create an entire wardrobe. In April 1780, Newark resident Gilbert Smith was apprehended carrying an enormous assortment of goods from British lines—more than thirty yards of French silk, twenty-one yards of linens, several bags of cotton, and dozens of buttons— all of which sold for $8,000 when auctioned by state officials.[18] When Revolutionary authorities apprehended Jasper Tenbrook returning from enemy lines in 1780, they seized, in addition to tea, multiple pairs of shoes, buckles, ribbons, gloves, and lace that he planned to sell.[19]

In exchange for these popular British commodities, Essex residents provided enemy soldiers and Loyalist refugees the valuable military supplies they needed to wage war and restore Parliament's authority. When British forces first arrived on Staten Island in late June 1776, its inhabitants welcomed General William Howe's army and readily sold British soldiers whatever they required. As the war progressed, however, Staten Island residents could not meet the material needs of the British garrison, and

the economic regulations imposed by British officers on the local population failed to produce adequate provisions for the soldiers. In particular,
eighteenth-century armies required large numbers of horses and oxen to
haul heavy carts loaded with artillery and other provisions. As a result,
draft animals were the most common targets of British raiding parties into
Essex throughout the war. Many Essex residents, however, willingly chose
to sell these vital resources to their enemies. On September 10, 1781, Caleb
Hatfield, a Newark farmer, traveled to Staten Island and sold one of his
horses before being apprehended upon his return.[20] One year later, Elihu
Woodruff of Elizabethtown was captured while bringing one ox to Staten
Island.[21] Some residents were willing to sell entire teams of animals. In
1781, Abraham Van Riper tried to bring three oxen and two cattle to British
lines, but militia units apprehended him and seized his animals.[22]

British soldiers desired other military provisions that were in short
supply, such as wagons, flatboats, baggage, tar, pitch, and soap, but the
item they coveted most was food.[23] British soldiers in New York or on
Staten Island did not have land to grow food or graze animals for themselves, and France's entry into the war placed even greater strain upon
supply shipments bound for British soldiers in America. Hungry troops,
therefore, paid handsomely for any type of meat, and numerous Essex
residents were eager to sell it. In late 1777, Joshua Winans of Rahway and
four other Rahway residents were apprehended by Patriot forces while
transporting a large quantity of beef to Staten Island.[24] That same year,
James Furlough transported twenty-two fowl and four quarters of mutton to
New York City before he was arrested.[25] The demand for food supplies by
British forces in New York and Staten Island persisted throughout the
conflict and was not significantly affected by the decision of British leaders
to shift their military efforts to the American South. In 1780, Rahway resident Lewis Brant attempted to transport ten sheep and ten ducks to Staten
Island before he was detained by militia forces along the coast and his
goods were auctioned to the public.[26] Continental soldiers and militiamen
regularly apprehended Essex residents traveling to and from enemy lines,
but they knew that countless others successfully eluded capture. American
quartermasters and commissaries struggled to feed their troops during
the war, and soldiers stationed in New Jersey were frequently reduced to
foraging for food or, in extreme cases like the winter of 1780, eating dogs

or tree bark to survive.[27] Essex residents nonetheless denied them access to the food they needed by transporting large quantities of it to those working to restore British authority throughout America.

The political leaders of Essex County, such as Continental Congress delegate Abraham Clark and Governor William Livingston, were infuriated by their constituents' willingness to assist America's enemies, and they repeatedly called upon the state legislature, courts, and military officials to make examples of smugglers by imposing severe penalties. The earliest New Jersey law dealing with the London Trade labeled as guilty of treason anyone who supplied "any Kind of Provision of Warlike Stores" to the "adherents of the King of Great Britain." This 1776 law called for the death penalty for citizens captured on their way to enemy lines, and subsequent laws continued to define this activity as a capital offense.[28] Local courts, however, were extremely reluctant to impose the death penalty in these cases, and by December 1780 the state legislature changed the law and no longer deemed illegal trade to be a capital offense. Instead, legislators prescribed nonlethal penalties that were designed to ostracize smugglers by stripping them of the economic and political rights necessary to be an active citizen. Those convicted of illegal trade would forfeit their "Estate, both Real and Personal," and they also faced additional punishments, such as imprisonment, public humiliation by being "cropped, whipped, or pilloried," or forced relocation from their hometown to a region farther from enemy lines.[29] Such penalties would bring economic ruin and political alienation, but Livingston refused to support any legislation that did not include the death penalty. He complained as late as 1782, "if any crime in the world deserve death, next to that of murder, it must be that of supplying an enemy in time of war, with the means of facilitating their continuing such war against one's own country."[30]

Livingston's frustration only grew as Essex residents exploited military customs and state laws governing travel across enemy lines as a means to continue their illegal commerce. Because of the small distance separating New Jersey's coast from the British garrisons around New York City, both American and British leaders found Essex County a convenient location to send or receive British agents traveling under flags of truce. International customs governing war stipulated that such individuals were to be respected as political and military envoys and suffer no harassment by the local population or state officials while conducting their business. British officials, however, frequently issued flags of truce to known or suspected Loyalists, and Livingston was convinced that these "dirty Villains" received their flags for the sole purpose of acquiring supplies from Essex residents. He complained in 1778 that individuals traveling under flags of truce were "intimately acquainted with Elizabethtown"; they knew where American soldiers were likely to patrol and could easily conduct their illicit trade elsewhere.[31] More important, they were familiar with the local population and could identify which residents, merchants, and even militia officers would be most willing to sell them the military resources needed behind British lines. Livingston honored British flags of truce so as not to give British officials cause to apprehend Americans traveling under them, but they were a tremendous vexation to the governor. He lamented to Washington in 1778 that after working for three years to prevent "the practice of our people carrying provisions to [our enemies], we shall have the mortification of seeing them fetching it from us."[32]

Flags of truce were not the only tools exploited by Essex residents interested in conducting trade with America's enemies. Some New Jerseyans had pressing interests behind enemy lines, such as the need to secure legitimate business investments, collect inheritances, or visit dying family members who had sought refuge with the British. These individuals had justifiable cause to travel to New York City or Staten Island, but the New Jersey legislature's efforts to guarantee their right to travel behind enemy lines were quickly abused by London Traders seeking safe passage. In 1777, New Jersey lawmakers granted Governor Livingston the power to issue travel passports into enemy-held territory. Livingston regarded this authority, which he shared only with generals within the Continental army and the state militia, as a powerful weapon that could stem the flow of vital military resources from New Jersey into enemy hands.[33] He studiously examined all the passport requests he received. He estimated that only "one in twenty" was justified and considered the rest to be the work of "venomous Tories" seeking a "cloak" for their illicit activity.[34] Although Livingston was, in his own words, "very sparing" in granting passports, he believed that others who possessed this authority did not "always use it with prudence."[35] He accused military officers of contributing greatly to the London Trade and the "inexpressible Mischief" within Essex by unnecessarily and illegally delegating this task to junior officers who were "incapable of resisting the solicitations of those eloquent and pernicious vagrants." He was particularly angered by the large number of approvals by Captain Burnet of the Essex militia and accused him of "Prostitution of Passports."[36]

As the war progressed, the number of political and military officials authorized to grant passports increased drastically, giving smugglers more opportunities to obtain permission to travel legally behind enemy lines to conduct their illegal activity. In 1777, the power over passports was shared by Livingston and several generals, but the legislature expanded this power in the spring of 1778 to include all twenty-three members of the New Jersey Council of Safety.[37] After the state legislature disbanded the council in October 1778, the power to issue passports to New Jersey residents was extended to both political and military officials within the state and those outside it. On August 13, 1778, the Continental Congress granted itself the authority to issue passports, and by April 1779 Congress also extended that power to the chief executives of every state, as well as any commander of any military department within the Continental army.[38] By the war's end, the power to grant passports in New Jersey had become so diluted that any representative in either house of the state legislature, as well as any justice of the peace willing to vouch for someone's character, could legally issue a passport.[39] Livingston complained to Washington that smugglers whose petitions he had denied could secure passports nonetheless by approaching multiple officials until they found one willing to grant the request.[40] By 1779, Livingston had grown so concerned over the abuse of passports that he ordered militia officers stationed in Essex and other coastal communities not to trust passports granted by other military officers and instead to direct petitioners to him, "that I may examine them and judge for myself."[41] In his mind, New Jersey residents who swore allegiance to his government yet traded with the British were no different from the Loyalists who fought against his government, and the countless hours he spent monitoring travel passports seemed like time very well spent.[42]

William Livingston was a popular wartime leader, reelected by the legislature to serve as governor from 1776 until his death in 1790, but the majority of his constituents within Essex did not share his ideological interpretation of the London Trade. The governor thought it unnatural for citizens of warring nations to trade with each other; the only logical explanation for such activity was either a lack of republican virtues or a lingering sense of allegiance to Great Britain. He frequently expressed these beliefs in his correspondence. Smugglers, in his view, were driven by "boundless avarice," "vain curiosity" for fine European commodities, or underlying Loyalist beliefs.[43] An examination of economic documents from Essex County, however, reveals that most participants in the London Trade were likely motivated by necessity rather than greed, personal weakness, or pro-British sentiment. As table 2.1 demonstrates, the vast majority of known smugglers within Essex were among the poorest members of their communities. These men and women were largely dependent upon others for their survival or, at best, spent their lives working small farms or businesses that stood little chance of profit. For example, in April 1780, Cornelius Edison was apprehended as he smuggled several yards of checkered linen from British lines into his hometown of Aquackanonk.[44] Edison owned no taxable property, was not the head of his own household, and probably survived by living with his parents and working their land.[45] Similarly, Continental army veteran John Alling was also charged with smuggling goods to and from enemy territory. Alling owned twenty-five acres in Newark, which made him far more economically autonomous than Edison, but he could never truly profit from cultivating such a meager plot.[46] Only a few of Essex County's convicted smugglers came from the upper tiers of society, and it is not surprising that the impoverished members of these communities would be attracted to the economic opportunities presented by illegal commerce. They probably believed that they had given all they could in pursuit of American independence and shrugged at Whig arguments like Livingston's that linked patriotism with selflessness and sacrifice.

The London Trade undoubtedly appealed to the lower classes of Essex because it offered them a semblance of the economic stability that had been missing from the region and from America as a whole since 1776. Parliament's economic regulations of the 1760s were extremely unpopular throughout colonial America, but legislation such as the Currency Act of 1764 helped minimize inflation and maintained a stable currency by prohibiting colonial governments from issuing paper money to serve as

TABLE 2.1

Average Wealth of Essex Taxpayers Charged with Illegal Trade

Tax rates, 1779	% of Essex taxpayer population (total number of taxpayers)	% of taxpayers apprehended/ prosecuted (total number)	Average number of acres owned by the accused
0–£1	24.4 (434)	17.5 (10)	2.8 (7 of 10 owned zero acres)
£1.05–£2	21.5 (382)	26.3 (15)	12.9
£2.05–£3	11.6 (206)	5.2 (3)	29.0
£3.05–£4	10.1 (177)	14.0 (8)	43.1
£4.05–£5	7.2 (128)	10.5 (6)	77.3
£5.05–£7.5	12.8 (228)	14.0 (8)	106.0
£7.55–£10	4.7 (84)	1.7 (1)	0 (tavern owner)
£10.05–£12.5	2.9 (52)	7.0 (4)	146.0
£12.55+	4.3 (77)	3.5 (2)	581.0

Source: Tax Ratables, box 99, Essex County, Aquackanonk, Newark, and Elizabethtown Townships, March 1779, New Jersey State Archives, Trenton.

legal tender.[47] That stable currency disappeared under the tidal wave of paper money printed by the Second Continental Congress and the thirteen state governments as they attempted to meet the tremendous costs of war. After the first year of the conflict, the value of these new currencies depreciated to the point that their use for economic transactions proved impractical. The exchange rate between Continental bills and specie fell to 5:1 in December 1777 and plummeted to 50:1 by December 1779. Congress's effort to stabilize values by replacing old bills with a new paper currency in 1780 met little success, and state-issued currencies were essentially worthless by 1781.[48] The lack of a reliable form of currency brought economic chaos throughout the country. Residents of Massachusetts saw the price of beef increase from $0.04 per pound to $1.69 per pound between 1777 and 1780.[49] In October 1781, Continental soldiers could receive the nominally impressive bounty of $1,200 from slave owners eager for the return of slaves who had sought refuge with Cornwallis's army at Yorktown, but this amount was enough to buy only a single quart of rum.[50] Within Essex County, the cost of livestock rose between 400 and 500 percent between 1777 and 1779.[51] The American Revolution was fought under a cloud of hyperinflation and economic uncertainty, and both the impoverished and the affluent residents of Essex who participated in the London Trade regarded the highly sought-after European goods available behind enemy lines as a financial lifeline. Tea, fabrics, and other coveted items were valuable resources in an economy that increasingly relied upon barter.

The London Trade also offered Essex residents something that their economy had lacked for a long time: specie. Parliament's economic regulations helped maintain a stable currency throughout its empire, but its mercantile policies had steadily drained specie from the American colonies for decades, making it nearly impossible to find gold or silver within rural settlements. America's alliance with France provided valuable military resources to Washington's army and saved the national government from bankruptcy, but it did not inject much-needed specie into the American economy. Even though the French government loaned 28 million livres to the American government by 1781, much of that money never left Europe and was instead used to settle debts already contracted by Congress.[52] Americans hungered for hard currency, and the invading British army had both a considerable amount of specie at its disposal and the desire to use it. Captain John Bowater of the British army noted as early as 1776 that Americans were eager to sell "their things to the Soldiers at the most Reasonable Terms" because they liked "our Gold & Silver better than the Congress paper money."[53] Popular demand for specie only increased as inflation grew rampant, and more Essex residents saw illegal trade as the only available means to acquire a stable currency and a just price for their goods. For example, in January 1778, William Pace of Morristown publicly complained to Elizabethtown resident Amos Swan about the depreciated prices offered by local quartermasters and merchants. Pace informed Swan that he had recently tried to sell a large quantity of beef to quartermasters but had "been offered half a Dollar Continental Money per pound weight for the beef, and [I] could not take it for damn the money. I did not want it; if I cannot get a shilling per pound weight in hard money at [Rahway] I will carry it to Staten Island where I can get it."[54] Pace did not want to sell his beef to the British. He was willing to try several American venders in

Essex and considered the London Trade only as a last resort in his quest for fair compensation for his goods. Similarly, nineteen-year-old Morris Hetfield of Elizabethtown attributed his participation in the London Trade to his desire for specie rather than any pro-British sentiment. During a conversation with several neighbors concerning the local economy, Hetfield brazenly drew several British coins from his pocket, told his companions they were "got by the London Trade," and asked "who amongst you have So Much? I have carried Beef to the Enemy and Can Carry one or two Quarters when I please, and as often as I please."[55] As a veteran of the 1776 Battle of Long Island, Hetfield clearly was no supporter of Parliament's efforts to restore New Jersey's colonial government, but he was also one of the poorest residents of Elizabethtown; he owned just six acres and resided in another man's household. Smuggling offered him the best means to secure the hard currency and economic stability that was widely absent within his community.[56]

Contrary to the wishes of William Livingston and George Washington, Essex courts seemed to sympathize with individuals accused of trading with British forces and rarely enforced state laws to their fullest extent. Between 1776 and 1780, judges refused to impose capital punishment in these cases, and they seldom used their power to detain smugglers or remove them physically from their communities. Forty-one Essex residents were charged with illegal commerce during this period, and all but two were released on their own recognizance rather than sent to prison while awaiting trial.[57] If judges seriously questioned the loyalty of the accused or regarded this crime as a major offense, they would not have allowed the defendants to return to their homes and resume their lives. Similarly, judges showed leniency during the sentencing stage of these trials; only two of those convicted of trading with America's enemy were sentenced to prison for their crime.[58] The law prescribed a wide range of penalties for illegal trade; depending on the year, convicted smugglers faced capital punishment, imprisonment, or conscription into the navy. Essex judges, however, relied almost exclusively upon economic penalties. They issued fines ranging from £5 to £1,000 between 1777 and 1779 and always accounted for inflation to make sure that the penalty was economically significant.[59] Nonetheless, those convicted remained within their communities following their trials, pursued their economic interests, and enjoyed the comfort of their family and friends despite the public's knowledge of their guilt.

William Livingston occasionally received petitions from Essex residents asking for a more vigorous enforcement of state laws prohibiting trade with the enemy, but the political and social climate within the region demonstrates that most inhabitants shared the judges' opposition to harsh penalties for smugglers.[60] Throughout the Revolution, the Essex population was frequently willing to use violence and intimidation against individuals who were suspected of maintaining their allegiance to the king and Parliament, but these measures were never employed against known smugglers within their communities.[61] Rather, Essex residents responded to convicted smugglers with widespread indifference and allowed the guilty parties to return to their former lives without any fear of social reprisal. For example, local business owners continued to welcome London Traders such as Joseph Baldwin and Francis King into their stores. Baldwin and King were convicted of illegally traveling to enemy territory in 1779 and 1780, respectively, and Baldwin received a larger than average fine of £300 for his crime.[62] Following their trials, however, both men continued to frequent the same local blacksmith as many of their neighbors and did so without shame.[63] Similarly, Joshua Winans remained a welcomed customer at the Sign of the Unicorn Tavern in Elizabethtown despite the public's knowledge of his participation in the London Trade. Winans was convicted of transporting a large quantity of beef to Staten Island in 1777, but he still felt comfortable visiting the tavern even though it was a popular destination for Elizabethtown's most prominent Whigs, such as Colonel Elias Dayton of the Continental army.[64]

The Essex population was so tolerant of illegal commerce with nearby British forces that upstanding citizens with no record of dubious behavior throughout the conflict were willing to call upon convicted smugglers to serve as character witnesses on their behalf before state officials. In December 1780, the New Jersey legislature attempted to curb illegal commerce by requiring all merchants in counties that bordered enemy territory to secure a license from the Court of Quarter Sessions. Petitioners needed to present a minimum of fifteen signatures from "reputable and well-affected" freeholders of the same county who would vouch for their loyalty.[65] Because of their close proximity to British forces, all merchants within Essex were subject to the provisions of this law; but even though these shopkeepers could look to hundreds of respectable, law-abiding citizens to serve as character witnesses, many of their petitions bear the signatures of convicted smugglers. For example, Anthony Sayre was a twenty-six-year-old resident of Springfield with an exemplary record of military service on behalf of the Revolution when he petitioned for a shopkeeper's license in January 1781. Unlike many Essex residents, Sayre provided frequent service to the county militia and served as a private every year between 1776 and 1780. He risked his life in June 1778 to assist the Continental army as it secured a hard-fought draw against the British army at the Battle of Monmouth.[66] The thirty-seven signatures he collected on his license petition were more than twice the number needed and demonstrated his popularity within his hometown. In fact, by the time he approached fellow Springfield resident and convicted London Trader Joshua Winans, Sayre already had nineteen signatures. Yet he included Winans's testament to his reputation along with those of several respected officers of the Continental army and the Essex militia, such as Captain Joseph Badgely and Colonel Samuel Potter.[67]

In 1781, Jesse Baldwin of Newark also presented to the Essex Court of Quarter Sessions a petition signed by both reputable military figures and known smugglers. Baldwin had served as an artificer and lieutenant in the First Regiment of the New Jersey Continental Line between 1776 and 1779. Like Sayre, he fought against the British at Monmouth and was respected by prominent military figures within Essex. His shopkeeper's license petition was signed by Robert Nichols, a former minuteman and Essex County militia captain, and Captain Abraham Lyons, a five-year veteran and officer in the Essex militia, the New Jersey state troops, and the Continental army.[68] Jesse Baldwin, however, also asked Joseph Baldwin to sign his petition, even though Joseph was guilty of the same crime the new law concerning merchants' licenses was designed to prevent.

Baldwin and Sayre were not unique in their view of convicted smugglers as respectable political figures within their communities; seven of the forty-three individuals who submitted petitions for merchants' licenses to the Essex court acquired the signature of at least one known London Trader. Although William Livingston would have questioned the political character of individuals who voluntarily sold materials to the British army, the Essex County Court of Quarter Sessions found no irregularity with petitions like Baldwin's. On April 10, 1781, Justice of the Peace Robert Ogden issued Jesse Baldwin the shopkeeper license he desired.[69]

WHEN ARMED CONFLICT erupted between Massachusetts colonists and British soldiers in 1775, Americans overwhelmingly and enthusiastically took up arms to protest this latest and most egregious of Parliament's transgressions. America's leaders celebrated the people's willingness to sacrifice their time, money, and even their lives in defense of the liberty that they saw at the heart of this conflict; but the ideological fervor and *rage militaire* that swept through the colonies proved to be short-lived. Americans' desire to make the sacrifices necessary to defeat their enemies and achieve independence decreased significantly after 1776, as demonstrated by the widespread and persistent nature of the commerce that existed across American and British lines. Prominent leaders such as George Washington attributed this illegal and militarily detrimental conduct to rampant selfishness and disloyalty; it made him want to "curse [his] own Species for possessing so little virtue and patriotism."[70] The residents of Essex County, New Jersey, however, would have vehemently rejected any argument that associated wartime smuggling with a lack of patriotism or loyalty. For ordinary Americans like them, years of high wartime taxes, devastating inflation, widespread property damage, required military service, and loss of loved ones in combat were enough to transform the war from a noble and worthwhile adventure into a disheartening, malicious, and seemingly endless conflict. The people of Essex embraced the London Trade as a means of surviving the numerous problems that the Revolutionary War brought to their doorsteps; unlike their leaders, they regarded it as no more than an unfortunate necessity or a forgivable offense that did little to harm their communities, government, or dreams of independence. Governor Livingston spent his seven years as New Jersey's wartime governor in a fruitless crusade to end this commerce and reform the behavior of his constituents, but no act by his government or its military forces could stop the flourishing trade between military adversaries. Washington succinctly summarized Americans' steadfast determination to trade with their enemies in October 1782 when he informed Congress's secretary of war that "allotment of the Whole Continental Army . . . would not prevent the practice" in places like Essex.[71]

NOTES

1. "Hendricks, Baker," New Jersey Department of Defense, Adjutant General's Office (Revolutionary War), Service Abstracts [Cards], ca. 1776–1783, New Jersey State Archives, Trenton (hereafter cited as NJSA); and Phillip Papas, *That Ever Loyal Island: Staten Island and the American Revolution* (New York: New York University Press, 2007), 86–88.

2. William Livingston to George Washington, January 28, 1778, in *The Papers of William Livingston*, ed. Carl E. Prince et al., 5 vols. (Trenton: New Jersey Historical Commission; New Brunswick, NJ: Rutgers University Press, 1979–1988), 2:194–195.

3. Ibid.

4. Papas, *That Ever Loyal Island*, 87.

5. Nicholas Murray (1802–1861) Papers, Manuscript Group 384, New Jersey Historical Society, Newark (hereafter cited as NJHS).

6. Peter Andreas, *Smuggler Nation: How Illicit Trade Made America* (Oxford: Oxford University Press, 2013), 58.

7. Ibid.

8. Ibid., 22–28.

9. The time frame of several hours for round-trip travel between the Essex coast and the British garrison on Staten Island was deduced from the timetable of events that led to General Philemon Dickinson's failed 1778 invasion of Staten Island. Dickinson was concerned with the threat of British spies in Essex and therefore kept his plan to attack from his troops until 8:00 p.m. the night of the invasion. However, a single Essex resident saw the Continental army forces preparing their invasion and managed to cross the channel and reach the British commanders so quickly that the British army had hours to strengthen their defenses before Dickinson's forces arrived in the middle of the night.

10. Philipp Waldeck, *A Hessian Report on the People, the Land, the War as Noted in the Diary of Chaplain Philipp Waldeck*, trans. and ed. Bruce E. Burgoyne (Bowie, MD: Heritage Books, 1995), 59.

11. New Jersey Council of Safety Records, 1776–1781, box 1, folder 149, NJSA, and "Account of Public Vendue, Essex County, December 1780," Bureau of Archives and History, Legislative Records, box 1–37, folder 93, NJSA.

12. "Account of Public Vendue, Elizabethtown, June 4, 1781," Bureau of Archives and History, Legislative Records, box 1–37, folder 96, NJSA.

13. "An Act of free and general Pardon and for other Purposes therein mentioned," *Acts of the Council and General Assembly of the State of New Jersey*, June 5, 1777.

14. "An Act for taking Charge of and leasing the Real Estates, and for forfeiting the Personal Estates of certain Fugitives and Offenders, and for enlarging and continuing the Powers of Commissioners appointed to Seize and dispose of Such Personal Estates, and for ascertaining and discharging the lawful Debts and Claims thereon," *Acts of the Council and General Assembly of the State of New Jersey*, April 18, 1778; and Ruth M. Keesey, "New Jersey Legislation Concerning Loyalists," *Proceedings of the New Jersey Historical Society* 79 (1961): 88–89.

15. T. H. Breen, *The Marketplace of Revolution: How Consumer Politics Shaped American Independence* (New York: Oxford University Press, 2004), 65–70.

16. Ibid., 281–282; and James H. Levitt, *New Jersey's Revolutionary Economy*, vol. 9 of *New Jersey's Revolutionary Experience*, ed. Larry R. Gerlach (Trenton: New Jersey Historical Commission, 1975), 20.

17. New Jersey Supreme Court Case Files, Judgment and Process Book N, #134, May 1776–June 1782, No. 28, Case #34621.

18. "Account of Public Vendue, Newark, April 29, 1780," Bureau of Archives and History, Legislative Records, box 1–37, folder 88, NJSA.

19. "Account of Public Vendue, Elizabethtown, June 4, 1781," Bureau of Archives and History, Legislative Records, box 1–37, folder 96, NJSA.

20. New Jersey Supreme Court Case Files, Case File #35947, NJSA.

21. "Accounts of Public Vendue, Essex County, April 1780–March 25, 1783," Bureau of Archives and History, Legislative Records, box 1–37, folder 86, NJSA; and New Jersey Supreme Court Case Files, Case File #39556, NJSA,

22. "Accounts of Public Vendue, Essex County, April 1780–March 25, 1783," Bureau of Archives and History, Legislative Records, box 1–37, folder 86, NJSA; and New Jersey Supreme Court Case Files, Case File #34016, NJSA.

23. David Alan Bernstein, "New Jersey in the American Revolution: The Establishment of a Government amid Civil and Military Disorder, 1770–1781" (Ph.D. diss., Rutgers University, 1970), 275; and Papas, *That Ever Loyal Island*, 71.

24. *Minutes of the Council of Safety of the State of New Jersey* (Jersey City: J. H. Lyon, 1872), 186.

25. New Jersey Supreme Court Case Files, Case File #35313, NJSA.

26. "Accounts of Public Vendue, Essex County, April 1780–March 25, 1783," Bureau of Archives and History, Legislative Records, box 1–37, folder 86, NJSA; and New Jersey Supreme Court Case Files, Case File #34094, NJSA.

27. James Thacher, *Military Journal of the American Revolution* (1862; repr., New York: New York Times and Arno Press, 1969), 172, 182.

28. "An Act to punish Traitor and disaffected Persons," October 4, 1776, and "An Act for rending more effectual two certain Acts therein mentioned," June 4, 1777, in *Acts of the Council and General Assembly of the State of New Jersey*, vol. 8. The latter revises "An Act to punish Traitors and disaffected Persons" as well as the laws concerning the New Jersey Council of Safety.

29. "An Act to more effectually to prevent the Inhabitants of this State from trading with the Enemy, or giving within their Lines, and for other Purposes therein mentioned," December 12, 1780, in *Acts of the Council and General Assembly of the State of New Jersey*, vol. 9.

30. William Livingston to George Washington, January 26, 1782, *Papers of William Livingston*, 4:373.

31. William Livingston to George Washington, April 15, 1778, *Papers of William Livingston*, 2:291.

32. William Livingston to George Washington, September 21, 1778, *Papers of William Livingston*, 2:444–446.

33. Editor's note concerning "An Act for constituting a Council of Safety," September 20, 1777, *Papers of William Livingston*, 2:104.

34. William Livingston to George Washington, December 21, 1778, *Papers of William Livingston*, 2:518–520.

35. William Livingston to John Sullivan, August 19, 1777, and editor's note, *Papers of William Livingston*, 2:37.

36. William Livingston to George Washington, December 21, 1778, and August 15–16, 1777, *Papers of William Livingston*, 2:519 and 34.

37. Bernstein, "New Jersey in the American Revolution," 286.

38. Editor's note, *Papers of William Livingston*, 3:117.

39. Editor's note, *Papers of William Livingston*, 4:310.

40. William Livingston to George Washington, December 21, 1778, *Papers of William Livingston*, 2:519.

41. William Livingston to Israel Shreve, May 24, 1779, *Papers of William Livingston*, 3:97.

42. William Livingston to George Washington, October 5, 1777, *Papers of William Livingston*, 2:85. Livingston writes, "I really pity your Excellency's Situation with respect to the Tories. In my small Department, I have infinite Troubles with them. A Tory is an incorrigible Animal: And nothing but the Extinction of Life, will extinguish his Malevolence against Liberty."

43. Edward A. Fuhlbruegger, "New Jersey Finances during the American Revolution," *Proceedings of the New Jersey Historical Society* 55, no. 3 (July 1937): 173

44. "Account of Public Vendue, Aquackanonk, April 27, 1780," Bureau of Archives and History, Legislative Records, box 1–37, folder 87, NJSA.

45. Tax Ratables, box 99, Essex County, Aquackanonk Township, March 1779, NJSA.

46. Tax Ratables, box 99, Essex County, Newark Township, March 1779. NJSA. Farmers needed at least thirty acres to turn a profit because anything less would not be enough to maintain a house, barn, and sufficient wooded areas. John Rutherford cited in Mark E. Lender, "The Enlisted Line: The Continental Soldiers of New Jersey" (Ph.D. diss., Rutgers University, 1975), 120–121.

47. Harry M. Ward, *The American Revolution: Nationhood Achieved, 1763–1788* (New York: St. Martin's Press, 1995), 31, 34.

48. Charles W. Calomiris, "Institutional Failure, Monetary Scarcity, and the Depreciation of the Continental," *Journal of Economic History* 48, no. 1 (March 1988): 47–68, 56; and Fuhlbruegger, "New Jersey Finances during the American Revolution," 172.

49. Robert Gross, *The Minutemen and Their World*, 25th anniversary ed. (New York: Hill and Wang, 2001), 140–141.

50. Woody Holton, *Unruly Americans and the Origins of the Constitution* (New York: Hill and Wang, 2007), 59.

51. Inflation rates calculated by comparing purchase prices at Loyalist personal estate sales. Department of Defense, Adjutant General's Office, Records of the Commissioner of Forfeited Estates, 1777–1795, box 2 and box 4, folder 1, NJSA.

52. William M. Fowler Jr., *American Crisis: George Washington and the Dangerous Two Years after Yorktown, 1781–1783* (New York: Walker & Company, 2011), 23–27.

53. Papas, *That Ever Loyal Island*, 70.

54. New Jersey Supreme Court Case Files, Case File #37502, NJSA.

55. New Jersey Supreme Court Case Files, Case File #39544, NJSA.

56. Tax Ratables, box 99, Essex County, Elizabethtown Township, Rahway Ward, March 1779; and Elizabethtown Township, Westfield Ward, March 1779, NJSA.

57. New Jersey Supreme Court Case Files, NJSA. The only two who were not released on recognizance were Benjamin Spinning and Nathaniel Bond. Their imprisonment while awaiting trial was probably the result of the New Jersey Council of Safety, which was led by Governor William Livingston, getting involved in the case. In April 1778, Bond was fined £5 and Spinning fined £10. *Minutes of the Council of Safety of New Jersey*, 226–228.

58. New Jersey Supreme Court Case Files, Case File #37046, NJSA,

59. New Jersey Supreme Court Case Files, Judgment and Process Book N, #134, May 1776–June 1782, No. 28, NJSA. Three Essex residents were convicted of smuggling in 1777 and received an average penalty of £11.5. Nine Essex residents were convicted in 1778 and received an average fine of £32.5. Twenty-seven residents were convicted in 1779 and received an average fine of £250.

60. "Petition of Inhabitants of Essex County to the Legislative Council & General Assembly Concerning Trading with the Enemy, June 8, 1781," Bureau of Archives and History, Legislative Records, box 1–14, folder 69, NJSA.

61. In the summer of 1776, a group of Essex men entered the home of Edward Vaughn Dongan, a successful Elizabethtown lawyer, and physically carried him from his bed six miles out of town. Similarly, in July 1779, Daniel Marsh, a quartermaster in the Continental army, led a group of men to confront William MacLeod and warn him that he had four days to leave Elizabethtown. MacLeod was a captain in the British army and had purchased land in Elizabethtown following the French and Indian War. He was arrested in 1775 to prevent him from rejoining British forces and placed on parole.

62. *Minutes of the Council of Safety of the State of New Jersey*, 269; New Jersey Supreme Court Case Files, Case Files #36382 and #34023, NJSA; Minutes of the Essex County Court of Oyer and Terminer, March 13, 1779, NJSA.

63. Newark Blacksmith Account Book, 1775–1795, pp. 12, 56, Manuscript Group 1325, NJHS.

64. Sign of the Unicorn Tavern (Graham's Tavern), Elizabeth, NJ, Records, 1765–1794, Manuscript Group 107, NJHS.

65. Essex County, Court of General Quarter Sessions of the Peace, Shopkeepers' Petitions and Licenses, 1781, Anthony Sayres, NJSA.

66. "Sayres, Anthony," New Jersey Department of Defense, Adjutant General's Office (Revolutionary War), Service Abstracts [Cards], ca. 1776–1783, NJSA.

67. *Minutes of the Council of Safety of the State of New Jersey*, 186.

68. "Nichols, Robert" and "Lyons, Abraham," New Jersey Department of Defense, Adjutant General's Office (Revolutionary War), Service Abstracts [Cards], ca. 1776–1783, NJSA.

69. Essex County Court of Quarter Sessions of the Peace, Shopkeeper' Petitions and Licenses, 1781, Baldwin, Jesse, April 10, 1781, NJSA. It is unclear if or how Jesse Baldwin and Joseph Baldwin were related. Baldwin was a remarkably common surname within Essex County: sixty-six men named Baldwin rendered military service, paid taxes, or were tried in Essex courts during the war.

70. Andreas, *Smuggler Nation*, 47.

71. Richard P. McCormick, *Experiment in Independence: New Jersey in the Critical Period 1781–1789* (New Brunswick, NJ: Rutgers University Press, 1950), 11.

3

Blasting, Scraping, and Scavenging

Iron and Salt Production in Revolutionary New Jersey

ELEANOR H. McCONNELL

On November 21, 1776, Joseph Hoff of the Hibernia Iron Works wrote to the Philadelphia Committee of Safety about a supply problem that endangered the ability of the furnace to manufacture ordnance for the Continental army. The Hibernia works "are now employ'd in makeing Canon, large Round Shott, Grape Shott, 8ic., for the publick service, and 'tis expected the Works will continue in Blast 'till late in January, but as it is now the time to lay in a stock of provisions, and I have no Salt to cure it with I must beg that you will be pleas'd to send me 30 bushels . . . otherwise I must immediately putt the Works out of Blast."[1] Salt was just as essential for the war effort as iron; without it, meat and other foodstuffs could not be preserved, and both soldiers and civilians would go hungry. An examination of the difficult conditions for workers and managers at iron and saltworks can offer an unusually vivid sense of the daily round of uncertainty, monotony, and stress that were pervasive among New Jerseyans on the battlefront and the home front throughout the Revolution.

Economic development in colonial New Jersey had often been hampered by political, social, and geographical obstacles. Records for the early proto-industries—most notably iron—mention some of the barriers to economic growth, such as transportation problems, harsh conditions, prolonged land disputes, and shortages of labor. When these fledgling enterprises mobilized to supply the Continental army with essential goods, they suffered from the chronically uneven distribution of resources and the logistical inability to command or coordinate supplies and production. These frustrating conditions differed only in degree from the types of problems experienced by early New Jersey industrialists both before the mid-1770s and again after peace returned in the early 1780s, but the exigencies of war made the consequences of these problems significantly more dire.

In the late colonial era, proto-industrial sites for extracting minerals developed mostly in the two most isolated parts of New Jersey: the rocky and forested Appalachian foothills in the northwest, and the flat, sandy pine barrens of the southeastern coast. Both regions were lightly settled in the late eighteenth century. While market farming was well established in the long-settled middle of the colony, the foothills and the coastal plain were still backcountry, peppered with small hardscrabble settlements and far removed from centers of trade. These lands were poor for farming, but rich in timber and minerals. The need for iron and salt production during the war made these New Jersey backwaters and backwoods just as economically important as the productive farmland in the war-torn middle of the state. But their remoteness (and the many logistical shortcomings on the American side) made it difficult to maximize the regions' productivity during wartime. In addition, life at these iron and saltworks was often a desolate, dreary experience in a crude, uncivil environment that tested the wills of managers and workers alike. The difficult conditions during the war also reveal long-visible trends in the area: prolonged tenancy, the presence of squatters, rent protests, absentee landlords or proprietors, and the persistent use of slave laborers. These conditions created an economic culture in which ownership was unstable, authority was diffuse and impotent, and the fruits of the land were hotly contested.[2]

The development of iron production required concentrated investment and intensive land exploitation. Usually groups of elite stakeholders—mainly urban entrepreneurs—established iron furnaces, not lone individuals or local farmers. Indeed, because these enterprises needed large supplies of timber and an itinerant labor force, they *had* to be situated in areas without firmly entrenched independent farmers. Peter Wacker and Paul Clemens note that the number of single men without property in New Jersey increased over the last quarter of the eighteenth century and first quarter of the nineteenth.[3] These marginal people with uncertain financial prospects and unstable residences were more likely to seek employment in frontier areas where new extractive industries were emerging. Neither the mining entrepreneur nor the day laborer fit the familiar description of the prosperous New Jersey farmer found so frequently in travel accounts.[4] In fact, these extractive industries were often operated in the same way large landlords administered property, that is, by agent-managers who hierarchically organized one or two discrete economic activities on behalf of investors. This pattern of hinterland development occurred in other remote parts of the mainland British colonies as well. Speculators and proprietors promoted preliminary extractive industries such as timbering and iron production ahead of settlement to gain profit from their holdings prior to land sales to settlers. These extractive efforts were often contentious and difficult, with laborers, speculators, and agents disputing ownership.[5]

Letters from the Hibernia Furnace in Morris County offer a particularly revealing glimpse of how the dangers, difficulties, and contingencies of the early iron industry in New Jersey were magnified during the war. Founded in 1767, the Hibernia works became a major supplier of ordnance to the Continental army during the Revolutionary War. The shortages and expediencies of wartime heightened the stakes for production at this operation. Isolated works like Hibernia were consistently challenged by an insufficient labor force, lack of timely supplies, and unreliable methods for transporting the iron pigs and iron bars they manufactured.

Hibernia was owned by a prominent, sometimes absentee gentleman, William Alexander, Lord Stirling. At the beginning of the conflict, Stirling vested his extensive estate (including Hibernia) with the state as a means to repay his numerous debts and, he hoped, to recoup some profit from iron production for the American cause. The everyday operations of the furnace during the wars years fell to two often beleaguered brothers from Hunterdon County, Joseph Hoff and Charles Hoff Jr. The Hoffs' correspondence with merchants and factors in New York and Philadelphia and with Lord Stirling provides a vivid picture of how mineral extraction was anything but easy and not nearly as profitable as the owner had hoped.[6]

Getting paid and obtaining supplies were problems even before the war started, especially because ship sabotage, closed ports, and other forms of economic disruption were already a reality. In March 1775, Joseph Hoff wrote one of his many letters to the merchants of Murray, Samson, and Company of New York. The firm had recently sent him a payment of £30, which would be a "temporary Relief" but would not solve his main problem: supplies for the furnace and his workers. "I this day sent one of our teams to Elizabeth Town for the powder and mollasses [but] I fear from [your letter] now before me it will return empty."[7] For basic goods, Hoff had to depend on port towns like Elizabeth, over forty miles away, because there was so little agricultural production nearby. The gunpowder was needed to blast the iron ore out of the rocks, while molasses was a staple for the workers and provided the means to make rum. Without more supplies, Hoff was "afraid the Minors will leave me as they have been idle some days."[8] Several months later he was again "distressed for powder and obligd to pay the minors for being Idle."[9]

By April, the furnace was in full blast, but several logistical issues still concerned Hoff. First, he worried he would not be able to find carters to transport his pig iron and iron bars. Also, the land itself was letting him down: "I find that the Oar takes much more powder to raise it than formerly & that my estimation will be far short." His miscalculation about gunpowder troubled him because he could sense what was coming: "[A]s matters is like to turn in America I dread the Scarcity of it."[10] Further, Hoff had to take measures to protect the Hibernia property from invasion by British forces.[11] Exhausted, Hoff confessed to Lord Stirling that "next year [I hope] to go into some other business for myself less perplexing and as profitable if possible" while still serving his lordship, to whom he is bound "in duty and Gratitude."[12] The Hoffs clearly looked to Stirling as a patron and hoped to be set up in business through their connection to him. Although most of Hibernia's output in these years was for public use, war production connected the Hoffs to influential people who could possibly assist their private interests later on. Therefore, the brothers were managers, estate agents, public servants, and potential future entrepreneurs.

When the port of New York was temporarily closed in June 1775, Hoff redirected his pleas for supplies to Philadelphia merchants, with as little success and much more distance for goods to travel. When New York commerce became permanently closed to New Jersey during most of the war (at least officially), he became ever more desperate to find the goods he needed. If he could not get paid for his pig iron, he would again be unable to purchase supplies, the workers would continue to desert him, and iron production would cease. He ruminated on the complications: "if Barr Iron will bring no money of course forge masters cant command Cash from any thing else to buy pig with[.] Since no pork is to be had I must endeavour to get beef but it will not be so much to our interest."[13] In other words, without some cash for his iron pigs, there will be no pigs to eat. It made sense for Hoff to prefer pigs to cattle, since pigs would roam the forest and feed themselves, whereas cattle would require purchased fodder. But first he needed to find ready cash, which was already scarce and would become even more so as the conflict escalated. Throughout the rebelling colonies, the war caused "a disruption of the paper currency and an inflation so rapid that it crippled the price system, with severe consequences for . . . the operation of the economy."[14]

By the spring of 1776, the ironworks needed not only food but also clothing, as "the people here [are] almost naked." Even though "the Coal [charcoal] is coming in Briskly," Hoff declared that "our people are so Distressed for Rum that I believe wee must have one hogshead let the price be what it will."[15] As it was, he could hardly pay them, at least in actual money: "the chief of my engagements with the workmen are for one half in goods the other half in cash if above 10 at 6 months and under that sum at 3 months." That is, he issued promissory notes payable in six or three months. But with "Cash, Goods being so Scarce," meeting these obligations seemed unlikely.[16]

Because of the shortages and the unpredictability of the local environment, figuring out how to balance resources, save money, and make the best use of time were pressing considerations. In March 1778, Charles Hoff wrote to Lord Stirling about how to proceed with blasting for the year ahead, laying out the advantages and drawbacks of alternative plans. By this time, the furnace had been completely commandeered by the Continental army to provide ordnance and other iron supplies, which made a production plan especially important. At the same time, Hoff was running out of workers, and he believed "it won't be possible to have more Wood Cutt, than will make out a blast of 4 or 5 months." The workers who had not simply deserted the operation had been persuaded to join the army and had not been allowed to return to Hibernia to cut wood or perform the other essential tasks that would enable the furnace to keep in blast. Because it would be so difficult to get started on time (that is, after the spring thaw, so that the streams that powered the bellows that fed the blast were no longer in danger of freezing), Hoff suggested holding off the blast for a few weeks, a plan that would save money and time in the long run:

> Since the Blast is not likely to continue so long as usual, [we could] put off blowing 'till the pasture becomes good, so that the Teams can get their liveing in the woods, without being at the expence of Feeding them—To begin early to draw in the Coal, & draw as much as the Teams can bear from the Woodfeed . . . & from the time of begining to go on with spirrit, will be much better than to begin so early under the present circumstances?—as by putting it off 'till then, will enable us to make all the necessary preparations completely before hand.[17]

By waiting, nature could provide the fodder for the horses and oxen that carted the wood and charcoal, saving resources while there were not enough carters, miners, and choppers to produce much anyway. Because of the limitations of wartime and weather, Hoff strategized about how to create a more productive blast in a shorter amount of time by coordinating the complex components of iron production.

But this plan hinged on Hoff's other plea to Lord Stirling: that he use his influence as a major general in the Continental army to order laborers back from nearby army barracks (and military prisons) to work at the furnace. Specifically, he suggested that Stirling send him deserters, both "Regular and Hessian." They would be preferable to his current rag-tag employees, whom he described as mostly farmers who "have left their Farms & come here, solely" to receive an exemption from militia service "& from no other motive:—This I have experienced as I find they are determin'd to Shuffle away the time they are exempt."[18]

Hoff apparently never had an opportunity to implement his grand strategy. Four months later, after he had "Strain'd every nerve with the few hands I had," he realized that to begin the blast "when hands were so Scarce" would run the risk of having to stop the blast if the situation worsened, which would be more wasteful than not starting it at all. On the other hand, if he could find workers, he would be able to manufacture not only cannon and other ordnance, but also valuable goods needed by New Jerseyans at home: "I find hallow ware [pots, pans, kettles] wou'd be in great demand here [and] would fetch almost any price."[19] Hoff hoped that by making hollowware too, he could begin to pay back the considerable debts owed by the furnace company to various individuals and other local ironworks.

Andover Iron Works in Sussex County experienced some of the same labor and production problems as Hibernia. Apparently it was a successful enterprise before the war, situated "Scarcely a Mile from . . . an inexhaustible Body of Ore" that produced "Iron of a superior Quality to any other in America."[20] The furnace owners, however, were Loyalists, so it was confiscated by the state early in the conflict. By 1778, the Board of War reopened it to resume production of pig iron for the Patriot effort. When the furnace and forge were advertised for lease two years later, included in the list of assets were "Some NEGROES belonging to said Works, To be SOLD."[21] A prewar advertisement from the *Pennsylvania Gazette* noted that there were six slaves at the works "who are good Forgemen, and understand the making and drawing of Iron well."[22]

Although wartime records for Andover are lacking, we can get a sense of the daily concerns at this operation just a few years later by examining the daybooks of furnace manager Archibald Stewart from 1786 to 1792. He described some of the hard labor that went into constructing and maintaining the operation, such as when his workers "began to ditch the Cranberry pond," "stayed to haul loggs," and began raising a dam.[23] The remote location meant food had to be brought in, and some workers spent their time gathering and gardening for lean times. For instance, in November 1789 "John Robinson wrought 3 days raisng potatoes."[24] Haymaking also took up at least a few days in late summer; feed for the carting teams had to be produced on site.[25] Because the forest near the works must have been chopped clean at this point to make charcoal for the blast, Stewart often dispatched men to try to obtain necessary supplies, such as millstones, planks, and shingles. His workforce seemed erratic: sometimes only three or four men worked on a given day, sometimes more than a dozen. And many did not stay long. In July 1793, Stewart paid James Waters and then "that night he ran away; he was to thrash [thresh] and his share [was] to be 18 bu. in 6 days."[26] Some of his workers were not worth keeping, such as whichever man stole from "negro Caleb" the "victuals he brought with him."[27] And of course, every month the workers were absent at least one day for militia training.

The historian Thomas Doerflinger has called early industrial production sites like Hibernia and Andover "forest factories"—self-contained enterprises with their own dwellings, blacksmiths, and other basics, but heavily reliant on outside supplies of food and cloth to supplement the one-dimensional production at the site. They look quite different from the later, urban image of a factory, yet their laborers were wage employees of an "industrial complex that was owned by capitalists, run by a professional manager, and tightly linked to the market economy."[28] The wartime challenges faced by these sites continued well into the Early Republic: these were places dependent upon markets for basic supplies, but they produced goods that could be made only in isolated areas with poor prospects for farming, little settlement, and no markets.

LOGISTICAL QUANDARIES ARE especially apparent in Patriot salt-making ventures during the war. With the British blockade on the West Indian trade, Americans were deprived of their usual source of salt. Therefore, from the beginning of the conflict, domestic salt production was considered essential by the Continental Congress and new state governments. But records from wartime saltworks on the New Jersey shore reveal the difficulties of manufacturing this staple and getting it to market.[29] Compared with the Jersey iron furnaces, the saltworks were small, primitive operations. However, both types of industry displayed the features and dynamics that would come to define a factory for processing natural commodities: a centralized manufactory on the periphery troubled by a lack of basic access to supplies, absentee ownership, and long-suffering agents with an erratic labor force.

Patriot leaders certainly understood the value of salt production, but seemed to be less able to comprehend the logistical and managerial realities that hindered success. Indeed, the historian Michael S. Adelberg has noted that the troubled salt-making ventures sponsored by Congress and the states reveal a kind of persistent naiveté and the fundamentally "amateur nature of government during the Revolutionary War."[30] In October 1777, General George Washington made a special point of telling Brigadier General David Forman that he was excused for his lateness in coming to reinforce the army on the Delaware because of his effort to thwart "the intent of the Enemy, [which] is to destroy the Salt works upon the Sea

Coast of Monmouth County." He believed these saltworks were "so truly valuable to the public; that they are certainly worth your attention."[31] But if Washington had known how unreliable most of these salt operations were, he might have questioned the value of the endeavor. Forman himself ran what seems to have been a scam salt operation in Monmouth County in 1778, which caused considerable local resentment. Several residents complained that no actual salt was being produced with the money and resources Washington had allocated to Forman and that the whole operation was only "aiding the Purposes of private Interest."[32]

There were several legitimate saltworks on the outer coastal plain during the Revolutionary War, but their ability to produce was consistently undermined by the same problems the Hoffs experienced at Hibernia Furnace: abundant natural resources that could not be effectively transformed into needed commodities. There was no shortage of saltwater at the shore, just the labor and infrastructure necessary to make it into salt and send that salt to market. The pine barren region was a prime location for these activities, not only because of the availability of saltwater but also because of the abundance of cordwood needed to keep the pans boiling.[33] But once again, abundant cordwood would be present only in an undersettled region, far from where the salt was needed.

Beginning in August 1780, Thomas Hopkins of the Friendship Salt Company kept an intermittent journal about the activities (and inactivities) of his workers and associates as they slogged through the marshy, mosquito-infested tidewaters of Great Egg Harbor and produced salt for Philadelphia. The process was arduous. Hopkins and his workers pumped saltwater into pans, cut and hauled wood from the nearby forests, tended the fires as the water boiled into "pickle" and eventually dried into salt, and then packed the salt into barrels, which likely also had to be made on site. Finally, the barrels of salt had to be hauled thirty miles across the pine barrens to Cooper's Ferry (now Camden) and transported to Philadelphia.

The chronic shortage of labor made this difficult work even worse. Beyond the fact that many able-bodied men were still actively mobilized for war, the working conditions were unpleasant and monotonous. The people Hopkins was able to hire were often hardly worth the trouble. On August 14, "the Woodcutters refusg to cut inducd me to offer them 2/6 p.

Cord which they agreed to fearing we should be out of Wood and obligd to stop the Pans." But the next day, "the 3 Wood Cutters elopd before Day & stole an Ax & a Loaf of Bread."[34] Woodcutting was apparently a much-dreaded task; supplies constantly needed to be replenished, which required chopping and hauling over rugged terrain from ever-greater distances. However, Hopkins learned that insubordination did not require specific reasons. Another laborer, Martin Nelson, was habitually drunk and would disappear during work hours, returning "so very quarelsome with Cursing & Daming that I could hardly keep my hands of[f] him."[35] Yet Hopkins only threatened to fire Nelson, which points to his desperate need for workers, no matter how odious. Hopkins continued to contact people whom he thought might be able to send more workers, but few came and fewer stayed. The whole region existed in a constant state of transience. Sometimes the workforce included slaves, such as the day when there were "11 Hands Cutting wood to Day, two of them Capt Stephens's Negroes."[36]

As at the Andover Iron Works, production at the Friendship Salt Works halted whenever the camp needed basic provisions. Some workers tended the company's garden, while others spent days gathering clams, often the company's only food between infrequent shipments from Philadelphia. Equipment (wagons, pans) broke frequently and took time to repair. The company produced anywhere from six to twelve bushels of salt on a good day, but sometimes barely anything at all due to truancy, insubordination, green wood, diseased horses, or food shortages.

Colonel John Neilson's Salt Works at Toms River seemed an equally wearisome and unpredictable endeavor, but it was perhaps more closely tied to merchant connections nearby. Neilson maintained his store in New Brunswick while his agent, Major John Van Embergh, supervised production at the works and acted as his main scout for coastal business ventures. In July 1778, Van Embergh reported that salt production had stalled: "There seems to be no Salt making on the Shore Scarcely since the Last alarm of the Enemy going through the State[.] People who belonged to the Country have Remained there to Harvest—& the Musquitoes are so excessive Plenty that those belonging to the Shore will not Work & has been Idle this 2 Weeks last[.] Hope to get them going Tomorrow."[37] The correspondence indicates that Neilson and Van Embergh were concerned not only with salt production but also with finding any possible opportunity to obtain goods to trade. This practice, as the historian Leonard Lundin notes, allowed many Patriot merchants "to make very acceptable profits as prices rose and a scarcity of goods began to be generally felt."[38] Indeed, Neilson seemed to focus on profit in any form, not just one commodity. In their correspondence Neilson and Van Embergh make few distinctions between increasing their supply of trade goods and providing salt to the army. Certainly both the military and the general population needed salt, and merchants like Neilson attempted to supply both.

Colonel Anthony White wrote to Neilson in September 1778 from Union, practically begging him to advance some salt, "as we are quite out haveing lived upon the borrow for some time past." If Neilson had none to send, White asked him to borrow some from another merchant in New Brunswick and repay him "when yours comes up [from Toms River]." He added that if Neilson is away, Mrs. Neilson should "apply to Mr. Van Embergh or Some other person for Some as I cannot go without Some at present."[39]

Just as the army was running low on salt, the situation in the cities was also critical. In November, John White in Philadelphia wrote to Neilson, desperate for some kind of salt trade. He proposed a complex scheme for purchasing a salt-laden vessel in British-held New York, claiming to British authorities that it was bound for Newfoundland, and then sailing it to Toms River. This "speculation," he suggested to Neilson, is "worth your Notice [and] hard money could be purchased here [in Philadelphia]." Clearly, White had low expectations about how much salt could be produced at Toms River, the ability to transport it, the availability of financing, and the return he could expect on his investment—so much so that smuggling a major vessel out of New York Harbor began to seem like a reasonable idea. No evidence suggests that this plan was actually attempted.[40] At this time, Van Embergh was so desperate for supply that he considered buying salvaged "fine Imported Salt" at a much higher price, just to have something to sell.[41] All of these prices were somewhat theoretical, however, since Neilson and his agents bought on long-term credit, borrowing not only money to buy goods but also goods to sell to their own customers.

Even if there was salt at Toms River, no one had the ability to pay for it. As noted above, paper currency issued by Congress and the states had become almost worthless, making it impossible to buy and sell on consistent, reliable terms. Van Embergh tried to pay the "Marshall" at Toms River with two conditional notes valued at "1000 dollars," but the marshal refused to accept them.[42] A week later he sent Neilson fifty-nine bushels of salt (probably salvaged from a captured British ship), having "borrowed" it from the appropriately named Major Gamble, because Neilson's own works had produced only one wagon-load. To supply Neilson's store, he indebted himself to Gamble to obtain the salt he could not produce at his own operation. Presumably, when Neilson finally got paid (and if he was selling to the Continental army, that would take a while), he would then pay Gamble. From the nature of the exchange, the loan's terms might have been usurious; yet these possibly shady exchanges based on confiscation and credit often seemed to be the best bet for getting goods to market. Piracy was easier than production.

Unrealistic expectations persisted about the availability of salt in Toms River, the ability to transport it, the possibility of financing, and the return Neilson could expect on the investment. His agent John White claimed that the operations by the seaside would be cheap and yield good returns in the coastal trade, as long as they could find a "Man we trust" to carry out the business.[43] But only a day later Van Embergh, whom Neilson seems to have trusted, wrote that he was sending nineteen bushels from the works, "which is all they have." Van Embergh wants to know how it is selling in New Brunswick, "as price is here very uncertain." His restlessness grows as the prospects for production and profit wane. In November 1778 there is "No Salt at Works" save what small amount he has sent to New Brunswick: "pray how does it Sell?—with us dull at 13 dolls."[44] The cogs of production refused to run smoothly in this isolated, desolate region.

Labor problems continued to vex Neilson and his associates as well. Van Embergh reported problems with a smuggling trip to the Caribbean: "a great extortion prevails among our hands on account of wages which they Insist on receiving in the W. Indies & [I] shall tomorrow settle with them— they at present Insist on £20 pr month paid them in the West Indies or priviledge equal to it which is In my opinion very extravigant."[45] Unfree laborers seemed just as intransigent. Neilson purchased a slave from a captured British ship, and Van Embergh reported in September that he had spoken to the man, "who is now Willing to go to the works & promises to be there tomorrow morning."[46] But by November, Van Embergh wrote that he had "Sold our Negro . . . for 1000 dollars . . . [I] found him a very Indifferent fellow & am glad we are Clear of him." He needed more workers at Toms River, or "the Works must Stop"; but even if workers could be found, "the price [of wages?] is such [that] the Works will not defray the Charges."[47]

Transportation was as big a problem as production. Even when Van Embergh could find workers to haul the salt, he feared they would steal it or let it be confiscated by the enemy. When he hired John Strickler and John Johnston to haul thirty bushels of salt to New Brunswick, he took the precaution of having them sign a promissory receipt with their X marks "to make them carefull."[48] A few days later, Van Embergh simply gave up (for the time being) and rented the saltworks for six weeks to an unnamed party, who would receive one-third of the salt produced during that time in exchange for operating the works.[49] It was more cost-effective (or at least less annoying) for Van Embergh to let someone else deal with the headaches of salt production, even if his two-thirds return turned out to be meager. The frustrations of producing salt affected more than just his pocketbook: "[I] Am Sir . . . impatient for Relief from this place."[50]

By late December, a harsh storm and a British landing on a nearby beach "has proved fatal to us. . . . The People have been oblidged to leave" while the "men to whom we Rented the Salt Works have Quit them as nothing can be done along shore in that way for some time now."[51] Throughout the winter of 1778–1779, inclement weather and enemy ships made production at Toms River nearly impossible. By the spring of 1779, however, conditions had improved enough for people to return to the area. Van Embergh seemed to find it easier to obtain salt and other provisions from passing vessels to convey to Neilson for market. He sent 150 bushels of salt purchased from the captured *Love and Unity*, and he declared that he would keep at it: "[I] shall not be Bashfull in bidding for the salt at Squan [Beach] if I like it." But the local people at Toms River were unwilling to work for him in flush times and became "Negligent of any thing but dividing & determining their shares in prizes" from captured vessels.[52] Whether Van Embergh's efforts continued into the last years of the war is unclear. By 1781, Colonel Neilson was no longer just a de facto factor; he had been appointed an official quartermaster for the army in Trenton. He continued to operate his private trading ventures, and the saltworks near Toms River went on supplying the military and the market with salt, however fitfully.

The men who invested in these hapless salt ventures, like Hopkins, Neilson, and Van Embergh, certainly hoped to help the Patriot cause—and expected to make money doing it. But the risks and annoyances certainly seemed to outweigh the benefits; profits were elusive at best. Perhaps they hoped for long-term gain. After the war, elite Patriots took the opportunity created by disorder, a political power vacuum, and unstable property ownership to further their own projects. Many became speculators in western lands. Land grants were awarded based on influence and patronage, allowing large landowners to set the terms of settlement for a large number of less privileged people. The Continental army's larger benefactors, like Lord Stirling of Hibernia Iron Works, would have certainly expected to be treated with favor if the Americans were victorious.[53] Whether this expectation for reward on investment was present among smaller entrepreneurs is less clear. However, war gave these investors in iron and salt production the unusual opportunity to justify their private aggrandizement in patriotic terms.

The continuing frustration of not being able to buy and sell at advantageous times, prices, and places was a central problem for all traders and producers during the war. Even during peacetime, schemes for regional trading ventures required a level of stability and predictability that was always hard to come by in the early Atlantic circuit, but especially difficult during times of war, when former trading partners were blockaded and specie was even more scarce than usual. War disrupted merchant control over the supply of goods and promoted the increase of economic practices that thrived on the volatility of conflict: profiteering, scavenging, and price-gouging. Merchants and other investors took advantage of opportunities to reap personal rewards while also winning praise for supplying the glorious cause. Laborers often resisted employment in the grim conditions at iron and saltworks, but they also tried to take economic advantage of the disruptions of war to better their own situations. The proto-industrialists of Revolutionary-era iron and salt production contended with the same chaotic environment that made the war years stark and difficult for all New Jerseyans. Their gains were tempered by frustration, bitterness, and endless logistical complications.

NOTES

1. *Pennsylvania Archives*, 1st ser., ed. Samuel Hazard, 12 vols. (Philadelphia: Joseph Severns, 1852–1856), 5:72. Excerpted in Charles Boyer, *Early Forges and Furnaces in New Jersey* (Philadelphia: University of Pennsylvania Press, 1931), 95–96.

2. For a detailed analysis of New Jersey's cultural and economic geography, see Peter O. Wacker and Paul G. E. Clemens, *Land Use in Early New Jersey: A Historical Geography* (Newark: New Jersey Historical Society, 1995). For a discussion of land disputes in the late colonial period, see Brendan McConville, *These Daring Disturbers of the Public Peace: The Struggle for Property and Power in Early New Jersey* (Ithaca, NY: Cornell University Press, 1999), 1–3, 92, 164–176.

3. Wacker and Clemens, *Land Use in Early New Jersey*, 98.

4. See especially Thomas Thompson, *A Letter from New Jersey, in America, Giving Some Account and Description of that Province by a Gentleman, Late of Christ's College, Cambridge* (London, 1756), 8, 12, 21–22; *Peter Kalm's Travels in North America: The English Version of 1770* (ed. Benson, 1937), excerpted in *Historic New Jersey Through Visitors' Eyes*, ed. Miriam V. Studley (Princeton, NJ: Van Nostrand, 1964), 19–20, 27, 31–32.

5. For the situation in Maine, see Alan Taylor, *Liberty Men and Great Proprietors: The Revolutionary Settlement on the Maine Frontier, 1760–1820* (Chapel Hill: University of North Carolina Press, 1990). The New Jersey situation was somewhat different because, unlike Massachusetts (Maine), Virginia, North Carolina, and other colonies, it possessed no frontier reserves granted by the crown. Proprietor lands in the barrens were still unsettled and ripe for exploitation, but there were limits to how much proprietors and prospective settlers could hope to gain within the confines of the colony/state.

6. Boyer, *Early Forges and Furnaces in New Jersey*, 95–98.

7. Joseph Hoff to Murray, Samson and Co., March 15, 1775, "Transcription of the Hoff Correspondence" (1775–1778), Works Projects Administration Historical Records Survey, 1935–1936, typescript copy at Special Collections and University Archives, Rutgers University Libraries, New Brunswick, NJ (hereafter cited as THC-WPA, RUSC).

8. Joseph Hoff to Murray, March 21, 1775, THC-WPA, RUSC.

9. Joseph Hoff to Murray, August, 25, 1775, THC-WPA, RUSC.

10. Joseph Hoff to Murray, April 29, 1775, THC-WPA, RUSC.

11. The campaigns of 1777 would bring British forces the closest to Hibernia, as General William Howe established a string of outposts across the state. See David Hackett Fischer, *Washington's Crossing* (New York: Oxford University Press, 2004).

12. Joseph Hoff to Lord Stirling, May 21, 1775, THC-WPA, RUSC.

13. Joseph Hoff to Murray, Samson and Co., September 23, 1775, THC-WPA, RUSC.

14. John J. McCusker and Russell R. Menard, *The Economy of British America, 1607–1789* (Chapel Hill: University of North Carolina Press, 1985), 359.

15. Joseph Hoff to Murray, May 21, 1776, THC-WPA, RUSC.

16. Joseph Hoff to Murray, May 27, 1776, THC-WPA, RUSC.

17. Charles Hoff Jr. to Lord Stirling, March 20, 1778, THC-WPA, RUSC.

18. Ibid.

19. Charles Hoff to Stirling, July 10, 1778, THC-WPA, RUSC.

20. *Pennsylvania Gazette*, October 2, 1770, THC-WPA, RUSC.

21. *Pennsylvania Packet*, December 2, 1780, excerpted in Boyer, *Early Forges and Furnaces in New Jersey*, 30.

22. *Pennsylvania Gazette*, October 4, 1770, excerpted in Boyer, *Early Forges and Furnaces in New Jersey*, 31.

23. Dorothy A. Stratford, ed., "Andover Furnace Work Book, 1786–1792," *Genealogical Magazine of New Jersey* 76, no. 1 (January 2002): 1–10, at 2; 77, no. 2 (May 2002): 61–72.

24. Ibid., 64.

25. Ibid., 66.

26. Ibid., 4–5, 70.

27. Ibid., 2.

28. Thomas M. Doerflinger, "Rural Capitalism in Iron Country: Staffing a Forest Factory, 1808–1815," *William and Mary Quarterly*, 3d ser., 59, no. 1 (January 2002): 3.

29. Michael S. Adelberg, "'Long in the Hand and Altogether Fruitless': The Pennsylvania Salt Works and Salt-Making on the New Jersey Shore during the American Revolution," *Pennsylvania History* 80, no. 2 (2013): 216–218.

30. Ibid., 234–235.

31. George Washington to David Forman, October 19, 1777, Neilson Family Papers, box 1, folder 4, Special Collections and University Archives, Rutgers University Libraries, New Brunswick, NJ (hereafter cited as NFP-RUSC).

32. Leonard Lundin, *Cockpit of the Revolution: The War for Independence in New Jersey* (Princeton, NJ: Princeton University Press, 1940), 289–291. The quotation is from a resolution of the legislative council, March 11, 1778; see William Livingston to George Washington, March 14, 1778, *The Papers of George Washington Digital Edition*, ed. Theodore J. Crackel (Charlottesville: University of Virginia Press, Rotunda, 2008), http://rotunda.upress.virginia.edu/founders/GEWN-03-14-02-0145.

33. Wacker and Clemens, *Land Use in Early New Jersey*, 76.

34. "Journal of Thomas Hopkins of the Friendship Salt Company, New Jersey, 1780," *Pennsylvania Magazine of History and Biography* 4 (1918): 47.

35. Ibid., 48.

36. Ibid., 55.

37. John Van Embergh to John Neilson, July 12, 1778, July 24, 1778, box 2, folder 4A, NFP-RUSC. There were apparently several saltworks near Toms River at various

points during the war. One source mentions the "Pennsylvania Salt Works" at Coates' Point, the "Union Salt Works" at Squan, and other saltworks at Shark River and Barnegat Bay. Whether Neilson's saltworks was one of these is unclear. In 1782, after Neilson's involvement appears to have ended, British and Loyalist forces destroyed the block house, an unspecified saltworks, and other structures at Toms River, killing several of the town's defenders and then hanging an American army captain, Joshua Huddy. See William S. Stryker, *The Capture of the Block House at Toms River, New Jersey, March 24, 1782* (Trenton: Naar, Day & Naar, 1883), 9–10.

38. Lundin, *Cockpit of the Revolution*, 92.

39. Anthony White to John Neilson, September 24, 1778, box 2, NFP-RUSC.

40. John White to Neilson, November 7, 1778, November 16, 1778, box 2, NFP-RUSC. This scheme is explained in Robert T. Thompson, "Colonel Neilson: Salt Merchant," *Journal of the Rutgers University Library* 1, no. 1 (1937): 15.

41. Van Embergh to Neilson, November 13, 1778, box 2, NFP-RUSC.

42. Van Embergh to Joseph Potts, November 8, 1778, box 2, NFP-RUSC.

43. John White to Neilson, November 16, 1778, box 2, NFP-RUSC.

44. Van Embergh to Neilson, November 17, 1778, box 2, NFP-RUSC.

45. Van Embergh to Neilson, November 30, 1778, box 2, NFP-RUSC.

46. Van Embergh to Neilson, September 13, 1778, box 2, NFP-RUSC.

47. Van Embergh to Neilson, November 18, 1778, box 2, NFP-RUSC.

48. Van Embergh to Neilson (letter and enclosed receipt), November 18, 1778, box 2, NFP-RUSC.

49. Van Embergh to Neilson, November 21, 1778, box 2, NFP-RUSC.

50. Van Embergh to Neilson, November 17, 1778, box 2, NFP-RUSC.

51. Van Embergh to Neilson, December 27, 1778, December 30, 1778, box 2, NFP-RUSC.

52. Van Embergh to Neilson, May 5, 1779, box 2, NFP-RUSC.

53. Lord Stirling himself did not live to benefit from his service. He was basically insolvent at the time of his death in 1783, possessing only worthless Continental currency. Boyer, *Early Forges and Furnaces in New Jersey*, 98.

4

A Nest of Tories

The American-versus-American Battle of Fort Lee, 1781

TODD W. BRAISTED

Fort Lee today is a thriving borough of some 35,000 residents, located in New Jersey's Bergen County, nestled atop the Palisades, overlooking the Hudson River and Manhattan. It is a diverse community, reflecting cultures from around the world; residents are often drawn to it because of its close proximity to New York City. In some ways, the Fort Lee of 1776 was little different. A part of Hackensack Township's English Neighborhood, the area was sparsely settled by Dutch, Huguenot, English, and other European families. The ferry owned by Peter Bourdet plied pettiaugers, small river craft, between Manhattan and the landing bearing his name at the foot of the Palisades. The boats carried both passengers and Bergen County's agriculture to the east side of the Hudson, bringing grains, vegetables, cattle, and other items of local produce to sell in lower Manhattan and returning with imported European goods and manufactures. This close connection with New York made Fort Lee an area of strategic importance in war.[1]

War came to the lower Hudson Valley in the summer of 1776, when Lieutenant General William Howe, commanding a force of more than 20,000 British, Hessian, and Provincial soldiers, landed unopposed on Staten Island in early July. Over the next two months Howe conquered Long Island and New York City, aided by the warships of the Royal Navy commanded by his brother, Admiral Lord Richard Howe. The threat of these warships led to the construction of Fort Lee (originally and often concurrently referred to as Fort Constitution) and its sister redoubt on the east side of the river, Fort Washington. Designed to work in conjunction, the forts never prevented the Royal Navy access northward on the river, despite the placement of submerged river obstructions and some punishing barrages from the heavy guns of Henry Knox's Continental artillery. On November 16, 1776, Howe's troops completed their conquest of Manhattan by storming Fort Washington, killing and capturing more than 2,700 troops in perhaps an hour. Realizing that Fort Lee no longer held any value, General George Washington determined upon an orderly evacuation of that post and commenced sending its valuable stores to the New Jersey interior. To thwart any such recovery, 5,000 troops under Lieutenant General Lord Charles Cornwallis scaled the Palisades six miles above Fort Lee four days after the fall of Fort Washington. The surprised American garrison abandoned most of its artillery, baggage, and stores in its headlong flight across the Hackensack River at New Bridge to the west. Cornwallis and his men pursued Washington across New Jersey while other British forces removed all the stores and demolished the works. By Christmas 1776, Fort Lee ceased to exist. Its role in the American Revolution, however, was just beginning.[2]

By 1781, four and a half years after Washington's troops had abandoned their bastion on the Palisades, Britain's military focus had shifted toward the southern states and toward its more traditional European foes, France and Spain. For Washington, New York City still remained the prize; its capture, he was certain, would finally defeat the British and secure independence for the United States of America. The goal seemed within reach in the summer of 1780, when Washington moved his 14,000 men into Bergen County, eager to cooperate with a powerful French land and naval force that had arrived in Newport, Rhode Island, that July. But the dream dissolved in a rapid succession of disappointments. The French force was only half the number promised, and many of the troops were too ill for any sort of action; the southern army under Major General Horatio Gates was virtually destroyed by Cornwallis's smaller force at Camden, South Carolina; and perhaps most unnerving, Major General Benedict Arnold's plot to surrender West Point to the British was uncovered, sending shockwaves through the army. The war continued with New York City firmly in British control.[3]

There, the British had enough problems of their own. The war around the city had been an endless series of raids and counter-raids, sometimes involving Continentals and British regulars, but more often left to the state militia on one side and the Refugees on the other. The term "Refugees" could refer to Loyalist families who sought shelter behind the British lines, but more commonly was used by both friend and foe to describe armed Loyalists organized in corps outside of the Provincial establishment. From the earliest days of the war, the British had employed thousands of Americans in their service, primarily in regularly established corps that could be deployed anywhere in America alongside their British compatriots. Known as Provincials, these troops received the same pay, clothing, arms, and provisions as the British and served under the same discipline and authority. New Jersey contributed several thousand men to the Provincial Forces, primarily in the New Jersey Volunteers under Brigadier General Cortland Skinner, the province's last attorney general under the crown. As opposed to Provincials, Refugee corps came later in the war and took a more aggressive approach toward fighting. Soldiers in all armies typically did more garrison chores—guard duty, the building of fortifications, and any number of mundane tasks—than fighting. Many Loyalists, however, desired to wage war on a far more active scale than usually allowed by serving in the ranks of a Provincial unit. Several prominent Loyalists, including William Franklin and William Tryon, royal governors of New Jersey and New York, respectively, began in 1779 to tap into a pool of Loyalist resentment and frustration. They organized corps and "associations" of Refugees that would serve the British more in a way that provided for their families' needs than assisted military utility.[4]

One such corps, the Loyal Refugee Volunteers, raised in the winter of 1779–1780 by Abraham Cuyler, former mayor of Albany, New York, was intended to appeal to those Loyalists who "are inclined to be employed on ample wages to cut FIRE-WOOD, for the use of his Majesty's Garrison at New-York."[5] Though the fledgling corps was organized too late to aid effectually in supplying fuel during that brutally cold winter, the British command took steps to put it in a position to start filling up British wood magazines.[6] Cuyler was the business head of the corps rather than its commander in the field. After signing a contract with the British Barrack Master General's Department, the civil branch of the army responsible for firewood, Cuyler established a post in (then) Bergen County at Bull's Ferry, about eight miles north of the British fort at Paulus Hook (modern Jersey City).[7] Cuyler gave command of the post to Captain Thomas Ward, a rather colorful figure who lived at the Clove in Orange County, New York, near the Bergen County border. Ward had not started the war on the side of King George, even though he later claimed to the British that "from the Commencement of the late Rebellion in America, and through every stage of the War, he was uniformly and Steadily Attached to His Majesty's Person and the Government and Constitution of Great Britain, and opposed to the measures of the American Congress."[8] In fact, Ward enlisted on April 3, 1777, as a sergeant in Colonel William Malcom's Additional Continental Regiment, serving at the Clove under a young Lieutenant Colonel Aaron Burr.[9] When exactly Ward joined the British is unclear. In an undated memorial he said he "Joined the Brittish Troops at New York the 16 of June 1777";[10] but a muster roll of his company in Malcom's Regiment listed him as deserting on April 26, 1778.

Ward quickly set his men, numbering about 110 of all ranks, to work building a blockhouse. By the beginning of July, they had created a work capable of defense against any surprise infantry attack, but not against heavy cannon.[11] The blockhouse would prove crucial to the survival of the corps. On July 21, 1780, General Anthony Wayne, at the head of over a thousand Pennsylvania Continental infantry, artillery, and cavalry, appeared before Ward's blockhouse. Despite the disparity in numbers and quality of troops, Wayne's force was bloodily repulsed, losing nearly seventy killed and wounded in the attempted takeover.[12]

Despite the spectacular and altogether unlikely victory, the damage done to the blockhouse and the proximity of even more Continentals led to the evacuation of Bull's Ferry over the next few weeks.[13] At the same time, Cuyler and Ward began to feud openly, with the former accusing the latter, probably not without reason, of circumventing their contract and selling wood clandestinely on the black market in New York City. The result was an end to the wood contract and a schism in the unit. Some officers and men started anew under Cuyler at Smithtown, Long Island, while the remainder stayed with Ward to establish a new post at Bergen Point.[14]

For the next eight months, Ward's corps continued to grow in size and scope while providing wood to the New York garrison, conducting raids into the New Jersey countryside, and fending off numerous attacks from Continentals and militia alike. Seeing better prospects to the north, both in terms of wood and neighborhoods to raid, Ward determined to set up a new base of operations. At first, the circumstances seemed benign, as reported in the May 9, 1781, edition of the Chatham *New Jersey Journal*: "We hear that banditti of refugees, that were at Bergen-Point, evacuated it last Sunday." The fortification at Bergen Point had indeed been evacuated. Ward boarded his men on the numerous armed and unarmed vessels that made up his naval force and brought them over to New York City before heading for their next destination: Fort Lee.

Since Fort Lee's evacuation in 1776, troops had been stationed there for only a few days at a time while operations took place nearby, such as the British "grand forage" in September/October 1778 and George Washington's similar errand in the county two years later. The northern parts of Bergen County had seen less of the war since the post at Bull's Ferry had been evacuated. Once winter quarters for the army had been established, no Continental troops were ever closer than Pompton, the Clove, and Morristown, and those left once the spring campaign season approached. The duties of the militia and state troops (militia embodied for a fixed period of three, six, nine, or twelve months, as opposed to the one month allowed by law) were primarily to prevent the residents from selling goods to the British, a practice then known as "London Trading."[15] Bergen County had more than its share of Loyalists and British sympathizers living within its borders. In 1776 it had raised an entire battalion of troops for Cortland Skinner's New Jersey Volunteers, and in July 1777 the state's governor, William Livingston, referred to it as the "almost totally revolted County of Bergen."[16] Despite scores of property confiscations by the state, families of Loyalists serving with the British still permeated the countryside, providing intelligence and hiding any number of British spies, Continental army deserters, and escaped prisoners. Ardent Patriot militiamen served under Colonel Theunis Dey of Preakness, at the western edge of the county. Colonel Dey was fully aware of the fractured nature of the county: his daughter Jane was married to Abraham Van Buskirk of Teaneck, the lieutenant colonel commandant of the Fourth Battalion, New Jersey Volunteers.

To date, the militia had a mixed record. During the British invasion of 1776 and Sir Henry Clinton's grand forage of 1777, they remained spectators rather than defenders of the state. However, as the war progressed, the militia improved in effectiveness and spirit, principally from having gained experience as levies (drafts from the militia used to serve temporarily in Continental regiments) or in the state troops. In all previous actions in the war, the militia had served only in scattered detachments, never as a whole regiment.[17]

On May 14, 1781, Captain John Pray of the First Massachusetts Regiment, commanding a detachment at Nyack, up the Hudson River in Orange County, reported to his superior, Brigadier General John Paterson, that "15 Saile of Shiping and twenty flat bottom boats lays off of Fort Lee." Pray initially worried that the Dobb's Ferry blockhouse was the object of this flotilla, but by midnight he further reported that the Refugees were establishing a post, with artillery, at Fort Lee.[18]

Indeed, Ward's force had arrived in a small fleet a few miles below Fort Lee. Ward disembarked at least a part of his men, to the number of 140, and marched the three or four miles north to Fort Lee.[19] After scouring the English Neighbourhood, the Refugees took possession of the ground that had been Fort Lee some four and a half years before and started constructing a blockhouse similar to the ones they had built at Bull's Ferry and Bergen Point. Before Ward's men could start work, however, a hundred Bergen County militiamen occupied an unidentified stone house and engaged the Refugees until forced to retreat.[20]

One of two men made prisoner in this action on May 14 was John Devoe, an eighteen-year-old militiaman serving in Captain Samuel Demarest's company and resident of the town of Hackensack. He had entered militia service on April 1, 1781, and Fort Lee was his first taste of action. John Brower, a young boy at the time and a friend of Devoe, later recalled the militiaman's harrowing experience that May afternoon, describing in detail how he was sabered by a cavalry sword, clubbed with a musket in the head and ribs, bayoneted, and grazed with a musket ball. Left for dead, he was taken prisoner by the Refugees and imprisoned briefly in New York City.[21] Devoe would be exchanged and returned home on May 26, 1781, where for the next two months he would recuperate while lamenting the loss of his musket and cartridge box to the enemy.[22]

Retiring to the Liberty Pole (modern Englewood), the militia licked its wounds but did not disperse for home; instead, the alarm call went out across the county. Scores of men from more than ten companies, led by Colonel Theunis Dey himself, rushed to renew the fight. Reinforced to a strength of some 400 militia and state troops, Colonel Dey's men advanced upon the Loyalists on May 15. Harmon Blauvelt of Harrington Township, a militiaman in Captain Abraham Haring's company, was one of those in the attack on that "nest of Tories."[23] The results, however, were little different than on the day before. Private Cornelius H. Post of Franklin recalled joining the regiment at Tenafly, after which they attacked the Refugees but were repulsed.[24] Sergeant Peter Van Allen of Franklin "recollects of being in an engagement with the British & Refugees at Fort Lee on the Hudson River and at which time his cousin John Van Allen, a member of the same company, was wounded."[25] The Loyalist press in New York City gloated that "the enemy . . . faced to the right about, and fled in great confusion."[26]

The attacks, although not successful, certainly set back the Refugees' timetable; as noted by Thomas Ward himself, the continuous skirmishing had prevented their efforts to fortify the site.[27] With so many enemies nearby, Ward took the precaution of keeping his men on the river overnight. Indeed, one Continental officer noted, "They are amphibious animals, keep on board Their craft by night and come on shore every morning with great precaution."[28] This situation guided the strategy for yet one more attack by the militia.

May 18 dawned very warm. Thomas Ward's men had been mostly left alone the past two days, and they had no reason to believe this day would be any different. The militia had been defeated twice that week, and it was unlikely they would risk another encounter. Unbeknownst to the Refugees, their unfinished works had been occupied during the night by Colonel Dey's militia, who then lay in ambush for them. It was a moment of exultation for the militia. John H. Post of Franklin, a militiaman in Captain Peter Ward's company, happily recalled that he "and his Brother in law John Ackerman were the first that entered the fort at fort Lee."[29] Lieutenant (or Captain) James Hamilton, an Ulster County Loyalist, led an advance guard of about ten men from the ferry landing at the base of the cliffs through a cut up the steep incline toward the unfinished works.[30] When almost within the works, Lieutenant Hamilton and one of his men were instantly captured as the militia rose up from their hiding spots.[31]

Recovering from their surprise, the remainder of the Refugees' advance guard fired and scampered back down the hill. Seeing the militia in hot pursuit of his men, Captain George Harden, on the shoreline, "ordered a field piece to be placed in such a position which, with the fire from a gun boat, and the musquetry, obliged them to return up the hill. Captain Harden advanced thro' a valley that led up the hill, and gained the right flank of the enemy, whom he instantly charged, and obliged to quit the works they were in possession of, retreating in great confusion, and leaving behind them 1 man killed and 1 wounded; they also took off with them several who were badly wounded; Captain Harden pursued the enemy to the heights of the English Neighbourhood, but was not able to come up with them."[32] The fighting was spirited and bloody. Private Daniel Banta of Captain John Outwater's company "was wounded by a musket ball which passed through both his thighs. He laid under the surgeons hands from the 18th May 1781 Until some time in Sept. following when he became able to help himself."[33] Paul Rutan, a militiaman in Captain John Willis's company, was also shot through both thighs. Daniel Van Horn, seeing the stricken Rutan, pulled him to safety inside the unfinished blockhouse. Abraham Vanderbeck, another comrade of Rutan's, placed him on a wood sled, which drew him off the battlefield. John H. Post, who had boasted of being first into the blockhouse, saw the wounded Rutan several days later at the home of his father, some eighteen miles from Fort Lee.

Although the fighting between the militia and the Refugees was at an end, both sides were about to turn this engagement into a much bigger and much bloodier fight. George Washington, from his headquarters at New Windsor, New York, sent instructions across the Hudson to Colonel Alexander Scammell, in command of a newly formed battalion of Continental light infantry. Scammell was to cross to the west side of the Hudson, gather up any New York and New Jersey militia he found, ascertain the strength of the Refugee post, and attack it as quickly as possible, "The sooner it is done the better, as the enemy, if they are fortifying will be every day stronger." Washington closed his orders by cautioning Scammell "to attempt nothing which may have the appearance of rashness and to guard well against being drawn into an ambuscade or being intercepted by a sudden reen-forcement from York Island."[34] Scammell's force was delayed at every turn, first in crossing the river and then in finding provisions, which eventually had to be drawn from Stony Point. At the same time, Captain Jonathan Lawrence, commanding a company of New York State levies, announced to Washington that he had visited Fort Lee on the May 15, after the second action, on behalf of Colonel Dey to negotiate an exchange of prisoners and to attend to the militia's wounded. Lawrence told Washington that he had conversed with Thomas Ward himself and that the latter was open to the idea of not only returning to the allegiance of the United States but also bringing all his men with him![35] Washington replied to Lawrence that he could not "place much confidence" in Ward's sincerity and surmised that the offer to switch allegiance again was a ruse.[36]

Thunderstorms rolled into the area by late afternoon on May 21 and continued until near midnight while Loyalist spies reported to Sir Henry Clinton on the movements of Scammell's light infantry toward Fort Lee. The danger prompted Clinton to some uncharacteristically quick action, moving troops and sending his adjutant general, Major Oliver DeLancey Jr., to Fort Lee to meet with Ward and ascertain the situation. This meeting would be the turning point of the enterprise, as Clinton ordered some two thousand British, Hessian, and Provincial troops in motion to support the Refugees and engage any force sent by Scammell. DeLancey, however, returned and reported to Clinton that the Refugees were not "inclined" to fortify themselves, prompting the commander in chief to order the post abandoned.[37] Ward reluctantly ordered his men to embark. They returned to Bergen Point to establish a new post, but not without much bitterness. People who had been on the scene when DeLancey arrived reported, "It appears that the order was very unexpected to Ward & his men, some of who flew into a violent passion and broke their Guns. . . . Various rumors (as is usual on such occasions) prevailed amongst them. One was that a body of french Forces had landed on the back of Long Island."[38]

Scammell, unaware of what was transpiring at Fort Lee, prepared his 400 light infantry for battle and moved to attack as the Refugees evacuated. At this point, nature intervened, preventing a further loss of life. Scammell reported to Washington that a "violent storm of rain" had rendered his men's weapons inoperative and forced him to retire to Closter. One of Scammell's officers then scouted Fort Lee and reported on the evacuation of the enemy force. Scammell's light infantry returned over the New York border to await developments. After three days of drying out, Scammell started his march toward Fort Lee once more, but scouts reported the Refugees had departed. The light infantry would keep an eye on the progress down river of the Refugee fleet, but the Battles of Fort Lee were over.[39]

A week of violence in Bergen County was at an end. After almost five years of experience in combat and hardship, Americans on both sides of the conflict had accepted, and in some cases become proficient in, the art of war. By 1781, some Patriot inhabitants of Bergen County had served as levies or otherwise in the Continental army; others had served for extended periods in the state troops. In either case, they had gained experience as soldiers, and they expected to fight at this point. They were men like Peter S. Van Orden of Schraalenburgh, who in upstate New York in October 1780 had "remained on the field all night [and] at break of day marched in pursuit of the enemy Forded the River and marched about twenty eight miles, hungry, wet, and weary, received about half a ration at Fort Herkimer that night and in the morning early marched in pursuit of the enemy in the wilderness, for about three days and a half without any sustenance except Roots, then returned with the capture of only one Indian."[40] The hard fighting led many militiamen to state inaccurately fifty years after the fact that they had actually won these battles. New Jersey's Patriot press could nevertheless report "the militia in that quarter [Bergen County] not liking such a Band of thieves for their neighbours, turned out with the spirit, and prevented them from erecting any works."[41]

For the Loyalists, there were a number of officers and men with recent service in the Provincial Forces. Mathew Benson served under David Babcock in the Provincial King's Orange Rangers and again under Thomas Ward.[42] James Hamilton had served a campaign as a lieutenant in the Guides & Pioneers. Ward's artillery was directed by Captains Anthony Hollingshead and Frederick Hauser, former lieutenant in the New Jersey Volunteers and warrant captain in the Loyal Foresters, respectively.[43] Indeed, Thomas Ward himself was recruiting men for a Provincial company at the time of the Fort Lee battles.[44] Their experience in regular units, the confidence in battle gained by defeating Anthony Wayne's Continentals in 1780, and a sense of pure resentment toward their foes brought on by property confiscations, fines, and prosecutions over the previous six years combined to make a motivated, if irregular, force commanded by a deserter from the Continental army. All circumstances conspired atop the Palisades of Fort Lee for a little over a week in 1781 to provide another chapter in America's first civil war.

NOTES

1. For an excellent account of Bergen County as it appeared at the start of the American Revolution, see Adrian Leiby's *The Revolutionary War in the Hackensack Valley: The Jersey Dutch and the Neutral Ground, 1775–1783* (New Brunswick, NJ: Rutgers University Press, 1962).

2. The story of New York City and environs during the war is well covered in Ruma Chopra's *Unnatural Rebellion: Loyalists in New York City during the Revolution* (Charlottesville: University of Virginia Press, 2011).

3. Washington laid the facts before his generals and solicited their advice while encamped at Steenrapie; they unanimously concurred that no attempt should be made to attack the city. George Washington, Council of War, Camp at Steenrapie, September 6, 1780, George Washington Papers, Series 4, General Correspondence, 26 August 1780–16 September 16, 1780, Library of Congress (hereafter cited as LOC).

4. "Governor Tryon's Reveries submitted to Sir Henry Clinton concerning the Embodying Loyalists etc." Enclosed in William Tryon to Sir Henry Clinton, June 30, 1779, Colonial Office, class 5, vol. 1109, fol. 160, National Archives, Great Britain (hereafter cited as TNA).

5. Recruiting notice of the Loyal Refugee Volunteers, New York, April 19, 1780, *Royal Gazette* (New York), April 22, 1780.

6. Thomas Ward to Lieutenant Colonel Oliver DeLancey Jr., December 1781, Sir Henry Clinton Papers, vol. 188, item 39, William L. Clements Library, University of Michigan, Ann Arbor (hereafter cited as CL). Thomas Ward and others occasionally passed to the New Jersey side of the Hudson for wood, such as on March 9, 1780, when Ward and nineteen other Refugees passed over to Weehawken. James Pattison Day Book, Royal Artillery Museum Library, Woolwich, Great Britain.

7. Major General James Pattison to Major Charles Lumm, New York, April 30, 1780, in *Collections of the New-York Historical Society for the Year 1875* (New York: Printed for the Society, 1876), 391.

8. Memorial of Thomas Ward to the Commissioners for American Claims, London, December 13, 1784, Audit Office, class 13, vol. 67, fols. 500–502, TNA.

9. Muster Roll of Captain John Santford's Company, Malcom's Additional Regiment, taken to September 1, 1777, in National Archives and Records Administration (NARA) microfilm publication M246, *Revolutionary War Rolls, 1775–1783* (Washington, DC: National Archives and Records Service, General Services Administration, 1980), reel 126, no. 140–1.

10. Memorial of Thomas Ward to unknown, undated, Clinton Papers, 232:16, CL.

11. Lieutenant William Fyers, a British sub-engineer, described the post as a "substantial, two story Blockhouse with two four Pounders in the upper story—a strong Stockade which runs, in right lines, from the Right and Left of the Blockhouse, to the edge of the Precipice, and, an Abbatis surrounding the whole at

the distance of nearly, sixty feet from the Stockade, which is form'd of Stakes about nine feet high, & eight or nine Inches in diameter, with Creneaux and a Banquette." Fyers to Sir Henry Clinton, July 11, 1780, Clinton Papers, III:4, CL.

12. Lieutenant Colonel Josiah Harmar of the Sixth Pennsylvania Regiment, serving under Wayne, wrote of the affair: "The Block House was commanded by a Refugee Captain & mann'd with about Seventy Negros, Tories & Vagabonds— Their defence was desperate, and we were obliged disgracefully to retire from this trifling Object with the Loss of Three Officers & Sixty six brave Soldiers kill'd & wounded; we ought certainly to have carried it at all Events." One of the most common period assertions was that the garrison under Ward consisted of only 70 men; the return made out by Ward of those in the battle was 110 officers and men. Regardless, the garrison was still outnumbered by a ratio of 10 to 1. Josiah Harmar Papers, Lt. Col. Josiah Harmar's Journal, No. 1, 11 November 1778 to 2 September 1780, pp. 113–114, CL.

13. *New Jersey Gazette* (Trenton), August 16, 1780.

14. Cuyler to Ward et al., New York, August 21, 1780, Clinton Papers, 118:11, CL.

15. A typical incident was described by militiaman Abraham Vanderbeck of Hackensack: "he being ordered out on the Bank of the Hackensack river to watch and detect London traders at which place he discovered a Boat in the said river of which he Informed his Capt when he the deponent, his captain and another of his comrades went with all speed to Capture the same on coming to it, the men had deserted and left the Boat containing twelve live sheep which they took as a prize which Boat with the sheep they towed up the said river and had the prize condemned before Jacob Terhune Justice of the peace." Pension application of Abraham Vanderbeck, October 12, 1833, no. S1130, in National Archives and Records Administration (NARA) microfilm publication M804, *Revolutionary War Pension and Bounty-Land-Warrant Application Files* (Washington, DC: National Archives and Records Service, General Services Administration, 1974), hereafter cited as NARA M804.

16. Livingston to George Washington, Newton, Sussex County, July 11, 1777, George Washington Papers, Series 4, General Correspondence, 30 May 1777–22 July 1777, LOC.

17. An example of the difficulties involved in maintaining troops for duty can be found in Captain John Outwater to Governor William Livingston, ca. 1779, Department of Defense, Adjutant General's Office (Revolutionary War), Numbered Manuscripts, document 22, New Jersey State Archives (hereafter cited as NJSA).

18. Pray to Paterson, Nyack, May 14, 1781, and Pray to Paterson, Dobbs Ferry, May 14, 1781, George Washington Papers, Series 4, General Correspondence, 24 April 1781–15 May 1781, LOC.

19. The total number of Refugees at Fort Lee was typically described as around 200. However, a provision order of the corps for their stay at the fort was listed as 350, while a return of the corps the following week showed just 299 officers and men. Return of Provisions received by John Truesdell, May 19, 1781, Clinton

Papers, 155:48, CL. Provision Return of the Loyal Refugee Volunteers, June 2, 1781, Clinton Papers, 156:46, CL. An unknown number of men certainly would have had to stay on board the ship, which may account for some of the disparity in the numbers guessed at by the militia.

20. *New York Gazette and the Weekly Mercury*, May 21, 1781.

21. Pension application of John Devoe, April 29, 1834, no. W20972, NARA M804.

22. Bills presented to the State of New Jersey by Andrew and John Devoe for the loss of musket and cartridge box, along with lodging, boarding, and medical expenses, April 8, 1783, Department of Defense, Adjutant General's Office (Revolutionary War), Numbered Manuscripts, document 16, NJSA.

23. Pension application of Harmon Blauvelt, June 27, 1833, no. S959, NARA M804.

24. Pension application of Cornelius H. Post, March 25, 1834, no. S29389, NARA M804.

25. Pension application of Peter Van Allen, October 31, 1832, no. S6301, NARA M804.

26. Quoted in William S. Stryker, *Official Register of the Officers and Men of New Jersey in the Revolutionary War* (Trenton: W. T. Nicholson & Company, 1872), 398.

27. Thomas Ward petition, 1782, Clinton Papers, 196:35, CL.

28. Alexander Scammell to George Washington, Clarkstown, May 24, 1781, George Washington Papers, Series 4, General Correspondence, 16 May 1781–24 June 1781, LOC.

29. Pension application of John H. Post, 1844, no. W866, NARA M804.

30. Memorial of James Hamilton to Lieutenant Governor John Wentworth, November 5, 1792, RG 20A, vol. 23, no. 1792–47, Nova Scotia Archives and Records Management, Halifax.

31. Pension application of George G. Ryerson, October 31, 1832, no. S1098, NARA M804.

32. *New York Gazette and the Weekly Mercury*, May 21, 1781.

33. Pension application of Daniel Banta, October 4, 1832, no. S2090, NARA M804.

34. Washington to Scammell, New Windsor, May 17, 1781, George Washington Papers, Series 4, General Correspondence, 16 May 1781–24 June 1781, LOC.

35. Lawrence to Washington, Rockland, May 16, 1781, ibid.

36. Washington to Lawrence, New Windsor, May 17, 1781, ibid.

37. Frederick Mackenzie. *The Diary of Frederick Mackenzie*, 2 vols. (Cambridge, MA: Harvard University Press, 1930), 2:526–527.

38. Scammell to Washington, Clarkstown, May 24, 1781, George Washington Papers, Series 4, General Correspondence, 16 May 1781–24 June 1781, LOC.

39. Ibid.

40. Pension application of Peter S. Van Orden, November 28, 1832, no. S11160, NARA M804.

41. *New Jersey Journal* (Chatham), May 30, 1781.

42. Mathew Benson was from Bergen County, New Jersey, and had joined the King's Orange Rangers the day Cornwallis invaded New Jersey in 1776. Babcock was from just over the border in Orange County, New York, and had served as a lieutenant in the same corps. Both had left the Rangers by 1778 and were with Thomas Ward by the time of Wayne's attack on Bull's Ferry in 1780. Muster Roll of Captain Lawrence Van Buskirk's Company, King's Orange Rangers, Paulus Hook, August 28, 1777, British Military and Naval Records (RG 8, "C" Series), vol. 1908, Library and Archives Canada, Ottawa (hereafter cited as LAC). Petition of Mathew Benson to Peter Russell, Kingston, May 22, 1798, Land Petitions of Upper Canada, "B" Miscellaneous, 1796–1799 (RG 1, L 3), vol. 66, no. 20, LAC. Memorial of David Babcock to the Commissioners for American Claims, Shelburne, 1786, Audit Office, class 13, vol. 25, fols. 28–29, TNA.

43. Return of officers in the New Jersey Volunteers, February 24, 1778, Miscellaneous Loyalist Muster Rolls, 1778–1782, a collection of photostat copies donated by Dr. Carlos E. Godfrey, accession no. 5066, LOC. Hauser to Sir Guy Carleton, New York, May 12, 1782, Headquarters Papers of the British Army in America, Public Record Office, 30/55/4586, TNA.

44. *Royal Gazette* (New York), May 16, 1781.

5

Rochambeau in New Jersey

The Good French Ally

ROBERT A. SELIG

Ever since the fall of 1776, when English- and German-speaking Continental army troops had hurried across the state toward Trenton and Philadelphia, pursued by English- and German-speaking crown forces, with a smattering of Welsh and Gaelic thrown in for good measure, the citizens of New Jersey had harbored multitudes of more or less friendly armed forces from the Old and New Worlds in their midst. Depending on their political convictions, religious or ethnic backgrounds, and reasons for emigrating to New Jersey, not to mention the need to survive in the vagaries of war, New Jerseyans had somehow found a way to coexist with these troops. Yet when French forces under Jean-Baptiste Donatien de Vimeur, comte de Rochambeau, entered New Jersey in the early morning hours of August 26, 1781, on today's Route 202, the Dutch settlers of Bergen County and, subsequently, their fellow citizens along the route the French took across the state to Trenton were faced with a new and doubly uncomfortable situation.[1] By the summer of 1781, five years of often painful experience had taught them to expect the worst from soldiers marching toward their homes, be they English, Hessian, or Continental. No one knew how the French forces would behave, especially since they had been the colonists' enemies in the French and Indian War (1754–1763) just two decades earlier. The few New Jerseyans who had ever met a French soldier had most likely eyed him down the barrel of a musket in upstate New York or in Canada. The same held true, at least figuratively, for officers among the French forces, who were aware of the May 1754 ambush on a small French

Canadian force by a company of Virginia militia led by a twenty-four-year-old George Washington, an action that precipitated the war with England and France's eventual loss of Canada.[2] Not surprisingly, even though the United States and France had signed treaties of friendship and alliance in February 1778, most Americans for a variety of political, cultural, historical, religious, or very personal reasons tended to look upon their French ally as a long-time enemy rather than a new friend.[3]

During the French and Indian War, the New Jersey General Assembly had resolved in early 1755 to raise and equip a battalion of five hundred men, called the New Jersey Regiment (the "Jersey Blues"), to counter the French threat. Until the fall of 1760, the regiment fought against French forces under Louis-Joseph de Montcalm-Gozon, marquis de Saint-Veran, in upstate New York around Lake George and at Fort Frontenac on Lake Ontario. Hundreds of them were captured as early as August 1756 and in the summer of 1757.[4] The tribulations of these New Jersey prisoners of war in Canada and among the Indians not only stood in a long tradition of captivity narratives but were also still very much alive in the memories of those who had lived through the conflict, and the barracks built at Burlington, Trenton, New Brunswick, Amboy, and Elizabethtown were only some of the most substantial reminders of the war.[5]

The French and Indian War had been over for only thirteen years when the colonies declared their independence in 1776. As the political situation moved toward a break with the mother country in the spring of that year, the leadership of the independence movement was acutely aware that the successful outcome of a war to achieve independence would depend on French support. Consequently, the Declaration of Independence was addressed not so much to the American people, many of whom already considered themselves to be independent and had already been shooting at British soldiers for a while, or to King George, who did not need to be informed that his colonies wanted to break away.[6] Although the document signed by the members of the Second Continental Congress was ostensibly "submitted to a candid world," it was first and foremost addressed to France and, to a lesser degree, to Spain and the rest of Europe. The settlers had started their war against Britain with empty coffers and without enough modern arms, supplies, or expertise to sustain that fight. Rebel leaders were well aware of their need for outside assistance and of the only places where that assistance could come from: the Bourbon kings Louis XVI of France (1754/74–1793) and Carlos III of Spain (1716/59–1788). But these monarchs would respond—clandestinely but positively—to the request for material support only if the colonists could succeed in portraying themselves as an independent nation fighting a common foe. Once the rebellion proved its viability, foreign support could be continued openly and become official with the acknowledgment of the United States as new member of the family of nations. Virtually all members of Congress shared the conviction that outside support hinged on Congress's ability to portray the rebellion as a war between two nations.[7]

In January 1776, Thomas Paine underlined the importance of that tactic in *Common Sense*: "Nothing can settle our affairs so expeditiously as an open and determined declaration for independence. . . . [neither] France or Spain will give us any kind of assistance . . . while we profess ourselves the subjects of Britain. . . . The custom of all courts is against us, and will be so, until, by an independence, we take rank with other nations."[8] Even John Adams, who privately wrote off Catholicism as a religion for the "simple and ignorant," admitted the need for treaties with France and Spain because the United States was "distressed for want of artillery, arms, ammunition, clothing."[9] At the same time, James Warren spoke for the vast majority of his fellow New Englanders when he wrote to Adams on May 8, 1776, that "I do not want a French army here, but I want to have one employed against Britain, and I doubt whether that will ever be done, till you make a more explicit declaration of Independence."[10]

Throughout the early 1770s France had been closely watching developments in the British colonies and was ready to assist the Americans. Between mid-March and early April 1775 a secret plan to aid the Americans was drawn up in Versailles. When news of Lexington and Concord reached Paris, the government of His Most Christian Majesty became the first foreign power to provide aid and support to the fledgling United States. In December 1775, Julien-Alexandre Achard de Bonvouloir, the emissary of the French foreign minister, Charles Gravier, comte de Vergennes, arrived in Philadelphia with instructions to establish semi-official relations and to evaluate the situation in the colonies. "They are more powerful than we could have thought, beyond imagination powerful," Bonvouloir reported back to Versailles. "Nothing shocks or frightens them, you can count on that. Independency is a certainty for 1776; there will be no drawing back."[11] Bonvouloir's enthusiastic report resulted in a major shift in French policy toward the rebels, which became obvious in a Council of State meeting on March 12, 1776, when Vergennes argued for providing arms to the Americans. The king agreed and decided on April 22, 1776, not only to provide funding to the American rebels but also to increase his country's naval budget to counter any hostile (British) reaction to France's support for the Americans.[12]

In an effort to hide France's involvement in the American rebellion and to prepare France for the possibility of war with Britain, Vergennes co-opted the playwright Pierre Augustin Caron de Beaumarchais, author of *The Barber of Seville*, into his service. As early as the fall of 1775, Beaumarchais had approached Vergennes with a plan to support the American rebels. In January 1776, Vergennes submitted the proposal to Louis XVI, informing him that the plan was "not so much to terminate the war between America and England, as to sustain and keep it alive to the detriment of the English, our natural and pronounced enemies."[13] After some hesitation, the king agreed to let Beaumarchais act as the secret agent of the crown.[14] Following the decision of April 22, 1776, military supplies were made available to Beaumarchais, who set up the trading company Roderigue Hortalez & Co. as a front to channel aid to the Americans. On May 2, 1776, the crown released one million livres to Beaumarchais to purchase supplies for the rebels, and Spain immediately matched the amount.[15] With this covert backing and financial support of the Spanish and French governments, Beaumarchais's ships carried much-needed supplies to the Americans, frequently via the Dutch island of St. Eustatius in the Caribbean.[16] By December 1777, France had dispatched clothing for 30,000 men, 4,000 tents, 30,000 muskets with bayonets, over 100 tons of gunpowder, 194 four-pound cannons and gun carriages, 27 mortars, almost 13,000 shells, and upward of 50,000 round shot.[17]

The Continental army put Beaumarchais's supplies to good use. The capture of General John Burgoyne and his army on October 17, 1777, by General Horatio Gates at Saratoga was a major turning point in the American War of Independence. It was won by American soldiers, even if 90 percent of the gunpowder they expended had been supplied by and paid for by France and was used in the French pattern muskets (model of

1763–1766) that had become standard in the Continental army. The victory at Saratoga proved to the French that the American rebellion could be sustained with a possibility of success. News of Burgoyne's surrender reached Paris on the evening of December 4, 1777; on December 17, Vergennes promised to recognize the independence of the thirteen colonies, with or without Spanish support. On January 30, 1778, the king authorized Conrad Alexandre Gérard de Rayneval, the secretary of the Council of State, to sign the Treaty of Amity and Commerce and a secret Treaty of Alliance on his behalf. Gérard carried out the order on February 6, 1778, while Silas Deane, Benjamin Franklin, and Arthur Lee signed for the United States. By these treaties, France offered "to maintain . . . the liberty, sovereignty, and independence" of the United States in case of war between that country and Great Britain. It would fight on until the independence of the United States was guaranteed in a peace treaty. The United States promised not to "conclude either truce or peace with Great Britain without the formal consent of the other first obtained."[18]

In 1776, both sides had been all too aware of the historical and cultural obstacles built up during decades of hostilities to assume an unqualified welcoming of French forces in the United States.[19] In spite of the crucial assistance after 1776, that assessment had changed but little by the time France acknowledged the independence of the United States in 1778. Yet the political and military outcome of the treaties of 1778—the first, indispensable diplomatic success of the new nation on its path to join the family of nations—depended to a large degree on changing the attitudes of the citizens of the nascent United States toward their erstwhile enemy. Would average Americans be able and willing to forget about the past and work with their new ally toward a common goal?

In 1778, France was hoping for a short war, and so long as no French forces were stationed on the mainland, any discussion of the potential risks was hypothetical. However, Sir Henry Clinton's successful foray into Georgia and South Carolina, combined with the failed sieges of Newport and Savannah in 1778 and 1779, dashed all hopes of a quick victory for the Franco-American alliance. Up until the summer of 1779, even Washington had had reservations about French ground forces in America. But in the fall of 1779, France and America needed a new strategy, and the decision in January 1780 to dispatch some 5,000 ground forces under the comte de

Rochambeau to be stationed on the American mainland formed the core of this new plan. On September 16, 1779, French minister Anne-César, chevalier de la Luzerne, met with Washington at West Point, New York, to discuss strategy for 1780. With an eye toward the deteriorating military situation in the South, he wondered "whether in case the Court of France should find it convenient to send directly from France a Squadron and a few Regiments attached to it, to act in conjunction with us in this quarter, it would be agreeable to the United States." Washington's reply, as recorded by Alexander Hamilton, indicated that the general "thought it would be very advancive of the common Cause." Washington repeated his views in a letter to the marquis de Lafayette of September 30, 1779, in which he expressed his hope that Lafayette would soon return to America either in his capacity as major general in the Continental army or as "an Officer at the head of a Corps of gallant French." Based on Luzerne's report of the September 16 meeting and an excerpt of Washington's letter to Lafayette, which the young Frenchman had sent to Vergennes on January 25, 1780, Vergennes decided that the time had come to send French ground forces to the New World.[20]

The initial welcome of Rochambeau's forces in Newport, Rhode Island, in July 1780 showed that the seventeen years since the Peace of Paris in 1763 had not been enough time to eradicate old prejudices rooted in a long tradition of Puritan anti-Catholicism, a century of British propaganda, accounts of émigré French Protestants (Huguenots), and memories of the battlefields of Canada.[21] Artillery lieutenant Jean-François Louis, comte de Clermont-Crèvecœur, believed that "the local people, little disposed in our favor, would have preferred, at that moment, I think, to see their enemies arrive rather than their allies." He thought the British were to blame. They "had made the French seem odious to the Americans . . . saying that we were dwarfs, pale, ugly, specimens who lived exclusively on frogs and snails."[22] Overcoming such prejudices would not be easy. In May 1779, more than a year after the signing of the Franco-American alliance, James Dana, pastor of the Congregational church of Wallingford, Connecticut, reminded the state's legislators that "the preservation of our religion depends on the continuance of a free government. Let our allies have their eyes open on the blessings of such a government, and they will at once renounce their superstition. On the other hand, should we lose our freedom this will prepare the way to the introduction of popery."[23]

Interpersonal contacts between French and Americans would be needed to whittle away these notions that tied Catholicism to absolutism, intolerance, and tyranny. The landing of Rochambeau's forces in Rhode Island in July 1780 began a process of "getting to know" one another that was repeated over and over again in the summer of 1781 in the villages along the French routes across New Jersey.

Even if, according to William de Deux-Ponts (1754–1807), *colonel-en-seconde* of his regiment, the French did not receive in Rhode Island "that reception on landing which we expected and which we ought to have had,"[24] all accounts by French officers emphasize the friendly response in New Jersey. Baron Luwig von Closen, a captain in the German Royal Deux-Ponts Regiment and one of Rochambeau's aides-de-camp, wrote that the "Jerseys, where we are now (beautiful country!) abound in all kinds of produce. The inhabitants (who are of Dutch origin) have kept it neat and have retained their gentle and peaceful customs, and have been very friendly towards the army. It is a land of milk and honey, with game, fish, vegetables, poultry, etc. after leaving New York State, where misery is written on the brows of the inhabitants, the affluence in the state of the Jerseys seems to be much greater."[25] Similarly, the abbé Claude Robin recorded upon arrival in Princeton on September 1, 1781: "The inhabitants, for the most part of Alsacian and Dutch descent, are gay, easy and engaging in their manners, and resemble the happy region they inhabit. Provisions are brought into our camp from all quarters; and those that bring them are commonly wealthy people."[26] Robin, like all travelers, commented about the wealth of New Jersey, a country that "abounds with orchards, fields of wheat, rye, barley, indian corn, and flourishing woods." Marie François Joseph Maxime baron Cromot du Bourg, Closen's fellow aide-de-camp, concurred upon entering New Jersey on August 26: "This is an open and well cultivated country, inhabited by Dutch people who are almost all quite rich. We arrived in good season, and the camps being set and the troops arrived, I thought I could do no better than to go to Totowa to see a cataract."[27] The Swede Axel von Fersen, another aide-de-camp to Rochambeau, wrote: "We crossed *Jersey*, which is one of the finest and most highly cultivated provinces of America."[28]

Accounts detailing the experiences of enlisted men during the campaign are extremely rare—only three are known to exist—yet their observations of life in wartime New Jersey provide the indispensable counterbalance to the descriptions recorded by their noble officers. One account, kept by André Amblard of the Saintonge regiment of infantry, contains few details about the march itself, though Amblard claimed, like his superiors, that "the fertility and beauty of that province causes it to be called the garden of America."[29] A more detailed account is that of Georg Daniel Flohr, an enlisted man in the Deutsche Königlich-Französische Infanterie-Regiment von Zweybrücken or Royal Deux-Ponts Regiment.[30] Upon entering New Jersey, he too noted that "this region is heavily settled by Dutch, but one also meets here and there a German already." A few days later he described Whippany as "a small town in the mountains in a beautiful area; there we had a rest day and again numerous visits from the inhabitants." Somerset was but "a little town in the plains and completely surrounded by fruit trees, a large number of them." In this case, "little town" means seven or eight houses, as opposed to the thirty houses of Whippany, which Cromot du Bourg called "quite a large place."[31]

All of these accounts indicate that French visitors believed that New Jersey was inhabited by either Dutch or Germans rather than Englishmen, that locals were remarkably friendly toward the troops, and that the state had achieved a high level of agricultural development and wealth. One reason for this perception was that about one-fourth of Rochambeau's men, the Royal Deux-Ponts and the volontaires étrangers de Lauzun (better known as Lauzun's Legion), were German or German-speaking troops from the Palatinate and along the Rhine in German-speaking Alsace and Lorraine.[32] Shared ethnicity colored the troops' reception. The closer they approached to Philadelphia, the more Germans they met and the friendlier their relations became with the locals, many of whom were anxious to learn news from back home, as evidenced by the frequent and "numerous visits from the inhabitants."[33] This welcoming reception was not without its downside; the perceived relative wealth and absence of class distinctions in the Middle Colonies seems to have provided a strong inducement for troops to desert. Flohr recorded that as his regiment entered New Jersey from Suffern, they found it a "very pleasant area where everybody would have loved to stay behind." This urge was reinforced whenever a soldier entered a house, because "the inhabitants would ask you if you wanted to stay with them and promised to hide you until the

French were gone!" This remark implies that the locals clearly distinguished between French and non-French allies. But when Flohr provides
an explanation for their behavior, he also shines a light on the havoc four
years of warfare had wreaked in northern New Jersey. On the return march
on September 13, 1782, he wrote that as his regiment set up camp in
Suffern, the women "expected us with great desire" and tried to buy out
the enlistment contracts of the soldiers since "the men were very rare
there. . . . very many had perished and most women had already lost their
husbands."[34] Not surprisingly, on the march across New Jersey toward
Philadelphia in 1781 and back in 1782, desertion among the German soldiers became a serious discipline issue; in Pennsylvania, according to
Flohr, half of the regiment met friends and relatives anxious to help a fellow countryman disappear. Of 316 deserters from Rochambeau's corps
who avoided recapture, 104 came from the Royal Deux-Ponts; another 186
deserters were German-speaking soldiers primarily from Lauzun's Legion.[35]
Shared religion may have played a role in the more favorable welcome of
the German soldiers as well: 269 (22.8 percent) of the men of the Royal
Deux-Ponts in America were Lutheran; another 180 (15.2 percent) were
Reformed Christians, whose presence posed no threat to the souls of the
Dutch (and fellow Reformed) settlers in New Jersey.[36]

The Dutch and German immigrants, like all immigrants before and
after them, had carried not only their culture, history, language, religion,
and prejudices with them into the New World, but also their family histo-
ries, which influenced their response to the French soldiers at their doorsteps. Many of the ancestors of the German settlers in New Jersey had
been forced to flee their homes in the Palatinate in the wake of the
devastation wreaked by the armies of Louis XIV during and after the War
of the Spanish Succession (1701–1714).[37] Shortly thereafter, the War of the
Austrian Succession (1740–1748) caused further devastation along
the Rhine, unleashing a new wave of emigration to the New World.
Survivors kept the memory of these hardships alive. Eight-year-old Eliza
Susan Morton remembered all her life that summer day in August 1781
when French troops stopped near her house in Basking Ridge to refresh
themselves at the spring. Her grandparents could not forget "the cruel
conduct of the French soldiers in Germany. . . . They refused to be
comforted and bewailed with tears the introduction of these allies."[38]

Providing supplies for man and beast occasionally created logistical headaches as the troops marched through communities not even half the size of a single French regiment. Washington and Quartermaster General Timothy Pickering had no funds and were forced to resort to impressment and confiscation almost the moment the Continental army entered the state. State authorities had long since turned to both collecting tax payments in kind and to handing out interest-bearing Continental loan certificates to farmers and merchants in exchange for their goods.[39]

But the French, and by extension their purchasing agents, had specie to pay for the vast amounts of supplies they needed. Strength numbers of armies on the move vary daily, but the ferry bills for the crossing of the Delaware at Trenton on September 2 and 3, 1781, provide firm data for those two days. Hugh Runyan ferried the First Division of the French army and charged Jeremiah Wadsworth for close to 4,800 officers and men (including the wagoners), more than 600 horses, and 399 wagons of all sizes drawn by

TABLE 5.1

Strength of the French Army on the March through New Jersey

Unit	Present NCOs and men	Detached	In hospitals along the route	Total
Bourbonnois	787	178	64	1,029
Soissonnois	896	116	44	1,056
Saintonge	851	115	77	1,043
Royal Deux-Ponts	842	172	29	1,043
Artillerie	239	240	31	510
Mineurs	0	23	0	23
Workers (*ouvriers*)	32	0	4	36
Lauzun's Legion	593	13	4	610
TOTAL	4,240	857	253	5,350

Source: National Archives and Records Administration publication M246, *Revolutionary War Rolls, 1775–1783* (Washington, DC: National Archives), microfilm, roll 136: Returns of the French Army under Count Rochambeau (six returns).

well over 2,000 oxen.[40] That number included almost 200 private wagons of the officers; that is, on the journey across New Jersey to Annapolis between August 25 and September 22, the French wagon train contained only 195 "official" teams with 1,170 oxen to transport supplies and equipment—plus 204 wagons belonging to officers drawn by over 1,200 animals.[41]

Once under way, the columns of soldiers and wagons stretched for miles across the countryside. As a comparison, during the Monmouth campaign of 1778, Sir Henry Clinton informed Lord George Germain on July 5, 1778, that "Under the head of the baggage was comprised, not only the wheeled carriages of every department, but also the bat horses, a train, which as the country admitted but of one route for carriages, extended near twelve miles."[42] Since Clinton's train consisted of about 1,500 wagons at the time, a train of twelve miles, including horses carrying baggage, averages out to about 42 feet per wagon or 125 wagons per mile. On their march through New Jersey, French army columns were not quite that long, but it is not unreasonable to assume a column stretching more than three miles along the road. Since the daily marching distance was between ten and fifteen miles, the troops at the head of the column had covered one quarter of their route before the last wagon left camp two hours later.

On August 18, 1781, the eve of the departure of the allied armies from Phillipsburg, Jeremiah Wadsworth, sole supplier of Rochambeau's forces during their stay in America, forwarded to his assistant David Reynolds an "Account of the Articles necessary to be provided at the different Posts where the french Army will march." The list begins with supplies needed at Suffern, the first stop once the French forces crossed the Hudson from Peekskill. Wadsworth ordered Reynolds to have stored at the campsite "15 Tons Hay, 20 Ton Straw, 230 Bushels of Corn, 5 Cords Wood. . . . If any Calves are to be got let four or five be procured at each Post."[43] Thereafter the same supplies were to be provided at every campsite across New Jersey, that is, at Pompton, Whippany, Bullion's Tavern, Somerset Court House, Princeton, and Trenton. No community along the route was large enough to supply such enormous amounts of foodstuffs; in 1781, the whole state of New Jersey had about 170,000 inhabitants. Trenton, the largest city along the route, had more or less one hundred houses with 500 inhabitants; Princeton, the next largest community, "peut avoir 80 Maison"; Whippany "peut contenir trente maison," that is, thirty houses with maybe 250 inhabitants; and Somerset Court House numbered all of seven or eight houses.[44] Put differently, the French army that camped and grazed across New Jersey with its close to 5,000 officers and men, their servants, horses, and cattle was five times the size of the largest town in the state (Burlington). They left behind roads ruined by deep ruts, devastated meadows, and tons of human and animal waste—but also thousands of gold Louis d'or and silver écus, which literally arrived by the wagonload. When the frigate *Resolue* sailed into Boston on August 25, 1781, it carried more than 400,000 écus worth 6 livres each. "Fourteen wagons hauled by fifty-six oxen and lead horses conveyed the specie" across Connecticut, New York, and New Jersey to Philadelphia.[45]

The importance of the French bullion for the wartime economy cannot be overemphasized. Historian Timothy R. Walton estimates that "on the eve of the American Revolution, about half the coins used in the British North American Colonies, some 4 million Pieces of Eight [21 million livres], were pieces of eight from New Spain and Peru."[46] Rochambeau had brought 2.6 million on board his fleet in July 1780; during the thirty months that French forces remained in the United States, he received nine additional shipments of specie for a total of about 10 million livres, plus a shipment of 1.2 million livres in Spanish pieces of eight that Admiral de Grasse brought with him to Yorktown from Cuba. James A. Lewis estimates that intergovernmental loans between France and Spain during the war, such as Admiral de Grasse's in August 1781, may have reached 10 million livres,[47] which adds up to even more than the 20 million historian Lee Kennett estimated French forces may have spent during their stay in the United States.[48] If loans arranged by private lenders, estimated at between 15 and 20 million livres, are added, Rochambeau's Expédition particulière may well have doubled the amount of specie circulating between Yorktown and Boston. Due to the relatively brief stay of French forces in the state, New Jersey received a smaller share of these funds than states where the troops took winter quarters; but after years of rapidly depreciating Continental currency, the infusion of vast amounts of specie provided a welcome boost to the local economy and was very much appreciated by the local populations everywhere.

John Howland of Newport, Rhode Island, remembered how paper money "ceased to pass, as the French Army under Count Rochambo paid all their expenses which were of a vast amount in specie, or in Bills on

France, and that supplyed the Circulation."[49] On December 31, 1781, John Jeffrey wrote to Jeffrey Whiting from Hartford: "Money is very scarce among the People in General, their daily Prayers are that the French Army may return soon to their part of the World that Money may again circulate amongst them."[50] As the French army was marching through Philadelphia in May 1781, George Nelson recorded the sale of his team "to some French Men for £110 hard money." That was "more Cash than I have been able to realize since the War."[51] A few miles down the road in Wilmington, Samuel Canby expressed his hope in November 1781 for a better future "as there is nothing but Specie now Circulating as a currency."[52]

New Jerseyans benefited from French largesse in multiple ways. Wadsworth's agents purchased supplies from dozens of farmers, who earned additional income for rental of the wagons required to transport these goods to the campsites. On August 17, Wadsworth had informed the French intendant that he needed to "be Monthly supplied with about four hundred thousand Livers—in Specie."[53] The availability of cash to pay for purchases made the French welcome guests not only in New Jersey but all along the route. By the summer of 1781, all faith in the Continental Congress, its money, and its agents was gone. New Jersey merchants had reverted to keeping their accounts in specie denominations rather than Continental dollars—and insisted that their own army too pay with gold and silver. From Pittsburgh, David Duncan assured Colonel John Davis, Assistant Quartermaster General for Pennsylvania, that he could "not do any thing without Money at this Place . . . they say they would not Trust their Father if in Public service, I cant blame them they have been Deceived so often since these times begun."[54]

As wagons broke down or drivers were discharged and returned home, the French army hired replacements both individually and in groups on the march through New Jersey. On September 2, a brigade of seven four-horse teams under Thomas Gardner was hired at 12/ (12 shillings, no pence) per day and driver. Gardner, who served as conductor at 10/8 per day, as well as the other drivers from around Chatham, were paid four days' expenses for their journey to Philadelphia, where they joined the French service on September 1.[55] One of the teams hired was driven by Peter Fisher but owned by Abraham Williamson of Amwell in Hunterdon County, who paid Fischer 3/9 per day, or £22 6/3 for the 119 days he spent in French service.[56]

While the enlisted men slept in tents, officers, especially if they traveled by themselves, took lodging with private citizens. That practice not only spread French specie farther across the state but also multiplied the personal contacts between Frenchmen and Americans. Riding from Suffern to Pompton, Commissaire des Guerres Claude Blanchard "passed the night . . . at the house of a Dutchman, John Van Gelder, who received me very well. The next day, at two, I dined at Whippany. . . . On the same day I came to spend the night at Bullion's tavern [Liberty Corner]."[57] These encounters on a personal level, many times repeated in 1782, when officers frequently stayed with their hosts of the previous year, did much to correct the prejudices that Americans may have had about France and Frenchmen.[58]

By September 3, 1781, the last French forces had crossed the Delaware into Pennsylvania. For the first time in their lives, thousands of New Jerseyans had been in close contact with French troops. Based on what we know about the relatively short interaction— August 25 to September 3, 1781, and September 5 to 14 in 1782—it seems fair to say that in the process their views of the erstwhile enemy changed for the better. As soldiers, the French compared favorably with the often undisciplined Continentals and British troops. As guests, they surprised pleasantly with their polite manners and refined culture. As customers, they and their silver were most welcome wherever they went. Looking back upon his first weeks and months in the New World, Charles Albert, comte de Moré, chevalier de Pontgibaud, identified mutual ignorance at the root of most problems "when Liberty was dawning over the land."[59] Personal encounters corrected many of those prejudices and misconceptions. As they celebrated the surrender of Lord Cornwallis, New Jerseyans had come to appreciate "the advantages already reaped from our alliance with that magnanimous Prince whose troops have had so great a share in executing the important enterprise." It was an "alliance now more firmly cemented by the united effusion of French and American blood."[60] In the crucible of war the old enemy had become a good ally and a friend.

NOTES

1. The historical background of French involvement as well as the marches of French and Continental army forces through New Jersey in 1781 and 1782 are analyzed in detail in Robert A. Selig, *The Washington-Rochambeau Revolutionary Route in the State of New Jersey, 1781–1783: An Historical and Architectural Survey,*

3 vols. (Trenton: New Jersey Historic Trust, Department of Community Affairs, 2006), CD-ROM.

2. See Marcel Trudel, "The Jumonville Affair," *Pennsylvania History* 21 (October 1954): 351–381.

3. An overview of mutual perception (and misperception) is Pierre Aubéry, "Des Stéréotypes ethniques dans l'Amérique du dix-huitième siècle," *Studies in Eighteenth-Century Culture* 6 (1977): 35–58. See also Jean-Jacques Fiechter, "L'Aventure américaine des officiers de Rochambeau vue à travers leurs journaux," in *Images of America in Revolutionary France*, ed. Michèle R. Morris (Washington, DC: Georgetown University Press, 1990), 65–82; Gilbert Bodinier, "Les Officiers du corps expéditionnaire de Rochambeau et la Revolution française," *Revue historique des armées* 3, no. 4 (1976): 139–164; and Robert A. Selig, "Old World Meets New: Franco-American Encounters and the Expédition particulière, 1780–1782," *The Brigade Dispatch: Journal of the Brigade of the American Revolution* 37, no. 1 (Spring 2007): 2–11.

4. See Charles M. B. Gilman, *The Story of the Jersey Blues* (Redbank, NJ: Arlington, 1962). The capture of some 300 of the Jersey Blues in late summer 1757 provided the historical background for James Fenimore Cooper's historical novel *The Last of the Mohicans: A Narrative of 1757*, published in 1826.

5. See Gayle K. Brown, "'Into the Hands of Papists': New England Captives in French Canada and the English Anti-Catholic Tradition, 1689–1763," *Maryland Historian* 21 (1990): 1–11.

6. The colony of Rhode Island and Providence Plantations had declared independence on May 4, 1776, and Virginia had followed suit on May 15, 1776.

7. American elites were under no illusion as to why France and Spain had entered war against Britain. In a letter to Silas Deane written in November 1781, Jeremiah Wadsworth told his fellow Connecticuter, "You seem to have supposed that France and Spain shou'd have entered into the War from no motives but to obtain justice for America—I had never such an Idea, Nations have other motives for making War than releveing the oppressed; and when France & Spain engaged in the present War, they intended to humble a haughty insolent and envious Neighbour, to do this effectually they will, if wise, continue the War so as to keep America interested in every event to its close." Jeremiah Wadsworth Papers, box 10, folder 3, Connecticut Historical Society, Hartford (hereafter cited as CTHS).

8. Thomas Paine, *Common Sense* (Mount Vernon, NY: A. Colish, 1976), 77–78.

9. Edmund C. Burnett, ed., *Letters of Members of the Continental Congress*, 8 vols. (Washington, DC: Carnegie Institution of Washington, 1921–36), 1:468–469. On October 9, 1774, Adams, "led by curiosity," attended a Catholic service at St. Mary's Church in Philadelphia. In a letter to his wife, Abigail, he described the service as "most awful and affecting; the poor wretches fingering their beads, chanting Latin, not a word of which they understood . . . everything [designed] to charm and bewitch the simple and ignorant." Charles Francis

Adams, *Familiar Letters of John Adams and His Wife Abigail, during the Revolution* (New York: Hurd and Houghton, 1876), 46.

10. *Warren-Adams Letters: Being Chiefly a Correspondence among John Adams, Samuel Adams, and James Warren*, vol. 1, *1743–1777* (Boston: Massachusetts Historical Society, 1917), 241.

11. The text of Bonvouloir's correspondence is printed in *New Materials for the History of the American Revolution*, trans. and ed. John Durand (New York: H. Holt, 1889), 1–16.

12. On Vergennes's desire to fight the war against England overseas rather than on the European continent, see Jean-François Labourdette, "Vergennes et la Cour," *Revue d'histoire diplomatique* 101, nos. 3–4 (1987): 289–321; and Orville T. Murphy, "The View from Versailles: Charles Gravier Comte de Vergennes' Perceptions of the American Revolution," in *Diplomacy and Revolution: The Franco-American Alliance of 1778*, ed. Ronald Hoffman and Peter J. Albert (Charlottesville: University Press of Virginia, 1978), 107–149.

13. Quoted in "Beaumarchais, Pierre-Augustin Caron de (1732–1799)," in *The American Revolution 1775–1783: An Encyclopedia*, ed. Richard L. Blanco, 2 vols. (New York: Garland, 1993), 1:107.

14. During a March 12, 1776, meeting the king told Vergennes that he "disliked the precedent of one monarchy giving support to a republican insurrection against a legitimate monarchy." Quoted in General Fonteneau, "La Période française de la guerre d'Indépendance (1776–1780)," *Revue historique des armées* 3, no. 4 (1976): 47–77, 48. Unless otherwise indicated, all translations are mine.

15. Claude Van Tyne, "French Aid before the Alliance of 1778," *American Historical Review* 31 (1925): 20–40; and Neil L. York, "Clandestine Aid and the American Revolutionary War Effort: A Re-Examination," *Military Affairs* 43, no. 1 (February 1979): 26–30.

16. In 1754, St. Eustatius became the first free port/free trade zone in the world. At the height of the American war in 1779, 3,551 vessels entered (and presumably also cleared) St. Eustatius for a total of 7,102; in London in 1777, only 627 entered and 342 cleared the port for a total of 969; in Providence, Rhode Island, the total was 1,661 vessels in 1773. Even if the numbers for St. Eustatius were inflated by the war, they were still multiples of any other harbor in the Western world. R. G. Gilmore, "St. Eustatius: The Nexus for Colonial Caribbean Capitalism," in *The Archaeology of Interdependence: European Involvement in the Development of a Sovereign United States*, ed. Douglas Comer (New York: Springer, 2013), 41–60, 44.

17. See Brian N. Morton and Donald C. Spinelli, *Beaumarchais and the American Revolution* (Lanham, MD: Lexington Books, 2003). Jean Langlet, "Les Ingenieurs de l'Ecole Royale de Génie de Mezières et les armes de la Manufacture de Charleville dans la guerre d'Indépendance américaine," *Revue historique Ardennais* 34 (1999–2000): 197–218, 200, estimates that more than 100,000 muskets and pistols were sent to America.

18. The text of the treaties is available in *Treaties and Other International Acts of the United States of America*, ed. Hunter Miller, vol. 2, *Documents 1–40: 1776–1818* (Washington, DC: Government Printing Office, 1931), 3–27 and 29–34.

19. That general hostility did not extend to individual French volunteers like the marquis de Lafayette, Presle du Portail, or Pierre l'Enfant, the Poles Taduesz Kosciuszko and Casimir Pulaski, or the German Barons Steuben and de Kalb. The individual officers who crossed the Atlantic after 1776 were much needed for the technical assistance and military expertise they brought to the Continental army. Their welcome constituted a big step forward when members of the Continental Congress such as Roger Sherman of Connecticut (1721–1793) had only recently clamored to keep Catholics from serving in the Continental army. The term "French volunteers" denotes service in the French military rather than the ethnic identity of an officer. Before the end of the war, Benjamin Franklin received 415 applications for employment in the Continental army; 312 applicants were French, the remainder came from all across Europe. See Catherine M. Prelinger, "Less Lucky than LaFayette: A Note on the French Applicants to Benjamin Franklin for Commissions in the American Army, 1776–1785," *Proceedings of the Annual Meeting of the Western Society for French History* 4 (1976): 263–270.

20. A concise analysis of the context of this decision can be found in Jonathan R. Dull, "Lafayette, Franklin, and the Coming of Rochambeau's Army" (lecture presented to the Washington Association in Morristown, NJ, February 18, 1980), available at http://xenophongroup.com/mcjoynt/dulltlk.htm.

21. Nicolas François Denis Brisout de Barneville, a forty-four-year-old *sous-lieutenant*, was one of many who thought that the negative image of the French had at least partly been formed "by numerous French refugees," that is, Huguenots who had settled in America. "Journal de Guerre de Brissout de Barneville. Mai 1780–Octobre 1781," *French-American Review* 3, no. 4 (October 1950): 217–278, 242. The Huguenots living around Mamaroneck and New Rochelle in New York, whose ancestors had fled France after the revocation of the Edict of Nantes in 1685, refused to cooperate with Rochambeau's troops.

22. Quoted from Clermont-Crèvecœur's journal in Howard C. Rice Jr. and Anne S. K. Brown, trans. and eds., *The American Campaigns of Rochambeau's Army 1780, 1781, 1782, 1783*, 2 vols. (Princeton, NJ: Princeton University Press, 1972), 1:15–100. Traveling through Canterbury in Connecticut, Rochambeau's aide-de-camp, the comte de Lauberdière (1759–1837), had a difficult time convincing his host that he was indeed a French officer: "he didn't want to believe me, and said to me that I had to be Scottish, that I was too white for a Frenchman." The "country squire" also thought that Lauberdière was too nice to be French: he knew that "people from that country were neither that polite nor that well mannered." See Robert A. Selig, "Lauberdière's Journal: The Revolutionary War Journal of Louis François Bertrand d'Aubevoye, comte de Lauberdière," *Colonial Williamsburg: The Journal of the Colonial Williamsburg Foundation* 18, no. 1 (Autumn 1995): 33–37. His unpublished journal is in the Bibliothèque Nationale

in Paris. Following Cornwallis's surrender, Colonel William Fontaine (1754–1810) of the Virginia militia wrote on October 26, 1781, that "the French are very different from the ideas formerly inculcated in us of a people living on frogs and coarse vegetables." Quoted in Henry P. Johnston, *The Yorktown Campaign and the Surrender of Cornwallis 1781* (1881; repr., New York: Eastern Acorn Press, 1981), 178.

23. James Dana, *A Sermon Preached before the General Assembly of the State of Connecticut at Hartford on the Day of the Anniversary Election, May 13, 1779* (Hartford: Printed by Hudson and Goodwin, 1779), 15.

24. William de Deux-Ponts, *My Campaigns in America*, trans. and ed. Samuel Abbot Green (Boston: J. K. Wiggin & W. P. Lunt, 1868), 91.

25. *The Revolutionary Journal of Baron Ludwig von Closen, 1780–1783*, trans. and ed. Evelyn M. Acomb (Chapel Hill: University of North Carolina Press, 1958), 111–112. The use of Dutch was so prevalent that Jean Baptiste Antoine de Verger (1762–1851), an eighteen-year-old Swiss officer in the Royal Deux-Ponts, recorded that most inhabitants "speak nothing but Dutch to one another." Rice and Brown, *American Campaigns*, 1:101–188, 164.

26. Abbé Robin, *New Travels through North–America: In a Series of Letters* (Philadelphia: Printed and sold by Robert Bell, 1783), 41.

27. Marie François Joseph Maxime baron Cromot du Bourg, "Diary of a French Officer, 1781," *Magazine of American History* 4 (May 1880): 376–385, 376.

28. "Letters of Axel de Fersen, Aide-de-Camp to Rochambeau written to his Father in Sweden 1780–1782," *Magazine of American History* 3 (1879): 300–309, 369–376, 437–448, 438.

29. Amblard, who enlisted at age nineteen in 1773, was discharged as a captain in 1793. His manuscript entitled "Histoire des campagnes de l'Armée de Rochambaud [*sic*] en Amérique" is located in the Archives Départementales de l'Ardèche in Privas, France. Passages from this journal can be found verbatim in the journal of an unidentified officer of the Soissonnois regiment in the Huntington Library, San Marino, CA (HM 621 U8 B3). The "Journal Militaire" of an unidentified grenadier in the Bourbonnois regiment is located in the Milton S. Latham Papers (MMC 1907) in the Library of Congress.

30. An illustrated history of that regiment can be found in Robert A Selig, "Das Deutsche Königlich-Französische Infanterie Regiment von Zweybrücken or Royal Deux-Ponts," *Journal of the Johannes Schwalm Historical Association*, part 1, April 1756–March 1780, in vol. 6, no. 4 (2000): 52–59; part 2, March 1780–June 1781, in vol. 7, no. 1 (2001): 43–53; part 3, July 1781–June 1783, in vol. 7, no. 2 (2002): 29–43; part 4, June 1783–21 July 1791, in vol. 7, no. 3 (2003): 42–52.

31. Georg Daniel Flohr's "Reisen Beschreibung von America welche das Hochlöbliche Regiment von Zweybrücken hat gemachtzu Wasser und zu Land vom Jahr 1780 bis 84" is located in the Bibliothèque Municipale, Strasbourg, France. See Robert A. Selig, "A German Soldier in America, 1780–1783: The Journal of

Georg Daniel Flohr," *William and Mary Quarterly*, 3rd ser., 50, no. 3 (July 1993): 575–590. Cromot du Bourg, "Diary of a French Officer," 376.

32. A history of Lauzun's Legion can be found in Robert A. Selig, *Hussars in Lebanon! A Connecticut Town and Lauzun's Legion during the American Revolution, 1780–1781* (Lebanon, CT: Lebanon Historical Society, 2004).

33. Selig, "A German Soldier in America."

34. Ibid.

35. Thirty-one men recruited as replacements for Royal Deux-Ponts from Hessian prisoners of war in the United States deserted as well. Selig, "Royal Deux-Ponts" (2001), 46.

36. Ibid., 46.

37. During the first large wave of immigration from the war-ravaged Palatinate in 1709–1710, Queen Anne had arranged for the transportation of almost 6,000 emigrants to New York and Pennsylvania.

38. Morton (1774–1850) wrote her reminiscences in 1821; her daughter Eliza Susan Quincy published them in 1861. *Memoir of the Life of Eliza S. M. Quincy* (Boston: Printed by J. Wilson and Son, 1861), 40.

39. On July 20, 1781, Pickering informed his deputy, Henry Dearborn (1751–1829), that in order to meet the needs of the artillery, Washington had consented to impress 100 large horses from "the disaffected" in Bergen County. A few days later, Pickering reported that the action had yielded only 52 horses. Letters sent by Pickering, May 10 to December 21, 1781, *The Papers of Timothy Pickering*, ed. Frederick S. Allem and Roy Bartolomeir (Boston: Massachusetts Historical Society, 1966), microfilm, reel 26, vol. 127. In the less than two years that John Neilson served as Continental deputy quartermaster general in New Jersey, he issued more than 10,000 certificates. They provide valuable insights into the wide variety of services required to move the Continental army across the state. His papers are stored with the Neilson Family Papers, Special Collections and University Archives, Rutgers University Libraries, New Brunswick (hereafter cited as RUSC).

40. Wadsworth Papers, September 1781, box 25, folder 5, CTHS. The bill for September 2, 1781, is in a private collection.

41. Once the equipment had been loaded on board vessels, Wadsworth discharged 85 teams at Annapolis, leaving 110 teams with 669 oxen to draw the empty wagons to Williamsburg. As the wagon train left Annapolis on September 21, 1781, Louis Alexandre Berthier wrote that "Lauzun's Legion, the artillery horses, and the army wagon train formed a column numbering 1,500 horses, 800 oxen, and 220 wagons," more than half of them private wagons of officers. Rice and Brown, *American Campaigns*, 2:83.

42. "State of the Forces under . . . Sir Henry Clinton," July 3, 1778, enclosed with Lieutenant General Sir Henry Clinton to Lord George Germain, July 5, 1778,

Sir Henry Clinton Papers, vol. 36, no. 5, William L. Clements Library, University of Michigan, Ann Arbor. Library of Congress, Mss. Division: PRO CO 5:96, 77.

43. Wadsworth Papers, box 24: Letter Book Folder 3: 1 to 25 August 1781, CTHS. Wadsworth did not ask for beef cattle since a large number of animals accompanied the troops.

44. All data from Selig, "Lauberdière's Journal."

45. Gregory D. Massey, *John Laurens and the American Revolution* (Columbia: University of South Carolina Press, 2000), 190–191.

46. Timothy R. Walton. *The Spanish Treasure Fleets* (Sarasota, FL: Pineapple Press, 1994), 183. Spanish milled dollars and French écus remained legal tender in the United States until 1857.

47. James A. Lewis, "Las Damas de la Havana, el precursor, and Francisco de Saavedra: A Note on Spanish Participation in the Battle of Yorktown," *The Americas* 37 (July 1980): 83–99.

48. Lee Kennett, *The French Forces in America, 1780–1783* (Westport, CT: Greenwood Press, 1977), 68.

49. "Recollections of John Howland" (ca. 1840–1849), p. 86, John Howland Collection (MSS 499), folder 2, Rhode Island Historical Society, Providence.

50. Wadsworth Papers, box 10, folder 3, CTHS.

51. Diary of George Nelson, 1780–1792 (AM 107), Historical Society of Pennsylvania, Philadelphia.

52. Diary of Samuel Canby, November 1779 to December 1796, Samuel Canby Collection, Delaware Historical Society, Wilmington (photostat from the original at Yale University Special Collections).

53. Wadsworth Papers, French army papers, CTHS. In order to pay the 2,700 troops under his command at Head of Elk on September 8, 1781, Washington borrowed 143,640 livres in French coin from Rochambeau; Robert Morris contributed the equivalent of 33,480 livres. These 177,120 livres were less than half the amount the French forces spent every month.

54. Papers of John Davis Papers, 1755–1783, 11 vols. (Library of Congress microfilm no. 17,137, reels 79–83). Forms part of the Papers and Collection of Peter Force (series 8D, entry 32).

55. Between September 29 and October 7, another five teams joined the brigade. The teams were paid off in Williamsburg on November 6, 1781. The receipt is in Wadsworth Papers, box 25, folder 6, CTHS. £1 = 20 shillings = 240 pennies = 480 halfpennies = 960 farthings. For an overview of currencies in use during the American War of Independence and their exchange rates, see Robert A. Selig, "Eighteenth-Century Currencies," *The Brigade Dispatch: Journal of the Brigade of the American Revolution* 43 no. 3 (Autumn 2013): 16–32.

56. Abraham Williamson, Farm Accounts 1778–1781, Williamson Family Papers, RUSC. Fischer entered the French service around September 4, 1781. For June 7,

1783, Williamson's account book contains the entry, "By driving Team in the french Service 3 months & 10 days a 3/9 pr day £18 15/."

57. *The Journal of Claude Blanchard, Commissary of the French Auxiliary Army Sent to the United States during the American Revolution*, trans. William Duane, ed. Thomas Balch (Albany: J. Munsell, 1876), 133–135.

58. That does not mean that there were no hold-outs. Thomas Foster, a private in the Seventh Massachusetts Regiment, wrote in his diary on May 31, 1782: "We had a grand rejoicing on the birth of a young dauphin. . . . Such a grand scene I never saw before and it was all for one little French pickaninny, a Roman Catholic. Oh strange this from what our forefathers fled from. Would they have done the like? No, by no means. We may now see what we have degenerated to and what I fear we are coming to." The unpublished diary spans May 1782–June 1783 and is in the collections of the Huntington Library, San Marino, CA (HM 643).

59. Charles Albert comte de Moré, chevalier de Pontgibaud, *A French Volunteer of the War of Independence*, trans. and ed. Robert B. Douglas, 2nd ed. (Paris: C. Carrington, 1898), 67.

60. *New Jersey Gazette* (Trenton), October 31, 1781. Quoted in *New Jersey in the American Revolution, 1763–1783: A Documentary History*, ed. Larry R. Gerlach (Trenton: New Jersey Historical Commission, 1975), 316.

PART TWO

The Impact of the Revolutionary Experience

6

Destitute of Almost Everything to Support Life

The Acquisition and Loss of Wealth in Revolutionary Monmouth County, New Jersey

MICHAEL S. ADELBERG

The Revolutionary War years were hard on many New Jersey families in Monmouth County's Middletown Township. Before the war, they lived peacefully on good farmland near the Raritan Bay, with easy access to markets at Amboy and New York. But the American Revolution created tumult in the township. Dozens of anti-independence residents joined the British in New York. Many returned as Loyalist raiders, robbing from and kidnapping some of their former neighbors and forcing others to flee to safer inland locations.[1]

Daniel Stevenson was part of an extended family that included both active Patriots (supporters of independence) and ardent Loyalists (supporters of British rule). The Stevensons lived comfortably on their 100-acre farm until their livestock were impressed by the British army in 1778 as it passed through Middletown. By the end of the war, were they able to rebuild their estate to a meager two head of livestock. Then, in April 1783, as the war was ending, the Stevensons' home was torched. A drive was advertised "to all charitable persons" to help the family. The broadside noted that Daniel Stevenson "is now left with a wife and three small children, [and is] destitute of almost everything to support life." The war had reduced a sturdy yeoman family of Middletown to poor relief.[2] This essay considers whether they were typical.

Several historians have suggested that the rebelling Atlantic seaboard colonies were an aggregation of semi-autonomous localities from which "power radiated upwards" to state and national governments.[3] Robert Gross (Concord, MA), James Lemon (Chester County, PA), and Sung Bok Kim (Westchester County, NY) have all demonstrated the localist orientation of agrarian areas on the eve of the American Revolution. They also note continuity in these communities through the Revolutionary period, at least in terms of maintaining local institutions, land ownership patterns, and leading families. Meanwhile, studies of laborers, such as those by Gary B. Nash and Billy G. Smith, reveal similar continuity among the poorer classes in cities and towns. Other quantitative studies, such as those of James Kirby Martin, Dennis Ryan, and Edward Countryman, note continuous stress points and levels of poverty through the Revolutionary period. As these studies of different localities tend to find continuity between the pre-Revolutionary and Revolutionary eras, they implicitly take issue with intellectual historians like Bernard Bailyn and Gordon S. Wood, who have suggested that the American Revolution "was as radical and revolutionary as any in history" because of "the transformative ideas" that reshaped the nation's governing elite.[4]

It is possible that the American Revolution was more radical in localities where the war was particularly violent, including the "military frontier" areas wracked by civil warfare—that is, the arc of land surrounding New York City, the eastern shore of the Chesapeake, and the Carolina upcountry. Writing two generations ago, Louis R. Gottschalk considered what makes a war of rebellion a "revolution." He suggested that a rebellion becomes a revolution when "a significant change in the structure of a nation or society is effected." He further discussed the replacement of elites and the redistribution of wealth as two potential manifestations of a revolution.[5] So, using Gottschalk's parameters, was the American Revolution "revolutionary" on the military frontiers? Did the military frontiers experience a "significant change" in structure even if more peaceful locales did not?

There is a small body of work that seeks to determine whether the American Revolution led to a large-scale redistribution of wealth. One historian who considered this question, Seymour Martin Lipsett, suggested that the American Revolution led to a dramatic redistribution of wealth because of the confiscation of Loyalist property. Paul H. Smith, whose research concluded that at least 20 percent of Americans were Loyalists, indirectly supports this assertion.[6] But, as noted above, a number of more recent historians have generally found continuity in the locales they have studied, which suggests a less "revolutionary" American Revolution.

Based on twenty years of archival research on the American Revolution in Monmouth County, New Jersey, I have compiled a biographical file of extant economic and political information on nearly every adult male in the county (nearly 6,000) and more than 1,000 females. This dataset was extracted to measure whether Monmouth County residents maintained, gained, or lost wealth during the American Revolution. The purpose of this study is to determine whether the American Revolution led to a substantial redistribution of wealth and to offer some insight into the larger question of whether or not the American Revolution was "revolutionary" in this military frontier locale.

REVOLUTIONARY-ERA MONMOUTH COUNTY consisted of the present-day counties of Monmouth and Ocean and stretched along seventy miles of Atlantic shoreline, from Sandy Hook (at the southern end of New York Harbor) to Little Egg Harbor, more than halfway down New Jersey's Atlantic coast. The swamps and pinelands near the shore were the least populated and poorest parts of the county due to sandy soil that was ill suited for farming. The northern and western parts of the county, which stretched thirty miles inland, offered superior farmland and so were wealthier and more thickly settled. Despite its long shoreline, the county lacked a true deep-water port and was largely agrarian.[7]

On the eve of the Revolution, Monmouth County was home to between 12,000 and 15,000 diverse people. There were five significant religious denominations: Anglican, Baptist, Dutch Reformed, Presbyterian, and Quaker. African Americans, roughly half of whom were free, accounted for more than 10 percent of the county's population. There were no cities in Monmouth County. The largest towns—Freehold, Middletown, Middletown Point, Shrewsbury, and Allentown—had no more than a couple dozen houses. The county had only one school (near Freehold) and two privately held libraries (at Middletown Point and Shrewsbury). The northern villages were linked to each other and the rest of the state by roads, including the state's primary east-west thruway, the Burlington Path (sometimes called the King's Highway); travel to the southern shore villages was by the so-called Cedar Road, which was less than its name might suggest.[8]

Monmouth County's proximity to New York and the relative affluence of its northern farms supported a small gentry class that followed politics and world events. When New York City's merchants mobilized to resist the Stamp Tax in 1765, sympathetic Monmouthers established Sons of Liberty groups at Freehold, Middletown, and Allentown. In 1769, when a handful of creditors (largely from outside the county) moved to foreclose on the mortgages of the county's indebted yeomen, dozens of angry landowners rioted and blocked the court from convening business at Freehold. A second riot in 1770 was even uglier and forced the royal governor's appointed attorney, Bernadus LeGrange, to flee for his safety out of the back window of the county courthouse. Although this agitation did not exceed that of urban centers, it does suggest that Monmouth County was among the more militant agrarian locales in the Middle Colonies.[9]

Pre-Revolutionary agitation in the county can be traced to a string of town meetings in 1774 and early 1775 that established committees of correspondence and inspection charged with coordinating anti-British dissent and enforcing a boycott of British goods. Monmouth County's committee formation ran parallel to the larger wave of anti-British dissent occurring across most of the Middle Colonies; but the Monmouth County committees showed a greater tendency for heavy-handed action, such as when the county committee at Freehold "ex-communicated" Shrewsbury Township from the rest of the county for not forming a committee of inspection.[10] As protest turned to armed rebellion, the people of Monmouth County aligned themselves across a continuum from ardent Patriots to neutrals to ardent Loyalists. In spring 1776, a half regiment (roughly 250 men) was raised from Monmouth County to help defend New York from the expected British invasion; in the latter half of 1776, 500 Monmouthers joined the New Jersey Volunteers, a Provincial Corps of the British army.[11]

In December 1776, Loyalists briefly controlled most of the county in a period commonly called the "Tory Ascendancy," but the nascent regime was toppled by detachments of Pennsylvania and Delaware Continentals in January 1777. The more active Loyalists retreated behind British lines to continue the war as embittered raiders. Over the next six years, from early 1777 through 1782, Monmouth's Patriots and Loyalists squared off against each other in localized civil war. The majority of the county was held by the Patriots, but Loyalists sheltered on Sandy Hook and Staten Island had easy access to the county's long shoreline and launched dozens of punishing raids. In addition, the county's coastal pine forests and swamps were lairs for Loyalist "Pine Robber" gangs that operated through the war. In total, well over one hundred armed clashes occurred in Monmouth County, and more than 1,100 of the county's men can be documented as having experienced bodily harm, loss of significant property, detention, or other negative event. Several of the county's towns and villages— Middletown Point, Middletown, Tinton Falls, Toms River—were razed. Nearly half of the leaders from Shrewsbury and Middletown, the two town-ships nearest to the British/Loyalist base at Sandy Hook, were captured, killed, or wounded during the war.[12]

Parallel to the civil war—perhaps because of the civil war—Monmouth County was the scene of numerous internal disorders and scandals. Three times, armed Patriot gangs intimidated voters at the county's annual elec-tion; the New Jersey General Assembly twice voided the election results and came within one vote of voiding them a third time. The county's highest-ranking military officer, David Forman, was implicated in a string of scan-dals and pressured by the state legislature into resigning his brigadier general's commission in the militia. From June 1780 through the end of the war, a secretive society, the Association for Retaliation, committed dozens of extralegal vigilante acts. Meanwhile, hundreds of the county's residents traded illegally with the British commissary at Sandy Hook or Loyalist middlemen in New York. Civil warfare in Monmouth County continued throughout 1782, longer than anywhere else in the northern colonies.[13]

TO DETERMINE WHETHER the people of Monmouth County maintained, gained, or lost wealth during the war, county tax ratables were examined for information on which individuals gained and lost wealth. With the exception of a single Freehold Township tax ratable from 1776, the earliest surviving tax ratables for the county were compiled in 1778–1779. The names in these tax lists were then compared against tax lists assembled at war's end, 1783–1784. This information was then cross-checked against political, legal, and military records on the county's residents. Only those individuals who appear in both sets of tax ratables were included in this case study. People who did not own taxable wealth (that is, slaves, married women, children) were excluded. But even among owners of taxable wealth, the dataset used in this study is bound by certain limitations. These are noted in table 6.1.

Furthermore, civil warfare and local vagaries (misspellings, unwillingness of tax assessors to venture into dangerous neighborhoods) lessened the number of people who could be identified on both lists, particularly in the shore townships. Sailors, itinerant farm laborers, and ne'er-do-wells existed largely outside of the tax lists and therefore are not included. Finally, certain names were frustratingly common (Monmouth County had at least five men named John Covenhoven); unless an individual was

TABLE 6.1

Data Limitations

Excluded or underrepresented groups	Reason for the exclusion or underrepresentation
Women-headed households	On remarriage, women are no longer listed in the tax ratables. Therefore, few woman-headed households are listed in tax ratables across a five-year time span.
Households headed by younger men	Many young men listed in 1783–1784 tax ratables were living with parents in 1778–1779 and are therefore excluded from this study.
Households headed by elderly	Many elderly persons listed in 1778–1779 ratables died prior to 1783–1784 and are therefore excluded from this study.
Households headed by small landholders	Small landholders, unable to support their families, were more likely to move out of the county between 1778–1779 and 1783–1784 and are therefore underrepresented in this study.
Households in the shore townships	Due to civil warfare, many shore residents moved inland between 1778–1779 and 1783–1784 and are hard to trace across the tax ratables. They are therefore underrepresented in this study.

Source: Extracted from Michael S. Adelberg, "Biographical File," on file at the library of the Monmouth County Historical Association, Freehold, NJ.

consistently assigned a secondary identifier (of Snag Swamp, son of Daniel), these names were excluded. Still, 1,251 distinct residents are listed in both the 1778–1779 and the 1783–1784 tax ratables. From these data, the question of whether the war helped Monmouthers maintain, gain, or lose wealth can be examined.[14]

Tax ratables list many sources of wealth: land, livestock, slaves, and income-producing types of property (sailing vessels, stills, mills, tanyards, and so on). Most of these types of wealth were limited to a very small number of individuals and therefore do not yield meaningful quantitative analysis. (For example, fewer than two hundred people in the county owned slaves, and fewer than ten owned sailing vessels.) Only landowner-ship and ownership of horses and cows were common enough traits to facilitate statistically significant observations. Therefore, the analysis in this essay focuses on the acquisition and loss of these forms of wealth.[15]

A dividing line was needed to differentiate between a "significant" and an "insignificant" jump or drop in wealth. For landownership, a sig-nificant gain or loss of wealth was defined as meeting both of the following criteria: a 25 percent change in acres owned between 1778–1779 and 1783–1784 *and* a change of twenty or more acres owned. For livestock: a 25 percent change in the number of horses and cows owned between 1778–1779 and 1783–1784 *and* a change of at least two head of livestock.[16]

A number of secondary analyses further subdivided the 1,251-person study group:

> *Leaders versus nonleaders:* More than three hundred Monmouthers held civil leadership positions (state legislator, county or township officeholder, or special commissioner) or military leadership positions (commissioned officer in the army or militia) during the war years. Because the majority of them are within the study group, it was possible to determine whether leaders generally fared better or worse than nonleaders.

> *Political disposition (support or opposition to the Revolution):* Approxi-mately two-thirds of the residents of Revolutionary-era Monmouth County can be assigned political disposition based on evidence found in military returns, court records, newspa-pers, loyalty oaths, and so on. Their political dispositions

ranged on a continuum from active Loyalists to active
Patriots, with less intense supporters on both sides and a
cohort of vacillating "trimmers" in between. The study population was examined to see whether political disposition can
be correlated with the acquisition or loss of wealth.[17]

Locale (by township): Monmouth County had six townships: Dover,
Freehold, Middletown, Shrewsbury, Stafford, and Upper Freehold. The townships differed in their ethnic and religious
makeup and proximity to civil war. All individuals in the tax
ratables are listed by township, making it possible to determine whether locale substantially influenced whether an individual was more likely to gain or lose wealth during the war.

Unfortunately, only 62 women are listed in the tax ratables across both
sets of years—too small a cohort to measure—so woman-headed households are not included in this study. Likewise, testing whether particular
religious denominations fared better or worse during the war could not be
conducted because church lists for Revolutionary Monmouth County are
regrettably incomplete; only 171 people in the study group can be tied to a
particular denomination, not enough for meaningful analysis.[18]

Of the 1,251 individuals in the study, large majorities neither gained
nor lost substantial amounts of wealth during the war years. More than
three-fourths of these individuals (951) emerged from the war with
approximately the same amount of land; nearly three-fourths (865)
emerged with approximately the same number of livestock. While the
data biases noted above might serve to exaggerate the level of economic
stability, these findings still suggest a high level of economic stability.

Among those who did gain or lose significant amounts of wealth or
livestock, more gained than lost: 175 gainers versus 125 losers of land; 203
gainers versus 183 losers of livestock. The net addition of wealth is likely
attributable to the confiscation and auction of 107 Loyalist estates
(involving both land and livestock), which created the opportunity for the
purchase of land and livestock at below normal market value. For example,
William Hendrickson of Upper Freehold entered the war as an early and
strong supporter of independence with a 125-acre estate. Armed Loyalists
took his gun and livestock during the December 1776 counter-insurrection.

He purchased a Loyalist estate at auction in April 1779 and took legal action to expel an aged Loyalist, William Grover, from a second estate in May 1780. In 1784, he became embroiled in another land dispute with Loyalist-leaning James Grover. By war's end, Hendrickson's estate had ballooned to 500 acres. He had also acquired two slaves.[19]

The fact that most Monmouthers, with the exception of active Loyalists, endured the war without losing wealth does not prove that the war was easy for them. At least one-third of the county's families suffered in some tangible way. John Whitlock provides a good example of a man who suffered great hardship and still acquired wealth. He was an ensign in the Middletown militia at the start of the war. In February 1777, he was captured by the British (along with his brother, Major James Whitlock, under whom he served) at the Battle of the Navesink. Whitlock was confined for about two years in the notorious Provost Prison in New York, where his brother died. On his release in 1779, he returned to militia service as a major (his brother's old commission) and was promptly captured again. He was paroled home in January 1780 and violated the terms of his parole by again rejoining the militia. For this action, he was kidnapped by Loyalist raiders in March 1780 and confined for another nine months. At war's end, Whitlock had his prisoner-of-war debts assumed by the Continental government, and the New Jersey legislature awarded him his dead brother's estate, despite his lack of legal title to it. Despite the hardships, Whitlock was wealthier at war's end.[20]

Leaders acquired and lost land at approximately the same the rate as the population at large. Interestingly, while fewer than 15 percent of the general population of Monmouth County lost livestock over the course of the war, more than 25 percent of leaders lost livestock. This significant difference likely reflects the impact of retribution-minded Loyalist raids against the leaders of the new government.

John and Barnes Smock of Middletown serve as good examples of leaders who suffered during the war. Both held numerous local leadership positions, including serving as the lieutenant colonel and captain in the township militia. In 1778, John owned twenty-six head of livestock and a slave; Barnes owned fifteen livestock and two slaves. Both men were captured and robbed in separate incidents in 1780. By war's end, their holdings had shrunk to fifteen and nine head of livestock, respectively;

TABLE 6.2

Wealth Gainers and Losers by Leadership

	Total	Land gainers	Land losers	Livestock gainers	Livestock losers
All leaders	167	24	18	30	46
Civil-only officers	87	10	9	12	27
Military-only officers	47	11	3	10	8
Civil and military officers	33	3	6	8	11
Study Population*	1,251	175	125	203	183

Source: Extracted from Michael S. Adelberg, "Biographical File," on file at the library of the Monmouth County Historical Association, Freehold, NJ.

*The preceding rows do not equal the study population row because the majority of the people in the study population were not leaders and therefore are not tabulated in this table.

all three of their slaves had run off. Their adult sons also lost livestock; their holdings were reduced from twenty-six head in 1778 to eleven in 1784.[21]

Of the three subcategories of leaders—those who held civil offices, those who held officer commissions in the militia or Continental army, and those whose leadership spanned civil and military offices—civil officeholders were especially likely to lose livestock. More than 35 percent lost livestock, more than twice the rate of the general population (under 15 percent). This outcome is likely because civil leaders (such as magistrates, assessors, collectors, and constables) performed duties that put them at odds with their disaffected neighbors and Loyalist refugees without much military protection. John Burrowes of Middletown Point provides an example of a civilian leader who was targeted. A comfortable merchant-farmer before the war, Burrowes served on the committees that enforced boycotts on British goods. He was an election judge at the county's first post-independence election and a known opponent of the Loyalist-leaning Kearney family, Middletown Point's wealthiest prewar family. His son John Jr. enlisted as a captain in the Continental army. Loyalist raiders captured John Sr. and burned down his store and warehouses in May 1778. After he was exchanged for a prominent Loyalist, another party of Loyalists robbed him again in September of that same year. Despite owning 700 acres—the third largest holding in the township—he possessed no livestock for the rest of the war.[22]

As noted above, the political dispositions of Monmouth County residents spanned a broad continuum. For the purposes of this study of wealth, they were assigned to the following categories.

Revolutionaries were the people who supported the cause of independence through voluntary and long-term military service in the Continental army or state troops, with all the sacrifices and dangers inherent to that service, or by holding an office (constable, magistrate, tax collector, and so on) that exposed them to retribution. These people voluntarily risked their personal safety and property to support the new government. Revolutionaries tended to gain land more often than the general population, likely the result of young soldiers purchasing land with service bounties and aging into greater land acquisition generally. Additionally, some revolutionaries, particularly officeholders or kin to officeholders, may have gained in wealth as a result of patronage from the new government—and outright corruption in a few cases.[23]

Supporters backed the Revolutionary cause by serving in the militia, signing pro-independence petitions, or joining associations with a pro-Revolutionary purpose. These people were dutiful citizens to the new government but are distinguished from revolutionaries because their actions did not involve the greater sacrifice of voluntary military service. Supporters fared slightly better than the general population in terms of gaining land and/or livestock during the war.

Trimmers were people who at various times took actions that, if examined individually, would place them alternatively in pro- or anti-Revolutionary camps. Due to the higher burden of proof needed to prove someone a trimmer, it is harder to document trimmers than other political categories. Most trimmers started the war as anti-Revolutionaries, participating in the Loyalist counter-insurrections of 1776. They then settled down as dutiful Patriots. Trimmers gained and lost wealth in approximately equal proportion to the general population (though previous research demonstrates that they endured legal punishments at a higher rate).

Disaffecteds were people who opposed the Revolution in a number of lesser ways, including committing misdemeanors with political underpinnings (for example, seditious words, unlawful assembly), joining one of the Loyalist associations in 1776, refusing to support the militia, or trading illegally with the British. Some disaffecteds may have been principled neutrals, but most appear to have been opportunists who might have nominally supported the new order in public settings but purposefully broke the law and took actions against the Revolution. Although these people demonstrated disaffection for the new government's laws, their opposition was limited and did not put their lives or estates at risk. Monmouth County's disaffecteds fared surprisingly well during the war; most notably, they gained land by a 3:2 margin. This outcome suggests that the primary economic advantage of being disaffected (for example, participating in illegal trade with the British) put enough money in their pockets to offset the fines and extralegal punishments that resulted from being caught committing anti-Revolutionary acts.

Loyalists were people who voluntarily supported the royal cause through serving in the British army's Provincial Corps, an irregular Loyalist partisan group, or by turning "refugee" and relocating to British-held New York. These people voluntarily risked their lives and estates to oppose the new government. The Loyalists counted in table 6.3 represent only a fraction of the total Loyalist population, most of whom are not considered because they lost their estates when they went within British lines. Understandably, most of these people did not fare well during the war, though, surprisingly, a few did.

Locale, more than any other factor examined, determined whether people gained or lost wealth in Revolutionary Monmouth County. The people of Middletown and Shrewsbury Townships (closest to the Loyalist base at Sandy Hook) lost livestock by a combined total of almost 2:1, with Middletown residents losing livestock by a ratio of more than 4:1. Meanwhile, the residents in the safer inland townships of Upper Freehold and Freehold gained livestock by a 2:1 margin. This improvement in prosperity is particularly pronounced in Freehold Township, the county seat and base of a clique of radical Patriots who enhanced their wealth (at least partially) through the vigilante Association for Retaliation, which confiscated property from the disaffected and the kin of Loyalist raiders still

TABLE 6.3

Gainers and Losers of Significant Wealth by Political Disposition

	Total	Land gainers	Land losers	Livestock gainers	Livestock losers
Revolutionary	131	21	13	25	26
Supporter	383	51	35	58	44
Trimmer	83	8	7	18	16
Disaffected	272	27	18	33	29
Loyalist*	54	7	9	7	11
Study Population**	1,251	175	125	203	183

Source: Extracted from Michael S. Adelberg, "Biographical File," on file at the library of the Monmouth County Historical Association, Freehold, NJ.

*These numbers do not include Loyalists who went and stayed behind British lines during the war.

**The preceding rows do not equal the study population row because some of the people in the study population cannot be assigned to a particular loyalty and are therefore not tabulated in this table.

living within the county.[24] Albert Covenhoven is one example of a Freehold Township "retaliator" who prospered during the war. Early in the war, Covenhoven left home to labor at a saltworks at Toms River. Returning home with cash in his pocket and perhaps supported by his large family, he purchased a 200-acre farm. But he was not initially wealthy. His estate was damaged during the Battle of Monmouth (June 28, 1778), and he owned only three head of livestock in 1779. But he was a staunch Freehold Patriot, testifying against Loyalists, signing pro-Revolutionary petitions, and joining the Retaliators in 1780. By war's end, his estate has grown to 304 acres (probably due to the purchase of a Loyalist estate at auction), eleven head of livestock, and a slave.[25]

The war was particularly hard on the residents of the Atlantic shore's Dover and Stafford Townships, where local residents lost property more often than they gained it (Stafford is not displayed in table 6.4 because of the unreliability and extremely small number of residents listed in its tax ratables). In these townships, indigenous Loyalist gangs of Pine Robbers

TABLE 6.4

Gainers and Loser of Significant Wealth by Locale

	Total	Land gainers	Land losers	Livestock gainers	Livestock losers
Dover	75	13	15	12	13
Freehold	244	42	23	72	21
Middletown	224	20	15	14	59
Shrewsbury	424	60	37	50	58
Upper Freehold	245	35	27	45	32
Study Population	1,251	175	125	203	183

Source: Extracted from Michael S. Adelberg, "Biographical File," on file at the library of the Monmouth County Historical Association, Freehold, NJ.

plundered local Patriots through to the end of the war. Many Whig leaders had to flee inland for safety. The level of dislocation and emigration from these townships is hard to measure, but likely was significant. One person who had to be excluded from the study because of emigration was Samuel Brown of Forked River. Early in the war, Brown opened a small saltworks and was elected captain of the local militia. Though militia companies from the lower shore were not well organized or consistently active, Brown led a party in taking a stranded Loyalist vessel in 1778 and then captured a second vessel operated by local Loyalists. With these acts, he apparently made enemies. Brown's home was plundered in fall 1779, and he was nearly captured by Pine Robbers. They then robbed his home two more times. He and his family relocated fifty miles north to Woodbridge (in Middlesex County), where Brown participated in the capture of two more Loyalist vessels in the Raritan Bay. Brown is absent from Monmouth County's wartime tax ratables.[26]

AS DEMONSTRATED ABOVE, civil warfare sapped the wealth of some Monmouthers, but most residents—despite war-related violence and plundering—maintained their wealth. Several county residents even prospered during the war. Though beyond the scope of this essay, the increase in wealth cannot be attributed solely to the confiscation of Loyalist estates and is likely the result of three activities: salt making, privateering, and illegal trade.

Salt making: The New Jersey shore was dotted with saltworks during the war, and the largest two were in Monmouth County:
the Union Salt Works at Manasquan and the Pennsylvania
Salt Works at Toms River. These works, though less productive than projected and ultimately destroyed by Loyalist
raiding parties, nonetheless brought wage-paying jobs and
capital to locales that were formerly sparsely populated and
poor. Other smaller saltworks were more successful.[27]

Privateering: During the war, dozens of privateers operated off the
New Jersey shoreline; these ranged from large vessels from
Philadelphia and Boston to small oar-powered local boats.
Over the course of the war, they captured well over one hundred prizes, many of which were towed into local ports for
sale (generally Little Egg Harbor and Toms River). Locals also
salvaged at least a dozen more stranded or wrecked vessels,
again bringing wealth into the county. The privateer and sal-
vaging activity was so prolific that it drew the notice of far-
away investors and merchants. Major John Van Emburgh of
New Brunswick, for example, visited in May 1779 to observe
"the busy season for the people on the shore, the late captures
has made them negligent of everything but dividing and
determining their share of prizes."[28]

Illegal trade: Illegal trade with the British is hard to document but
was probably the greatest source of wartime wealth for the
people of Monmouth County. The trade was so prolific that
even George Washington considered it a menace and felt com-
pelled to take action, writing in January 1779, "I have received
such repeated information of the trade that is carried on
between Monmouth and New York . . . that I find it an absolute
necessity of sending down a party to that quarter to put a stop
that intercourse." Washington and New Jersey Governor William Livingston collaborated on a string of military deployments
into Monmouth for the purpose of curbing the illegal trade.
While individual traders were arrested and their goods confiscated, the illegal trade flourished through the end of the war.
This illegal trading is probably the reason that Monmouth

County's disaffecteds—despite facing many disadvantages—
fared better than the county's population as a whole.[29]

DESPITE SIX YEARS of civil warfare resulting in more than a hundred
armed clashes and at least that many legal and extralegal property
confiscations, most Monmouthers maintained economic stability through
the war. Among the factors examined, locale was the most important
determinant. In particular, proximity to Sandy Hook (the epicenter of
local civil warfare) strongly correlated with loss of livestock. Leaders did
not acquire wealth more often than others; in fact, they were more likely
to lose livestock, probably due to retribution from Loyalist raiding parties. Civil officeholders (deprived of military association) were especially
likely to suffer the loss of property. While certain disaffected individuals
suffered brutal vigilante justice (an unarmed Loyalist, Stephen Edwards,
was hanged without a civil trial; illegal trader James Pew was murdered in
his jail cell while awaiting trial), the "disaffected," as a whole, fared well.
This outcome suggests that the so-called London Trade between the disaffected and the British was so lucrative that its economic advantages
outweighed the risks of flouting the new government.

While the American Revolution was a difficult period for most, more
Monmouthers gained than lost wealth during the war. This finding suggests that, despite all the difficulties and dislocation of the war, the economic opportunities that accompanied it—a lucrative illegal trade with
the British, handsome military bounties, the windfall that might come
from capturing a beached British ship or purchasing a prime Loyalist
estate at auction—counterbalanced the destruction.

In conclusion, these findings suggest that the American Revolution in
Monmouth County was not revolutionary. While the war certainly produced many individual hardships, a surprising level of economic stability
persisted. With perfect documentation, dozens more cases like the
Stevenson family might be known. Yet the forces of continuity—stable
leadership and landownership, incoming wealth to balance the destruction of property—remained intact. At least by the measures used in this
essay, the American Revolution in Monmouth County—despite six years of
punishing civil warfare—did not bring about a redistribution of wealth for
residents living along a military frontier line. This result dovetails with the

economic continuity noted by Robert Gross, James Lemon, and other historians who have studied communities elsewhere. All of this ongoing work suggests that the American Revolution was not particularly revolutionary in the military frontier areas, much less the new nation.

NOTES

1. Middletown Township stretched from present-day Matawan to Sandy Hook along the Raritan Bay and hosted dozens of bloody encounters during the American Revolution. In 1778, it had 456 households, making it the fourth largest of the six Monmouth County townships. Several of the events that occurred in Middletown Township during the Revolution are discussed in Franklin Ellis, *The History of Monmouth County, New Jersey* (Philadelphia: R. T. Peck, 1885), and Edwin Salter, *A History of Monmouth and Ocean Counties* (Bayonne, NJ: E. Gardner & Son, 1890). For further information on Middletown, see Michael S. Adelberg, *The American Revolution in Monmouth County: The Theatre of Spoil and Destruction* (Charleston, SC: History Press, 2010), and Dennis Ryan, "Six Towns: Continuity and Change in Revolutionary New Jersey" (Ph.D. diss., New York University, 1974).

2. Complete information on the activities of the Stevenson family during the American Revolution is in Michael S. Adelberg, "Biographical File," on file at the library of the Monmouth County Historical Association, Freehold, NJ. The announcement of a charity drive for the family of Daniel Stevenson is at the Monmouth County Historical Association, Oversized Manuscripts, closet 1, drawer 10, folder 3.

3. Jack Greene, "The American Revolution," *American Historical Review*, 105, no. 1 (February 2000): 93–102.

4. Generally, historians have noted continuity between the new American governments and the colonial British assemblies and courts they supplanted (with the notable exceptions of replacing a small cadre of crown-appointed executives with newly elected executives). These historians have noted that the more prominent of the Founding Fathers were nearly all members of the colonial elite. Crane Brinton, for example, said the aim of the American Revolution was not to overturn the existing "social and economic system," but rather only to "set up the English North American colonies as an independent nation-state." Other historians, including James Henretta and James Kirby Martin, have generally agreed, the former suggesting that local elites maintained power during the war and the latter suggesting the American Revolution switched out an entrenched elite for a "frustrated" near-elite that easily stepped into the vacated leadership slots. See Crane Brinton, *The Anatomy of Revolution*, rev. ed. (New York: Vintage Books, 1965), 22. Also see James Henretta, *The Evolution of American Society, 1700–1815: An Interdisciplinary Analysis* (Lexington, MA: D. C. Heath, 1973), and James Kirby Martin, *Men in Rebellion: Higher Government Leaders and the Coming of the American Revolution* (New Brunswick, NJ: Rutgers University Press, 1973). Works examining wealth

in Revolutionary-era America include: Peter A. Coclanis, "The Wealth of British America on the Eve of the Revolution," *Journal of Interdisciplinary History* 21, no. 2 (1990): 245–260; Lee Soltow, *Distribution of Wealth and Income in the United States in 1798* (Pittsburgh: University of Pittsburgh Press, 1989); John J. McCusker and Russell R. Menard, *The Economy of British America, 1607–1789* (Chapel Hill: University of North Carolina Press, 1985); Alice Hanson Jones, "Wealth and Growth of the Thirteen Colonies: Some Implications," *Journal of Economic History* 44, no. 22 (1984): 239–254; Alice Hanson Jones, *Wealth of a Nation to Be: The American Colonies on the Eve of the Revolution* (New York: Columbia University Press, 1980); Edwin J. Perkins, *The Economy of Colonial America* (New York: Columbia University Press, 1980); Gloria L. Main, "American Colonial Wealth," *Business History Review* 52 (1978): 408–410; Gary B. Nash, "Urban Wealth and Poverty in Pre-Revolutionary America," *Journal of Interdisciplinary History* 6, no. 4 (1976): 545–584. See also James T. Lemon, *The Best Poor Man's Country: A Geographical Study of Early Southeastern Pennsylvania* (Baltimore: Johns Hopkins University Press, 1972), and Peter Wacker, *Land and People: The Cultural Geography of Pre-Industrial New Jersey Origins and Settlement Patterns* (New Brunswick, NJ: Rutgers University Press, 1975), which distills his larger work on cultural geography of colonial New Jersey. A primary impediment to additional quantitative studies on Revolutionary-era wealth is the lack of broadly available datasets, without which each historian must start from scratch. One notable exception is the American Colonial Wealth Estimates project, supported by historians and economists at the University of Michigan and Washington University. It is a dataset of the estates of 919 Americans who died in 1774: http://www.icpsr.umich.edu/icpsrweb/ICPSR/studies/07329/version/1. Leading locality-based studies include: Robert Gross, *The Minutemen and the Their World* (New York: Hill and Wang, 1976); Sung Bok Kim, *Landlord and Tenant in Colonial New York: Manorial Society, 1664–1775* (Chapel Hill: University of North Carolina Press, 1978); Martin, *Men in Rebellion*; Edward Countryman, *A People in Revolution: The American Revolution and Political Society in New York, 1760–1790* (New York: Norton, 1989). Billy G. Smith concluded that throughout the latter half of the eighteenth century, "many, if not most" laboring Philadelphians "lived in poverty or on its edge." His research shows little evidence of social mobility or a shrinking of the laborer class. See Billy G. Smith, "The Material Lives of Laboring Philadelphians, 1750 to 1800," *William and Mary Quarterly*, 3rd ser., 38 (April 1981): 163–202. There is a diverse body of research on the military frontier areas of the American Revolution, but the most complete overview may be Harry M. Ward, *Between the Lines: Banditti of the American Revolution* (Westport, CT: Praeger, 2002). There are numerous synopses of the work of Bernard Bailyn and Gordon S. Wood, but few better than Wood's own *The Radicalism of the American Revolution* (New York: Vintage Books, 1993), which builds on Bailyn's and his own earlier work.

5. Louis R. Gottschalk, "Cause of Revolution," reprinted in *Why Revolution: Theories and Analyses*, ed. Clifford T. Paynton and Robert Blackey (Cambridge, MA: Schenckman, 1971), 27.

6. See Seymour Martin Lipset, *Continental Divide: The Values and Institutions of the United States and Canada* (New York: Routledge, 1990). Paul H. Smith's research on Loyalists is discussed in different works, but was most explicitly documented in his article, "The American Loyalists: Notes on Their Organization and Numerical Strength," *William and Mary Quarterly*, 3rd ser., 25 (April 1968): 259–277.

7. The best book on the cultural geography of colonial New Jersey is Peter Wacker's *Land and People*. See also Adelberg, *American Revolution in Monmouth County*.

8. For information on Monmouth County's roads, see Sarah Errickson, *The Trails, Roads, Highways of Old Monmouth* (Bradley Beach, NJ: Clarence W. Smith Press, 1924).

9. Evidence of the activities of the Monmouth County Sons of Liberty is fragmentary. A March 1766 document from the Maryland Sons of Liberty records the dispatch of a letter to the Sons of Liberty of Upper Freehold, including its three co-chairs; see *Memoir of the Life and Times of Major General John Lamb* (Albany: J. Munsell, 1857), 4. For a document sent by the Middletown Sons of Liberty to the New York Sons of Liberty, April 1766, see the John Lamb Papers, reel 1, no. 33, New-York Historical Society. The minutes of the Freehold and Upper Freehold Sons of Liberty meetings were also published in the New York *Mercury*, May 12, 1766. The most complete treatment of the Monmouth land riots is William Eisenring, "Monmouth and Essex Counties' 1769–70 Riots Against Lawyers: Predecessors of Revolutionary Social Conflict," *New Jersey History* 112 (Spring/ Summer 1994): 1–18. A comprehensive treatment of prewar agitation in the Middle Colonies is provided in John Neuenschwander, "The Forgotten Section: The Middle Colonies, 1774–6" (Ph.D. diss., Case Western Reserve University, 1971).

10. The proceedings of the Monmouth County and Freehold Township committees are published in Salter, *History of Monmouth and Ocean Counties*, 46–53, and other antiquarian sources. Additional minutes of the Shrewsbury Township committee are at the Monmouth County Historical Association; see Subjects Alphabetical, Revolutionary War, folder 1, and the Cherry Hall Papers, box 15, folders 7, 11. See also the Holmes Family Papers (MG 282), box 5, folder 6, New Jersey Historical Society.

11. See Adelberg, *American Revolution in Monmouth County*, for an overview of the Monmouthers who mustered under David Forman for the New York campaign of 1776. Also see Fred Andersen Berg, *Encyclopedia of Continental Army Units: Battalions, Regiments, and Independent Corps* (Harrisburg, PA: Stackpole, 1972). My previous research documented that roughly 600 Monmouthers eventually joined the Loyalist New Jersey Volunteers. See Adelberg, "An Evenly Balanced County: The Scope and Severity of Civil Warfare in Revolutionary Monmouth County New Jersey," *Journal of Military History* 73, no. 1 (January 2009): 9–48.

12. The most complete overview of Monmouth County's raid warfare is Adelberg, *American Revolution in Monmouth County*. The defining work on the Pine Robbers is David Fowler, "Egregious Villains, Wood Rangers, and London Traders: The Pine Robbers Phenomenon in New Jersey during the American Revolution" (Ph.D. diss., Rutgers University, 1987). The figure of 100+ battles and skirmishes (including maritime clashes) comes from David Munn, *Battles and Skirmishes of*

the American Revolution in New Jersey (Trenton: Department of Environmental Protection, 1976), available at http://www.state.nj.us/dep/njgs/enviroed/oldpubs/battles.pdf. For a discussion of Monmouth County's local leaders and the dangers they faced, see Adelberg, "The Transformation of Local Governance in Monmouth County, New Jersey, during the War of the American Revolution," *Journal of the Early Republic* 31, no. 3 (Fall 2011): 467–498.

13. The most complete account of Monmouth County's political scandals and disorders, as well as the rise of the Retaliators, is Michael S. Adelberg, "'A Combination to Trample All Law Underfoot': The Association for Retaliation and the American Revolution in Monmouth County, New Jersey," *New Jersey History* 115 (February 1997): 3–36.

14. Adelberg, "An Evenly Balanced County," contains a more complete discussion about limitations of using local Revolutionary-era records for quantitative research.

15. The tax ratables, in their original form, are at the New Jersey State Archives in Trenton. There are complete runs of tax ratables for the years in between 1778–1779 and 1783–1784. A single Freehold Township tax list from 1776 was published as "Freehold Township Tax List, 1776," in the *Monmouth Inquirer* on July 1, 1886.

16. Many individuals in the tax ratables are listed as "householders" (sometimes called cottagers) or "single men." Householders owned small plots of land; single men rented cottages. In this study, householders were assigned one acre of land and single men zero acres. Regarding livestock ownership, I considered treating horses and cows separately, but after looking at a number of estate inventories, I chose to lump the two together because their assessed value was similar, with horses being generally, but not always, somewhat more valuable. Several of the tax ratables also record hogs and sheep, but they are excluded from this study because their inclusion across all tax ratables is uneven.

17. Active Loyalists are problematic in this study because they were generally behind British lines, in prison, or dead by war's end. Only a few active Loyalists (generally prewar gentry who threw in their lot with the British early in the war and then, because of advanced age, were allowed to "retire" to their farms as neutrals) are traceable across both sets of tax ratables. Eleven hundred Monmouthers can be traced to serving in the county militia, and another six hundred can traced to serving in the state troops or Continental army. Six hundred Monmouthers can be traced to serving in the Loyalist New Jersey Volunteers, and another two hundred to serving in irregular Loyalist groups (for example, Pine Robber gangs and the Associated Loyalists). The military service of these men was compared with the 1,251-person study group to determine if particular types of military service correlated especially strongly with gaining or losing wealth. Service in the Revolutionary militia was compulsory, but because so much of Monmouth was weakly governed and wracked with civil war, militia service entailed genuine risk and service was inconsistently enforced. Therefore, faithful militia service can be equated with support for the Revolution.

Service in the Continental army or state troops (long-term militia units raised for local defense) was voluntary. The Loyalist New Jersey Volunteers eventually mustered more than 2,000 men, making it the largest Provincial corps of the British army. The core of its first and second battalions was raised from Monmouth County in July–August and November–December 1776. More than one-fourth of the Volunteers were ultimately raised from the county. There was also a collection of Loyalist irregular groups: Loyalist insurrectionaries briefly took over most of the county in late 1776, an ill-fated Loyalist militia recruited men in 1777, Pine Robber gangs started in late 1778 and continued along the shore through 1782, and the Associated Loyalists, composed of Loyalist refugees in New York, existed from 1780 to 1782 and included dozens of Monmouthers.

18. Monmouth County had several denominations. There were Dutch Reformed congregations at Marlboro and Holmdel, and the records for one of those congregations still exist. But those records are in Dutch, and it is difficult to match up these names with the Anglicized names in the tax lists. The county had one large Quaker meeting at Shrewsbury and a satellite meeting Manasquan; Quakers in the western and southern parts of Monmouth attended meetings in Burlington County. The records of these meetings still exist but do not include comprehensive lists of attendees, limiting their use for this study. There were Baptist congregations in Middletown and Upper Freehold Townships. Records exist of the Middletown meeting, but there are only a few congregants listed in surviving records of the Upper Freehold meeting. There were Anglican congregations at Freehold and Shrewsbury, but no attendee records for the former and incomplete congregants' lists for the latter. There were Presbyterian meetings in Freehold and Upper Freehold Townships; a prewar congregant list exists for the Freehold Township congregation, but no congregants' list exists for the Upper Freehold congregation. There was also a denominationally ambiguous meeting house at Good Luck, just north of Toms River, but no congregant list exists for it. Finally, the county had a few Jews, French Protestants, and Methodists, too few for analysis.

19. The collected Revolutionary War activities of William Hendrickson are in the Adelberg, "Biographical File."

20. The activities and sufferings of John Whitlock are collected in ibid. Whitlock was awarded title to this brother's estate by a special act of the New Jersey legislature. See *Votes and Proceedings of the General Assembly of the State of New-Jersey*, June 4, 1781, and October 4, 1781.

21. John Smock served as a captain and then lieutenant colonel of the Monmouth militia, overseer of highways, tax assessor, and purchasing contractor for the Continental army. Barnes Smock served as the Middletown Township overseer of highways in addition to serving as captain of the militia's "dress company" and, later, the state troops. Their compiled public service and other wartime activities are in Adelberg, "Biographical File." It is worth noting that other members of the Smock family who lived farther inland in Freehold Township prospered during the war.

22. The collected activities of John Burrowes Sr. are in Adelberg, "Biographical File." See also Mary Lou Koegler, *The Burrowes Mansion of Matawan, New Jersey, and Notations on the History of Monmouth County*, ed. F. Howard Lloyd Jr. (Eatontown, NJ: Snell Graphics, 1978).

23. No single source lists all of the scandals and irregularities that occurred in Revolutionary Monmouth County, but two of the author's previous articles cover the majority of the larger ones. See "Transformation of Local Governance in Monmouth County" and "A Combination to Trample All Law Underfoot."

24. See Adelberg, "A Combination to Trample All Law Underfoot."

25. The collected Revolutionary War activities of Albert Covenhoven are in Adelberg, "Biographical File," which also includes information on several other members of Covenhoven's immediate and extended family.

26. Information on Samuel Brown is found in several sources, but collected in Adelberg, "Biographical File." Also see the Revolutionary War Veteran's Pension Application of Thomas Brown, Samuel Brown's son, on file as "New Jersey–Monmouth County–Thomas Brown" at the National Archives, Washington, DC.

27. There are a number of antiquarian works on New Jersey's Revolutionary War saltworks; the most complete recent historical work is Michael S. Adelberg, "'Long in the Hand and Altogether Fruitless': The Pennsylvania Salt Work and Salt-Making on the Jersey Shore during the American Revolution," *Pennsylvania History* 80 (Spring 2013): 215–242.

28. There is no authoritative treatment of privateering in New Jersey during the American Revolution. Many incidents are spread across various archival and antiquarian sources. The most complete treatments are Arthur Pierce, *Smugglers' Woods: Jaunts and Journeys in Colonial and Revolutionary New Jersey* (New Brunswick, NJ: Rutgers University Press, 1960), and Robert Scheina, "A Matter of Definition: A New Jersey Navy, 1777–1783," *American Neptune* 39 (1979): 209–217. Van Emburgh's quote is in Leonard Lundin, *Cockpit of the Revolution: The War for Independence in New Jersey* (Princeton, NJ: Princeton University Press, 1940), 404–405.

29. There is no comprehensive treatment of the illegal trade between New Jersey and New York during the American Revolution, but a number of works discuss the topic, including Fowler, *Egregious Villains*; Judith L. Van Buskirk, *Generous Enemies: Patriots and Loyalists in Revolutionary New York* (Philadelphia: University of Pennsylvania Press, 2002); and Adelberg, *American Revolution in Monmouth County*. See also Michael S. Adelberg, "Factions, Contraband, and Civil War: The Historical Context of *Holmes v. Walton*," in *Holmes v. Walton: Case File Transcriptions and Other Materials*, ed. Paul Axel-Lute (New Brunswick, NJ: Rutgers University Library for the Center for Law & Justice, February 2010), http://njlegallib.rutgers.edu/hw, for its discussion of the confiscation of contraband goods.

7

Discharging Their Duty

Salem Quakers and Slavery, 1730–1780

BRUCE A. BENDLER

On the twentieth day of the third month in 1778, the Gloucester-Salem Quarterly Meeting of the Society of Friends convened in Haddonfield, New Jersey.[1] For the monthly meetings represented at that quarterly meeting, the clerk recorded the observance of a mandate issued in 1776 requiring Quakers to manumit all of their slaves. He reported compliance of the Salem Monthly Meeting as "wholly so," while noting that members of the Haddonfield Monthly Meeting still held seven slaves and those in Evesham still held two bondsmen.[2] The antislavery sentiment that led to these notations had long been developing in the Mid-Atlantic Quaker community. In 1776, the Philadelphia Yearly Meeting decreed that holding slaves would result in "disownment," an action similar to excommunication in other Christian bodies, and it so instructed the quarterly and monthly meetings under its care. Quakers in the Salem Monthly Meeting, under the care of the Gloucester-Salem Quarterly meeting, responded by complying with that directive, as indeed they had with earlier antislavery declarations. The upheaval of war, coupled with the efforts of Quakers to maintain their peace testimony, made this accomplishment even more remarkable and noteworthy.

Quaker communities in West Jersey and Pennsylvania held a position of social power and authority unique in British North America.[3] Although their faith was not established by law as was the case in Anglican Virginia or Congregational New England, Quakers were the dominant religious organization in those Mid-Atlantic colonies. Architectural historian

Michael J. Chiarappa posited the development of a "social umbrella" that manifested itself as a "socially controlling and territorial force" that was "pervasive and revealing across the region," one reflecting a degree of social control.[4] To enforce their values and in spite of their emphasis on an individual "inner light," Quakers developed a hierarchy of yearly, quarterly, and monthly meetings, which allowed them to impose stern discipline on their members. Yet that discipline was directed toward the ideals of equality and humanity, as became manifest in the emergent Quaker support for the abolition of slavery. Corporate efforts by Quaker meetings to enforce standards of behavior thus had a basis in respect for the spiritual value and dignity of each individual.[5]

Furthermore, the Quaker ecclesiastical structure permitted discussion of important questions and led to the enforcement of decisions emerging from those discussions. According to Jon Butler, Mid-Atlantic Friends crafted a "strong non-democratic leadership that fostered corporate unity and denominational order in well-structured disciplinary institutions despite the fact that important changes significantly altered the structure of that leadership after 1695." Such changes, some resulting from the Keithian schism of the early 1690s, had indeed strengthened the role of visiting "Public Friends" and the yearly meeting in enforcing behavioral standards, stimulating a "renaissance in disciplinary and institutional creativity" and allowing a "new legalism" to emerge. "Public Friends" from London and other meetings in America traveled from meeting to meeting, leading efforts to build consensus on behavioral and ethical standards within the Quaker community. Such visitations also encouraged unity and solidarity, as did correspondence between yearly meetings such as those in Philadelphia and London.[6]

Nevertheless, "well-structured disciplinary institutions" did not stifle debate and discussions of how to enforce Quaker ideals. Monthly meetings and quarterly meetings could present petitions to the Philadelphia Yearly Meeting, which exercised oversight of Mid-Atlantic Quakers. Furthermore, the Philadelphia Yearly Meeting communicated with its counterpart in London and would at times implement that meeting's advice and recommendations on this side of the Atlantic. The Philadelphia leadership gave its attention to and acted on the steady stream of petitions and queries from local and regional meetings under its care. Local leadership thus could and did play a role in shaping the response of Friends to social and cultural issues. If the structure was not totally democratic, it was not repressive or unresponsive.

The structure that provided the Quakers with unity had developed in spite of the society's "democratic" and "loosely knit" origins, a "common center" in London providing a unifying force. Circulation of literature, such as the works of George Fox, William Sewel, Robert Barclay, and William Penn, also "tended to stereotype the thinking on certain subjects throughout the colonies," as Henry J. Cadbury points out. Thus, a common faith and a sense of mutual respect within the Quaker community maintained and reinforced organizational unity. A more centralized structure could still remain consensual and open to dialogue. Such dialogue gave more attention to the question of slavery in the eighteenth century, when polemicists such as Anthony Benezet and John Woolman built on an already-established literary tradition and directed their polemics toward their fellow Quakers, urging them to end their involvement in the slave trade and to free the slaves they themselves owned.[7]

Friends in Salem became a part of this process of building and maintaining consensual unity. Salem, New Jersey, was among the first Quaker settlements in West Jersey, founded by Friends in 1675 under the leadership of John Fenwick. The meeting itself was organized in 1676. Quakers established a colony at Greenwich that same year, and both of these preceded settlement of Burlington, Cooper's Ferry (present day Camden), and Woodbury.[8] The Salem meeting acquired a permanent meeting house on the sixth day of the sixth month, 1681, when Samuel and Ann Nicholson deeded sixteen acres of land on Wharf Street (now West Broadway) to the Salem Monthly Meeting for payment of £12. A log house on the site was converted into a meeting house. By 1700, a new brick edifice was built, where the Gloucester-Salem Quarterly Meeting, with oversight over Friends in West Jersey, often met.[9]

Quakers in Salem first took formal notice of the issue of slavery in 1730, when the clerk at the monthly meeting there read, and entered into the minutes, an extract of the proceedings of the Philadelphia Yearly Meeting "concerning the legality of our friends importing Negroes and buying them when imported." Attendees at the Salem meeting concluded that "one as well as the other ought to be restricted."[10] That exhortation from Philadelphia had urged the monthly meetings to admonish and caution those who "may be or likely to be in that practice."[11] Salem Quakers did not dissent.

The Philadelphia Yearly Meeting repeated its admonition frequently over the next twenty years. In the meantime, the Gloucester-Salem Quarterly Meeting also took sporadic action on the question of slavery. On the seventeenth of the first month of 1737/38, the clerk reported that the yearly meeting had recommended two books to each monthly meeting: "Moses West's book and that relating to Negroes."[12] That same year, the quarterly meeting noted that monthly meetings in Gloucester and Salem Counties were "mostly clear of buying Negroes."[13] Salem Quakers thus demonstrated their compliance with such antislavery exhortations.

The movement against slavery in the Quaker fellowship then moved beyond the matter of buying imported slaves. In 1753, John Woolman wrote a groundbreaking tract against slavery, pointing out its inconsistency with both divine law and human ethics. Born in 1720 to a Quaker family near Mount Holly in Burlington County, Woolman became convinced of the evils of slavery as a young man. In 1742, his employer had asked him to draw up a deed of transfer for a slave. Although he complied with that request, he felt pangs of conscience. A journey in 1746 through New Jersey into Maryland and Virginia, colonies with slave populations far greater than that of New Jersey, confirmed his antislavery convictions.[14]

John Woolman was no stranger to Salem Quakers. He had visited them in 1746 as part of his efforts to arouse the conscience of the Mid-Atlantic Quaker community.[15] The Philadelphia Yearly Meeting published Woolman's work and arranged for its distribution to local meetings. On the twenty-fifth of the third month, 1754, the clerk of the Salem Monthly Meeting reported that there "came to hand 45 books set out by John Woolman Intitled Some Considerations on Keeping Slaves." The books were promptly "distributed to the several branches of this meeting."[16]

Indeed, by propagating these works, Salem Quakers linked themselves with the antislavery movement Woolman was building. Woolman journeyed far and wide across the Mid-Atlantic, New England, and the Chesapeake region, exhorting his fellow Friends to reconsider their toleration of slavery. Concurrently, he established contacts with Quakers in England. Anthony Benezet, who evidently never visited Salem, played an even greater role in building a trans-Atlantic community committed to extirpating slavery from Quaker ranks. Benezet and Woolman thus drew local meetings such as Salem into a much wider and well-coordinated effort to end Quaker participation in the slave trade and slavery itself.[17]

Woolman's exhortation did not lead to an immediate end to slavery in Salem or anywhere else, but it inspired a growing concern for those enslaved and a growing recognition of their humanity. In 1756, the Salem Monthly Meeting responded to a query from Philadelphia, stating that although local Quakers had ceased purchasing imported slaves, they "are not all so careful as to train [slaves] up in the principles of the Christian religion as they ought." A year later, in the twelfth month of 1757, the Salem meeting reprimanded one of its own members, Samuel Mason, for purchasing a slave. In response, although Mason "talked very calmly," he had "nothing to offer in respect to it."[18] A scarcity of labor and consequent higher wages, brought about by the Seven Years' War, had led some slave owners like Mason to delay or forgo manumission.[19] But Mason knew that such an excuse would not prove acceptable; he thus did not offer one.

In 1758, the Philadelphia Yearly Meeting ordered that any Friend who purchased or sold a slave would be barred from participation in the Society's business or administrative activities unless he openly repented for doing so and received pardon.[20] In Salem, Quakers had already dealt with cases like Mason's and, indeed, had virtually eliminated the practice within their meeting. John Woolman again visited Salem in 1759, soon after the Philadelphia Yearly Meeting had set forth its edict. There his "heart was enlarged in heavenly love, and [he] found a near fellowship in the brothers and sisters, in the manifold trials attending their Christian progress through this world."[21] Perhaps inspired by Woolman, the Salem meeting thereafter took a more proactive stance, initiating efforts to eliminate slave ownership within its spiritual jurisdiction.

Salem Quakers did not act alone. Their counterparts in Shrewsbury, Monmouth County, moved with even greater alacrity. Shrewsbury Quakers ended the practices of buying and selling slaves and began to manumit them, even before the Philadelphia Yearly Meeting made such actions mandatory. But not all New Jersey Quakers so acted. Quakers in Chesterfield, Burlington County, proved more resistant to directives from their spiritual leaders and continued to buy and sell human property.

Although immediate economic or social circumstances often determined a local constituency's response, John Woolman's account of events suggested that Quakers in Salem acted on conscience, in response to his exhortations.[22]

Throughout the 1760s, sentiment in West Jersey to go beyond the mandate of 1758 grew. On the twenty-third of the third month, 1764, the Gloucester-Salem Quarterly Meeting responded to a request for its "sense and advice" from the monthly meeting in Haddonfield about dealing with slaveholders in order to clarify the guidance received from Philadelphia in 1758.[23] On the twenty-first of the ninth month, 1764, the quarterly meeting recommended "brotherly care" to bring Quakers to a "sense of the evil of the practice."[24] By 1768, a new spirit had emerged. "A sense of the inconsistency of keeping slaves for term of life seems to increase amongst us," the clerk then reported.[25] This spirit manifested itself in Salem, where the monthly meeting initiated a program to visit slave owners, presumably to encourage them to manumit their human property.

Quaker concern for the spiritual well-being of enslaved African Americans likewise grew. Mark Reeve, a member of the Salem Monthly Meeting, initiated an effort to hold a meeting for worship "amongst the Negroes of Salem." At the monthly meeting held on the twenty-fifth of the seventh month, 1768, Reeve reported that the worship service for African Americans was "accordingly held," as suggested, to "a good degree of satisfaction."[26] Reeve again pressed the matter in 1769, even as Salem Friends were considering construction of a new meeting house to replace their old and by now overcrowded building.[27] The clerk reported that slave owners had been "generally visited," and "not any amongst us justified the practice of bringing [slaves] into bondage."[28]

Salem, along with other monthly meetings under the care of the Philadelphia Yearly Meeting, soon moved toward support for complete emancipation.[29] In 1772, the Salem Monthly Meeting received "43 printed epistles wrought by our Friend John Woolman." The monthly meeting took action to distribute them to the preparative meetings under its jurisdiction and "directed them to be read."[30] The "printed epistles" were probably Woolman's *Epistle to the Quarterly and Monthly Meetings of Friends*, published just before he embarked on a voyage to visit Friends in England, where he died in Yorkshire early in October 1772.[31]

Woolman's final epistle emphasized the need for firm but loving discipline within the Quaker community. He addressed the leaders of local meetings, "noted among the professors of Truth and active in dealing with such who walk disorderly." Citing a variety of scriptural passages, Woolman urged that humility and Christian love accompany firmness in the administration of disciplinary action. Woolman advised those who imposed that discipline to be motivated solely by "Divine Love."[32]

Salem Friends not only read John Woolman's epistle but they also put his principles into practice as they dealt with local slaveholders. In the fourth month of 1774, an overseer of the Alloway's Creek Preparative Meeting reported that one Richard Smith had purchased a slave. The monthly meeting dealt gently with Smith, concluding that he "appears willing to submit to the advice of his fellow Friends." A couple of months later, Smith remained "under care," receiving spiritual oversight and guidance from the leaders of his local meeting. Those leaders acted in the spirit suggested by Woolman's final epistle, even though dealing with a very recalcitrant member.[33]

Salem Friends also resumed the practice of visiting slave owners in 1774. William Goodwin, one of the committee appointed for that purpose, reported that Salem slave owners "are mostly disposed to set [slaves] at liberty, yet not all fully as could be desired." Goodwin added that the matter "may demand our future attention." Two months later, the committee reported "a good degree of satisfaction," but some "are putting off the time notwithstanding they appear to have attained their ripe years." Presumably, this meant the common practice of delaying manumission to exploit the strength and vigor of youthful slaves.[34]

Two years before the Philadelphia Yearly Meeting made slave ownership a "disownable offense" in 1776, Salem Friends had already begun the process of purging slavery from their ranks. At a monthly meeting on the twenty-sixth of the twelfth month, 1774, the clerk presented extracts from Philadelphia "relating to the detainure [sic] of slaves beyond the limited time proscribed by law for the freedom of white people," referring to laws regulating indentured servitude. The meeting again resolved to visit slaveholders and "treat further with them in brotherly love and affection" to achieve full compliance with the stated goal of ending slaveholding within its ranks.[35]

While they dealt with slaveholding within their own body, Salem Quakers sent a petition to Governor William Franklin, the Royal Council, and the House of Representatives, imploring New Jersey's government to restrict slavery throughout the colony. The petitioners merged the rhetoric of contemporary resistance to Great Britain with the rhetoric they themselves had employed against slavery. They invoked "the laws of God and nature, the inherent and universal right of man" on which "the laws of England are founded," even pointing out the "superior advantages" of the British constitution. The toleration of slavery "among a free people" was "inimical and destructive" of that constitution, which purportedly protected personal liberties.[36]

The Quakers in Salem supplemented such constitutional arguments with reasoning based on the Quaker interpretation of Christianity. They pointed out the moral consequences of slavery with rhetoric traceable to George Fox through Benezet, Woolman, and others who had crafted the testimony against slavery. Such rhetoric had come to differentiate Quakers from most other Christian bodies. Slavery corrupted in a "pernicious" manner "the morals of the people among whom it prevails." It was thus "inconsistent with the Spirit and whole Tenor of the Christian religion."

The petition stopped short of calling for the abolition of slavery, but it did propose severe restrictions. It urged Governor Franklin to bring before the colonial legislature "such measures as may be judged most effective to suppress this complicated evil." The petitioners called the governor's attention to the "cruelty and injustice of a trade whereby many thousands of our fellow creatures are yearly forced from the state of liberty assigned them by Providence." The Quakers urged enactment of a bill to prohibit the further importation of slaves into New Jersey. Furthermore, the petitioners called for an act to ease the process of manumission, presumably referring to the law enacted in 1713 that required slaveholders to post a bond of £200 for each slave set free. Seventy-eight of the "people called Quakers" in Salem County signed the petition.

Indeed, petitioners from Gloucester, Somerset, Middlesex, Hunterdon, Burlington, and Essex Counties also supported this effort. The session of the General Assembly that met between November 1773 and March 1774 received the first petition on this subject from Gloucester County on November 24, 1773. The clerk reported receipt of a petition from Salem

County on February 8, 1774. Only one petition, from the city of Perth Amboy, inveighed against efforts to ease the process of manumission. By that time, a committee chaired by John Hinchman of Gloucester County was preparing a bill "for the more equitable manumission of slaves." The bill did not win passage. On February 16, 1774, the representatives agreed to delay its consideration until the next session of the legislature, requiring that the text of the proposed act be appended to the published minutes. With New Jersey increasingly engulfed in the turmoil of revolution, the planned reconsideration did not take place.[37]

In spite of legislative inaction, Friends continued the work within their own body. Only two cases involving slave owners unwilling to make any commitment to freeing their slaves remained open in Salem by early 1775.[38] Efforts to resolve these persisted into 1776, when the Yearly Meeting in Philadelphia reached that momentous decision to require its members to free all of their slaves. In Salem, a committee delayed confronting slave owners, but by the eighth month of 1776, the "service of visiting such as hold slaves" was "now being performed." The two slaveholders remaining under the meeting's jurisdiction proved recalcitrant. John Roberts was "determined not to free his slaves on any terms," and William Oakford, "rather shifting and evasive," promised to free his slaves in his will.[39] Nonetheless, by the end of 1776, the meeting appointed three of its members "to proceed further in that service."[40]

By the fourth month of 1777, the Salem meeting claimed that the problem of slavery within its jurisdiction was "nearly gone." Indeed, slaveholders there recorded a spate of manumissions during that very month, confirming that fourteen slaveholders in Salem had freed thirty-eight slaves. Underage slaves would not attain freedom until reaching the age of majority: eighteen for females and twenty-one for males. Based on long-observed child indenture laws, this procedure for freeing young slaves had become common practice across the colonies and especially in the Mid-Atlantic. Each manumission document stated the owner's name, the slave's name, and the effective date of the manumission (see table 7.1). Two witnesses, "Friends of good standing," signed each of the certificates.[41]

As noted above, manumission was not an inexpensive process in New Jersey. The state legislature did not reduce the bond requirement until 1786, when, at the behest of Governor William Livingston, it enacted

TABLE 7.1

Manumissions by Salem Quakers

Owner's name	Slave's name	Slave's age
William Abbott	Edward	21
Jedediah Allen	Sam	27
Aaron Bradway	Cato	28
Joseph Brick	Lil	18
Joseph Brick	Kate	5
Preston Carpenter	Charlotte	10
Preston Carpenter	Jack	40
Preston Carpenter	Perfena	47
Preston Carpenter	Fillis	6
Preston Carpenter	Primas	28
Charles Ellet	Dina	24
Charles Fogg	Dick	56
Charles Fogg	Jude	3
Charles Fogg	Susannah	1
Charles Fogg	Grace	37
Charles Fogg	Lilley	1
Charles Fogg	Teena	17
Thomas Goodwin	Will	16
William Goodwin	Frank	13
William Goodwin	Harry	11
William Goodwin	Robin	13
William Goodwin	Fillis	16
William Goodwin	Hegro	26
	Daughters	
	Hegro	5
	Hette	7
Margaret Hall	Harre	45
Samuel Hewes	Mingo	24
John Mason	Cornelius	11
William Nicholson	Sidne	22
John Somers	Jone	27
Richard Smith	Belinder	24
Richard Smith	Bob	7
Richard Smith	Floro	3
Richard Smith	Primes	26
Richard Smith	Sidne	1
James Tyler	Frank	1
Bartholomew Wyatt	Bob	46
Bartholomew Wyatt	Dick	56
Bartholomew Wyatt	George	5
Bartholomew Wyatt	Hagar	19
Bartholomew Wyatt	Peter	21
Bartholomew Wyatt	Tobias	6
Bartholomew Wyatt	Rebecca	19
Bartholomew Wyatt	Zilpah	35

Source: Manumission Papers, Salem Monthly Meeting, SC/079, Friends Historical Library, Swarthmore College, Swarthmore, PA.

a new law banning the importation of slaves into the state. In spite of the substantial financial burdens still in force in 1777, Quakers complied with the mandate of their spiritual overseers and, presumably, their own consciences.[42]

By the ninth month of 1777, Salem reported only two unresolved cases involving slave owners who evidently had reneged on earlier commitments. At that same time, Haddonfield reported thirteen such cases and Evesham reported twelve.[43] The remaining cases in Salem proved difficult to resolve. At a meeting held in the eleventh month of 1777, the Salem Monthly Meeting dealt with Charles Fogg, who had sold two young female slaves "for such a number of years and under such circumstances that their freedom would be long delayed," thus "breach[ing] the rule of our yearly meeting."[44] The Salem Women's Meeting handled a case that emerged after a report of full compliance in 1778. In the seventh month of 1779, the women approached Grace Bassett "about her selling a Negro slave for life." The women visited Bassett, who pledged to set her male slave free "at age." Grace Basset herself was ultimately disowned, not for slave ownership but for marrying "out of unity," that is, marrying a non-Quaker.[45]

Overall, though, the manumission process had gone so well that, by the late 1770s, the prime concern had shifted from manumission to assistance for the newly free African Americans. By the first month of 1778, Mark Reeve, who had started a meeting for African Americans a decade earlier, began efforts to visit African American families who, despite their newfound freedom, remained in a "low and abject condition."[46] Later that year, the meeting expressed concern "respecting the education of Negro children" and resolved to instruct them about reading the scriptures and "other writings."[47]

In the tenth month of 1778, a committee appointed to deal with the question of education presented its report, which urged "care of [ex-slaves'] conduct and morals." The committee urged Friends to "discharge their duty to these poor neglected people," even if it meant travel into the remoter parts of Salem County.[48] About the same time, the Salem Friends held worship meetings for African Americans, one of which was praised for its "respectful and affectionate conduct."[49] By 1781, the meeting had expended its funds designated for "Negro schooling," and it urged the preparative meetings to raise more money, which two had already done.[50]

Indeed, Salem Quakers adopted a somewhat paternalistic attitude toward the slaves they had freed and toward the African American community in Salem County in general. A mixture of motives—genuine compassion, the burden of conscience, and at least a measure of condescension—guided the leaders of the meeting to search for means to improve the lot of a newly freed people who would still face discrimination as they sought to construct new lives. Education, based on faith, would presumably instill a greater sense of the moral devotion so valued by Quakers.[51]

As the American Revolution ended, Salem Quakers, like Quakers in the Mid-Atlantic and elsewhere, had often suffered grievously, mainly because of their refusal to serve in the military or even to provide supplies for troops on either side. In areas where fighting was heaviest, Quakers had to deal as well with property destruction. Nevertheless, the Quakers had led a revolution of their own, helping to bring about the ultimate demise of slavery in the Mid-Atlantic. The newly independent states of New Jersey and Pennsylvania eventually enacted laws for the gradual abolition of slavery within their bounds, in 1780 and 1804, respectively.

Because of the efforts of its members, the Philadelphia Yearly Meeting was, by the mid-1780s, able to shift its attention to the questions of educating African Americans and urging national legislation to end the slave trade.[52] In 1782 the annual extract from the proceedings of the Philadelphia Yearly Meeting, sent to meetings under its care, urged "assisting and advising" freed slaves. The extract sent out in 1785 set forth the "Christian necessity" of ending the slave trade.[53] Having purged slavery from their own ranks, Friends now sought to bring about a larger social transformation in the new republic, ending the slave trade throughout the nation while seeking abolition in the Mid-Atlantic. In Nathan Kite's words, "Christian zeal tempered with Christian prudence and forbearance" laid the groundwork for a much broader effort that only intensified as time passed.[54]

In New Jersey, the majority of African Americans in counties with sizable Quaker populations had already gained their freedom before the enactment of gradual emancipation in 1804. In Salem County, 374 of 546 African Americans were free by 1790. In 1800, 607 of 692 were free by the time census takers canvassed the county; only Gloucester County, another

Quaker stronghold, had a higher percentage of freedmen than Salem.[55] By comparison, 12,422 of 16,824 African Americans in the entire state remained in bondage in 1800.

African Americans in Salem County faced enormous obstacles in taking advantage of their newly acquired liberty. In 1797, the Salem County chapter of the New Jersey Society for the Abolition of Slavery appointed one of its members to collect data on the status of both slaves and free blacks in each township. The details provided in each locality varied. Some included only general information about economic circumstances and comments on lifestyle, with remarks on the level of education. Others reported details about each family and, in some cases, individuals. Comments were often condescending, but nonetheless reflected at least a measure of concern and compassion.

Gervais Hall, who reported from Mannington Township, found that most free black families lived in "tolerable circumstances," providing for "themselves and their families plentifully," even though others were often "drunken and not counted very honest." Education concerned Barzillai Jefferis, who reported on circumstances in Lower Alloway Creek Township. Jefferis lamented that while many freedmen were "pretty good to labor," others were "subject to weaknesses and failures too much prevailing among those of their color." In Upper Penn's Neck Township, Artis Seagrave blamed the lack of education on the freedmen themselves. They gave "little attention to education;" and few "seem to make any provision for their children." Furthermore, "few of them seem to have a return for religion."[56]

Reports from two townships mentioned some of the slaves set free by Quakers twenty-five years before. In Salem Township, Edward Burroughs reported that Sidne, aged one in 1774, was married to Edward Dunn and was the mother of three children. George Dunn, once the slave of Bartholomew Wyatt, now had a son and proved "careful," having saved the sizable sum of £50. Fillis, in 1774 the six-year-old slave of Preston Carpenter, was now a "young woman" with "one bastard child." Another Sidne, aged twenty-two in 1774, was now the wife of London Miller; though "advanced in years," the couple "made a good living by their industry." Cate, five in 1774, was married and kept house in 1797. Burroughs had less praise for other former slaves. Dina, once the slave of

Charles Ellet, lived with Cuff and Sally Miller, who kept a "disorderly house and are idle and lazy."

In Elsinboro Township, Clement Hall reported in similar fashion. Harry, once enslaved to Margaret Hall, had married Hagar, once the slave of Bartholomew Wyatt, and the couple had one child. Even though Harry was "very old and nearly blind," the couple were "rather fond of frolicking," particularly the more youthful Hagar. Harry Oaker, once enslaved to William Goodwin, and his wife "make out indifferently." William Emery, once enslaved to Thomas Goodwin, was the father of one child but nevertheless "fond of strong drink." Jude Clements, the three-year-old slave of Charles Fogg in 1774, was a "poor half-witted creature." Ten of the slaves manumitted in 1774 thus appeared in the detailed returns from Salem and Elsinboro Townships.

Quakers had been at the forefront of questioning and challenging the slave trade and the institution of slavery itself. The records of the Salem Monthly Meeting reveal that missives from the Philadelphia Yearly Meeting were not only read but also heeded, and sometimes even anticipated. At times, some members complied slowly, reluctantly, and even grudgingly. But the leadership of the Salem Monthly Meeting paid careful attention to directives from its superior authority, and at times they prodded that authority to be more proactive even as they urged their membership to comply with set standards. Such interaction played a role in the long, arduous, and ultimately bloody process of ending slavery in the American republic. Henry Cadbury noted that "the growth of Quaker conscience worked independently but uniformly."[57] Although the records of the Salem Monthly Meeting, read in the context of its counterparts, reveal that the Quaker conscience did not develop with such uniformity, Quakers in Salem were among those who listened to the exhortations they received and to their consciences before many of their peers did so.

NOTES

1. This essay employs the Quaker practice of identifying months and days by number rather than by name. Thus, March is the "third month;" Sunday is the "first day." Quakers believed that the names of months and days were of pagan origin, and should not be used for that reason.

2. Gloucester and Salem Quarterly Meeting Minutes, 1697–1775 (hereafter cited as GSQM), MR/Ph/580, microfilm, Friends Historical Library, Swarthmore College, Swarthmore, PA (hereafter cited as FHL).

3. West Jersey consisted of that portion of the colony south and west of a diagonal line extending northwestward from Little Egg Harbor, including all of the present-day counties of Cape May, Atlantic, Cumberland, Salem, Gloucester, Camden, and Burlington. It also included parts of present-day Mercer, Hunterdon, and Warren Counties.

4. Michael J. Chiarappa, "The Social Context of Eighteenth-Century West New Jersey Brick Artisanry," *Perspectives in Vernacular Architecture* 4 (1991): 31–43.

5. Numerous works have narrated the emergence of Quaker opposition to slavery. Those who opposed the emergent antislavery sentiment often expressed that dissent by employing delaying tactics when abolitionist proposals were set forth at Quaker gatherings. One of the most recent accounts is Maurice Jackson, *Let This Voice Be Heard: Anthony Benezet, Father of Atlantic Abolitionism* (Philadelphia: University of Pennsylvania Press, 2009).

6. Jon Butler, "Power, Authority, and the Origins of the American Denominational Order: The English Churches in the Delaware Valley, 1680–1730," *Transactions of the American Philosophical Society* 68, no. 2 (1978): 39–43.

7. Henry J. Cadbury, "Intercolonial Solidarity of American Quakerism," *Pennsylvania Magazine of History and Biography* 64, no. 4 (October 1936): 362–374. See also Jackson, *Let This Voice Be Heard*, and Geoffrey Plank, *John Woolman's Path to the Peaceable Kingdom: A Quaker in the British Empire* (Philadelphia: University of Pennsylvania Press, 2012).

8. Peter Wacker, *Land and People: A Cultural Geography of Preindustrial New Jersey Origins and Settlement Patterns* (New Brunswick, NJ: Rutgers University Press, 1975), 121ff.

9. M. Augusta Pettit, *A Short History of the Organization of the Religious Society of Friends at Salem, New Jersey* (Salem, 1922).

10. Records of the Salem (New Jersey) Monthly Meeting, transcription at the Historical Society of Pennsylvania, Philadelphia (hereafter cited as HSP).

11. Extracts from the Philadelphia Yearly Meeting, Salem Monthly Meeting Miscellaneous Papers, RG2/Ph/S24, FHL.

12. GSQM, 68. Moses West's pamphlet, *A Treatise Concerning Marriage* (Philadelphia: Bradford, 1730), was a warning to Quakers against marriage "out of unity" and did not address the question of slavery. The book "relating to Negroes" is not precisely identified.

13. GSQM, 70.

14. Plank, *John Woolman's Path to the Peaceable Kingdom*.

15. John Woolman, *The Works of John Woolman in Two Parts* (Philadelphia: Joseph Crukshank, 1774), 24–25.

16. Salem Monthly Meeting Minutes 1740–1768, 319, HSP.

17. Plank, *John Woolman's Path to the Peaceable Kingdom*, 68; Jackson, *Let This Voice Be Heard*, 142–153.

18. Salem Monthly Meeting Minutes 1740–1768, 414, HSP.

19. Gary B. Nash, "Slaves and Slaveowners in Colonial Philadelphia," *William and Mary Quarterly*, 3rd ser., 30 (1973): 253–254.

20. Jack D. Marietta, *The Reformation of American Quakerism, 1748–1783* (Philadelphia: University of Pennsylvania Press, 1984), 116.

21. *Works of John Woolman*, 99–100.

22. For motives, see Jean R. Soderlund, *Quakers and Slavery: A Divided Spirit* (Princeton, NJ: Princeton University Press, 1985), 127–140.

23. GSQM, 163–165.

24. GSQM, 166–168.

25. GSQM, 192–193.

26. Records of Salem Monthly Meeting, 1760–1788, 7–10, HSP. Henry J. Cadbury noted that Reeve's initiative was one of the first such efforts. See Cadbury, "Negro Membership in the Society of Friends," *Journal of Negro History* 21, no. 2 (April 1936): 156.

27. Pettit, *Short History*, 12.

28. Records of Salem Monthly Meeting, 1760–1788, 8, HSP.

29. Gary Nash and Jean Soderlund note that those other monthly meetings moved with differing degrees of alacrity. In Pennsylvania, the Philadelphia Monthly Meeting proceeded quickly, while meetings in Chester County acted with greater reluctance. In New Jersey, Quakers in Shrewsbury freed their slaves long before mandated to do so, while Cesterfield Quakers refused to comply until the late 1770s. See Gary B. Nash and Jean R. Soderlund, *Freedom by Degrees: Emancipation in Pennsylvania and Its Aftermath* (New York: Oxford University Press, 1991), 91–96, and Soderlund, *Quakers and Slavery*, 127–137.

30. Records of Salem Monthly Meeting, 1760–1788, 215–222, HSP.

31. *The Journal and Major Essays of John Woolman*, ed. Phillips P. Moulton (New York: Oxford University Press, 1971), 17–20.

32. John Woolman, *An Epistle to the Quarterly and Monthly Meetings of Friends* (Burlington, NJ, 1772), 1–2.

33. Records of the Salem Monthly Meeting 1760–1788, 230, HSP.

34. Ibid., 227, 233.

35. Ibid., 239.

36. Petition of the Quakers of Salem County to Governor William Franklin, RG2/Ph/S26, FHL.

37. *Votes and Proceedings of the General Assembly of the Colony of New-Jersey at a Session Began at Burlington, Wednesday, November 10, 1773, and Continued until the 11th Day of March Following* (Burlington: Printed by Isaac Collins, 1774), 25–26, 29, 70, 73, 79, 114, 123, 132, 135, 161–162, 211–215.

38. Records of the Salem Monthly Meeting 1760–1788, 243, HSP.

39. Ibid., 292.

40. Ibid., 307.

41. Manumission papers, Salem Monthly Meeting, SC/079, FHL. Manumission records in Delaware and northeastern Maryland often followed the precedent of granting full liberty when a slave child came of age.

42. Wacker, *Land and People*, 203; Graham Russell Hodges, *Root and Branch: African Americans in New York and East Jersey 1613–1863* (Chapel Hill: University of North Carolina Press, 1999), 149.

43. Minutes of the Gloucester-Salem Quarterly Meeting, 1776–1794, 12, MR/Ph/580, microfilm, FHL.

44. Records of the Salem Monthly Meeting, 1760–1788, HSP, 334. Nathan Kite noted that one of the slaves was actually freed, but the meeting was "not able to procure" the other's release. See *A Brief Statement of the Rise and Progress of the Testimony of the Religious Society of Friends, Against Slavery and the Slave Trade* (Philadelphia: Printed by J. and W. Kite, 1843), 41.

45. Salem Women's Meeting 1763–1792, 309–311, FHL.

46. Records of the Salem Monthly Meeting 1760–1788, 341, HSP.

47. Ibid., 354.

48. Ibid., 361.

49. Ibid., 367, and Kite, *Brief Statement*, 41.

50. Records of the Salem Monthly Meeting 1760–1788, HSP, 454.

51. Hodges, *Root and Branch*, 175–176, describes the difficulties confronting rural African Americans.

52. Salem Monthly Meeting Miscellaneous Papers, RG2/Ph/524, FHL.

53. Ibid.

54. Kite, *Brief Statement*, 57.

55. Wacker, *Land and People*, 194, 416–417.

56. Mss. #5, Abolition Box #2, Burlington County, New Jersey, Abolition Collection, 1752-1840, Burlington County Historical Society, Burlington, NJ. Photocopy at the Salem County Historical Society, Salem, NJ.

57. Cadbury, "Intercolonial Solidarity," 362.

8

Slavery, Abolition, and African Americans in New Jersey's American Revolution

JAMES J. GIGANTINO II

In 1688, Quakers in Germantown, Pennsylvania, released an antislavery petition that became the first in a series of discussions among Mid-Atlantic Quakers on the morality of owning slaves. For the next hundred years, the Philadelphia Yearly Meeting, with which most New Jersey Friends associated, debated the practice of enslaving Africans while believing that all individuals were spiritually equal. The tension created by the paradox grew over time and transformed Philadelphia and western New Jersey into hotbeds of abolitionist thought, protest, and activism that influenced how both non-Quaker whites and African Americans debated abolition as slavery became increasingly important in the late colonial period.[1]

The role of Quakerism in the growth of the eighteenth-century abolition movement was critical to the eventual enactment of gradual abolition laws across the North. Quakers, although in most cases far from racial egalitarians, became the first organized group to advocate against slavery consistently. They successfully orchestrated slavery's end among their own members and eventually moved their advocacy to a wider audience. The debate over slaveholding within the Society of Friends therefore influenced statewide discussions over slavery and fused together abolitionist rhetoric, Patriot discussions of Britain's tyrannical enslavement of the colonies, and slaves' own calls for freedom. Abolitionists and slaves took advantage of the Patriots' rhetorical use of "freedom" and "slavery" to make strong parallels between the struggle for freedom from Great Britain and the hypocrisy of continued African enslavement. The Revolution therefore made the idea of freedom a right that transcended race and forced white New Jerseyans to debate slavery openly and decide whether their fight for freedom from Britain should be seen as part of a wider freedom struggle.

However, abolition remained a highly contentious and disputed proposition, given that slavery was so deeply intertwined in colonial society. Retorts of racial amalgamation, race war, racial inferiority, and potential economic losses limited its impact. Slavery survived the Revolution because of New Jersey's status as a hotly contested revolutionary battleground. The Revolution's destructive power and disruptive influence on the state, coupled with the constant threat of British invasion, encouraged lawmakers and white citizens to decline to advance abolition even as it moved forward in Pennsylvania and New England. The fallout from the actual battles solidified opposition to abolitionism and effectively ended the initial efforts to end slavery. The destructive reality of the Revolution combined with a powerful anxiety over a potential race war as hundreds of slaves absconded to British lines and returned as Loyalist soldiers. Reports of ex-slaves murdering, raping, and pillaging their former hometowns delayed serious discussions of abolition as many Jersey whites believed themselves under attack by a ruthless and uncontrollable enemy.

IN 1754, JOHN WOOLMAN AND ANTHONY BENEZET authored an official warning to the Society of Friends about slavery that "ushered in a new phase in the Quaker fight against slavery." It had an "explosive impact" on Quakers in Greater Philadelphia and, along with Woolman's writings, declared slavery sinful and encouraged the Friends to reform. Woolman argued that the slave trade represented the root of slavery's evil because it separated families, eliminated the ability of Africans to have a relationship with God, and violated the Golden Rule.[2] The Philadelphia Yearly Meeting took up Woolman's emphasis on the Golden Rule and lamented the "dreadful scenes of murder and cruelty those barbarous ravages must occasion in these unhappy people's country." Yet many Friends continued to support slavery because it had become so vital to the economy.[3]

In the 1760s and 1770s, other Jersey Quakers began to associate the burgeoning abolition movement with the brewing discontent over British imperial policies and made that link a central focus of the Revolutionary period. In 1774, Burlington Quaker Samuel Allinson claimed that the call for abolition had never been louder "than at a time when many or all the inhabitants of North America are groaning under unconstitutional impositions destructive of their liberty." Allinson further questioned whether God would forgive Americans for their failure to treat African Americans humanely. Granville Sharp, one of Britain's leading antislavery advocates, echoed this idea when in 1774 he told Allinson that if the colonists "hope[d] to maintain their own natural rights . . . they ought not to deny the same rights to" slaves.[4]

Faced with increasing pressure from multiple angles on the eve of the Revolution, the Philadelphia Yearly Meeting banned all members from owning slaves by 1776.[5] West Jersey Quakers also called for a much larger debate on slavery in New Jersey by advocating for a legislative end to the institution and for limitations to the state's harsh slave code. In 1775, Chesterfield Quakers, wishing to "avert the judgments of God from our heads," urged gradual abolition. Burlington and Cumberland Quakers added their voices to the debate, arguing that Americans must "show to the World a conduct consistent with the principles of that liberty . . . we claim as our birthright," especially as the Revolution had begun.[6]

Calls for abolition provoked protests from non-Quakers, mainly in East Jersey, who were even more dependent on slave labor than their West Jersey neighbors. In 1774, eighty-one angry Perth Amboy residents warned Governor William Franklin of the "dismal consequences" of abolition, especially the possibility of a revolt if whites could not use slavery to control the state's black population. They believed blacks were "the most barbarous in human matters" and that only slavery kept their barbarism in check. Without that institution, blacks would "invade the inhabitants and accomplish that unhuman design . . . to bring the white people into the same state that the Negroes are now in." They pleaded for Franklin to preserve "the liberty of the white people of this province."[7]

Therefore, Jersey slaveholders used fears of insurrection and anxiety over the possibility of fighting hordes of barbarous blacks to quell Quaker attempts at abolitionism. Once the Revolution began, the rhetorical devices that Patriots employed to rally support for the war moved discussions of abolitionism to center stage as Americans appropriated the language of freedom and slavery to characterize their relationship with Great Britain. Slaveholding New Jerseyans positioned their own battle against the British as a crusade to free themselves from British bondage. For instance, in October 1776 the state's General Assembly, in describing the American relationship with Great Britain, called for "deliverance from the galling yoke of slavery, the unparalleled unanimity of the American states in refitting the encroachments of despotism."[8]

Jacob Green, a Morris County Presbyterian minister, employed this same type of rhetoric to support both the Patriots and abolitionism. In a 1779 "Fast Day Sermon," Green asked his parishioners if "a people contending for liberty should, at the same time, be promoting and supporting slavery." Green argued that slaves "never forfeited their right to freedom; 'tis as the Congress say, a natural right, and an unalienable one." With this sermon, Green entered into the debate on the paradoxical role of slavery in a nation founded on individual freedom and, like many others, expressed a conviction that Americans' hypocritical actions were sinful. Across the colonies, others like Green made the link between freedom for slaves and the freedom embodied in the Declaration of Independence and advocated for an increased engagement with the question of human bondage.[9]

In New Jersey, this abolitionist linkage with the American Revolution did prod some slaveholders to answer the call for black freedom. The most prominent example came on July 4, 1783, when Moses Bloomfield, the father of future governor Joseph Bloomfield, mounted a platform in Woodbridge to celebrate the birth of the young nation. He told the crowd below that "as a nation we are free and independent—all men are created equal and why should these, my fellow citizens—my equals, be held in bondage?" He then freed all his slaves. Although men like Bloomfield remained rare in both eighteenth-century New Jersey and the United States in general, they show that at least some adhered to what was the largest movement to date that concerned itself with the role of blacks in the new republic.[10]

However, pro-slavery advocates across the colonies quickly responded to these attempts to use the Patriot cause to support abolitionism by arguing that the two propositions were very different. In November 1780, "Eliobo" rejected Green's link between the Revolution and abolition in the *New Jersey Journal*, claiming that the bondage Great Britain imposed on the colonies had little in common with the enslavement of Africans.[11] A month later, Eliobo further advanced his proslavery argument by claiming that abolition would destroy white civilization and create a "kingdom of Cuffie." With apocalyptic flair, he predicted that freed slaves would ally with the Indians. The two savage races would "sweep our land with sallies of murder and rapine. Then will the shrieks and cries of murdered children and the lamentation of assassinated friends weltering in gore" force Americans to realize that abolition produced destruction.[12] Likewise, "Marcus Aurelius," another author writing in response to Green, claimed that even the discussion of liberty could "stimulate servants to insurrection." He too saw a clear difference between freedom from the British and individual freedom of slaves, claiming that Green "in his heart knows they are measured upon two scales and have no connection with each other."[13]

As Aurelius indicates, anti-abolitionism was largely motivated by fears that slaves would harness abolitionist rhetoric themselves. Like slaves in Massachusetts and New Hampshire, Jersey slaves knew about the debates flying around them in the state's newspapers and used them as negotiation tools with their masters. In Massachusetts, for example, slaves deployed Revolutionary ideas of freedom in a petition to the legislature demanding an immediate end to their enslavement. These slaves adapted Enlightenment principles as well as rhetoric employed by Patriot pamphleteers to show the utter disparity between their status and the goals of the Revolutionary movement. Indeed, petitioners in both Massachusetts and New Hampshire attempted to illustrate to their Patriot masters that in a republic founded upon freedom, slavery could not be sustained. No formal petitions from slaves came to the New Jersey legislature, though rural slaveholders definitely believed that the Revolution's ideas of liberty had influenced their slaves. These rural slaves had let it be known that "it was not necessary [for them] to please their masters for they should not have their masters long." Revolutionary ideas therefore emboldened slaves to negotiate from a stronger position by using language from the era that would evoke a strong emotional reaction from their masters.[14]

Abolitionist petitions and the newspaper debates they provoked helped anti-abolitionists drum up significant support, motivated violence against abolitionists, and allowed anti-abolitionists to establish clear reasons for all New Jerseyans to oppose black freedom. This latter group primarily argued that slavery could not be abolished because the Revolution had devastated the state economically and because the possibility of further destruction remained imminent. For instance, one abolitionist critic claimed that New Jersey could not follow its neighbors toward abolition because it had been "laid to waste and rendered desolate by the ravages" of the British army. Governor William Livingston claimed that the legislature, "thinking us rather in too critical a situation," assumed abolitionism was too radical a step in the midst of war and thereby derailed the wartime abolitionist agenda.[15]

Indeed, the reality of war in New Jersey hit the state's citizens hard, as New Jersey became "a ragged borderline between the two Americas, Loyalist and Patriot," and where the "neutral zone of eastern and northern New Jersey, especially Monmouth and Bergen counties" witnessed the "most brutal" violence.[16] War in New Jersey became a relentless foraging battle in which both armies scavenged for supplies, with major battles occasionally highlighting the daily struggle for food and influence. Defending the state against British attack preoccupied the minds of most New Jerseyans and therefore limited the abolitionist influence.[17]

After the British invasion of New Jersey in late 1776, news of the rape of three young Hunterdon County women by British soldiers stood as indicative of the cruelty and the distressed situation that preoccupied most New Jerseyans and swayed them away from supporting any substantive change in the state's racial hierarchy.[18] The effects of the Revolution on state residents were further exacerbated by the constant threat of slaves running to British lines. Thousands of slaves from across the colonies used the proximity of British troops for their own benefit. In New Jersey, slaveholders in the most heavily slave populated county, Bergen, saw hundreds of their bondsmen join the British army, depriving residents of a key agricultural workforce. One Bergen resident, Richard Varick, bemoaned in 1778 that two of his slaves joined hundreds more who heard the British promise of freedom. The fear that blacks could run away, disrupt New Jersey's slave system, and potentially serve in the king's army exacerbated the existing anxiety caused by the war and further damaged slaveholders' economic viability. When individual negotiations between master and slave failed, the act of "stealing" oneself inadvertently convinced whites of the dangers of wartime abolition.[19]

The British practice of offering slaves their freedom, thereby hurting Patriot masters economically while strengthening their own tactical position, began in 1775, when Lord Dunmore, the last royal governor of Virginia, promised freedom to any slave who would fight for the king. News of Dunmore's proclamation spread far, and soon slaves in New Jersey understood the British army to be a beacon of freedom. British commanders across the colonies issued similar declarations. In 1779, British General David Jones declared from New York that "all Negroes that fly from the Enemy's Country are Free," an offer that Jersey slaves quickly accepted.[20] Lutheran minister Henry Muhlenberg testified to the support that the British had among Jersey slaves, writing that they wished "the British army might win, for then all Negro slaves will gain their freedom." This sentiment, according to Muhlenberg, was "almost universal among the *Negroes* in America."[21] For the most part, he was right. Thousands of blacks ran toward British lines, covered by the disorder of war, especially in the Mid-Atlantic. The fugitive slave population of Philadelphia doubled, and that of New York nearly quadrupled.[22] Throughout the war, Lord Dunmore maintained that blacks would be the "most efficacious, expeditious, cheapest, and certain means of reducing [the Patriots] to a proper sense of their duty."[23]

The constant military maneuvering in the state transformed New Jersey into a battleground between slavery and freedom as British army lines and the freedom they offered ebbed and flowed throughout the war. Fleeing slavery was easy in New Jersey; as in other occupied areas, slaves could "simply walk out of their master's homes."[24] Some did not have to walk far at all, since passing British troops lured many slaves away with promises of freedom. Ennis Graham, for instance, claimed that a large body of Hessian soldiers carried off his slave Oliver on their way to the Battle of Trenton in December 1776, while Thomas Edgar of Woodbridge saw his thirty-five-year-old male slave flee to nearby British forces during the same campaign.[25]

The British foraging raids and the rising number of absconding slaves focused attention on the perceived threat that a radical change in the state's racial structure could bring. Thousands of New Jerseyans filed damage claims with the legislature in 1781 and 1782, detailing how the British army was, as Abraham Clark wrote, one of "the most savage known among civilized nations" and had "spread desolation through" New Jersey, precipitating an economic and social crisis. These damages had a direct impact on slaveholders' unwillingness to support freedom for their chattel. Between 1775 and 1783, 83 percent of slaves mentioned in wills statewide were sold or bequeathed to a slaveholder's heirs; only 17 percent gained freedom. Even as Quakers brought discussions of abolition to the forefront of regional consciousness, the revolutionary spirit did not animate the vast majority of New Jersey and New York slaveholders.[26]

More than just threatening wealth and status, however, runaway slaves also stoked already heightened fears of slave rebellion. The possibility of black revolt came alive in 1772, when, in the midst of abolitionist discussions, Somerset slaveholders learned that their slaves had congregated in mass meetings at night to discuss freedom. Masters in Somerset had feared just such discontent, having repeatedly observed their slaves disobeying the state's slave code. In 1771, for instance, Somerset justice of the peace Jacob Van Noorstrand recorded the convictions of ten slaves for violating the nine o'clock curfew and for theft.[27] Jersey slaves, absorbing the rhetoric of revolution from Patriot sources, forced the issue of slave freedom even further in 1774. Slaveholders in Shrewsbury and Middletown complained that their slaves increasingly ignored the curfew and, as in Somerset, met at night to create a plan to "cut the throats of their masters" and take over the state. In 1775, the Committee of Safety in Shrewsbury safeguarded against black revolt by banning all slave meetings and ordering the militia to conduct nightly slave patrols.[28]

The fires that ravaged Baltimore, Philadelphia, Savannah, and New York in December 1776 further inflamed tensions among whites already anxious over the possibility of revolt. New York City newspapers reported that "the minds of the citizens are in a state of agitation" because many believed rebellious slaves had set the fires.[29] As in New York, the danger of black revolt loomed more ominously as British forces crisscrossed New Jersey, making freedom for slaves that much more tangible. In August 1776, Jonathan Dickinson Sergeant, a member of the Second Continental Congress, wrote to John Adams that New Jersey had to call out its militia because the "slaves left at home excite an alarm for the safety of their families." In 1779, Sergeant's fears became reality as local Loyalists and British forces coaxed slaves near Elizabethtown to murder their masters.

Even though authorities discovered the plot in its planning stages and quickly suppressed it, the slaves' willing response highlights the important role that the British played as agitators in stoking fears of rebellion.[30]

Many Jersey masters saw British efforts to recruit blacks as particularly dangerous because the British army provided a ready training ground for ex-slaves to spread destruction and death in retribution for past wrongs. The practice had been discussed by Lord Dartmouth as early as May 1775. Indeed, in June 1775, General Thomas Gage advocated that "we must avail ourselves of every resource even to raise the Negroes in our cause." By July 1776, Patriot leaders received reports of large numbers of blacks mustering with British regiments, and British recruitment efforts in New York increased significantly after Henry Clinton's 1779 guarantee of freedom to all slaves who deserted their masters.[31]

The presence of black British troops signaled the elevation of black power in New Jersey and assaulted the state's racial hierarchy: for the first time, blacks held power over whites. Newark minister Alexander MacWhorter described the dangers of arming black men when he detailed the aftermath of a British attack on his city in 1777. The enemy force, which included black British troops, made the town "look more like a scene of ruin than a pleasant well cultivated village." Former slaves invaded and assaulted at least three men. One man was "cut and slashed" horribly, while "three women were most horridly ravished by them, one of them an old woman near seventy years of age, whom they abused in a manner beyond description, another of them was a woman considerably advanced in her pregnancy, and the third was a young girl."[32]

The Newark raid confirmed whites' most powerful fears, that ex-slaves would come back to kill, rape, and pillage among their former masters' homes and families. Even some British officers believed that marauding black troops were particularly dangerous because they "distress and maltreat the inhabitants infinitely more than the whole army at the same time that they engross, waste, and destroy."[33] Colonel Tye, or Titus, a slave from Colts Neck in Monmouth County, embodied these fears. After he fled from his master, Titus joined the British army and returned to New Jersey as Colonel Tye to lead a band of mostly black guerrilla fighters that operated out of Sandy Hook. Tye and his men attacked wealthy slaveholding Patriots, burned houses, seized guns, and foraged for food and supplies in order to disrupt Patriot activities and maintain the British war machine.[34]

Monmouth County residents decried these attacks by their former slaves and requested emergency assistance from Governor William Livingston. The county had already been devastated by the early years of the war and was even more battered after the Battle of Monmouth. John Fell, a delegate to the Second Continental Congress, wrote to fellow delegate Robert Morris that Monmouth County had been ravaged by the war "as bad as Bergen," the county that bore much of the brunt of British raiding parties.[35] Livingston declared martial law and requested additional supplies and troops from the legislature to stop Tye. However, in September 1780 Tye's unit made its most dramatic attack, a failed attempt to capture Monmouth militia officer Joshua Huddy. In the fierce two-hour battle at Toms River, Tye suffered a minor bullet wound to the wrist, which became infected and ultimately killed him a few days later. Even though he died before the war ended, Tye and his unit succeeded in bringing so much fear and destruction to New Jersey that whites dreaded the consequences of freeing their slaves.[36]

UNLIKE THE BRITISH army, the Continental forces never guaranteed freedom to slaves in exchange for service. New Jersey, like most states, did not allow slaves or freed blacks to join the militia, thereby reinforcing the state's existing racial boundaries.[37] Nevertheless, black troops did enter Continental service in New Jersey in various ways. Some Patriot commanders believed that black troops could play an important role as foils to black British troops. For example, Governor Livingston suggested to George Washington in 1777 that "it may not be improper to let loose upon [the British] a few of General Stephen's tawny Yagers, the only Americans that can match them in their bloody work." In Livingston's opinion, the black soldiers serving in Major General Adam Stephen's Virginia brigade could fight the black British troops on their own terms because of their perceived inherent barbarity.[38]

One New Jersey slave, Samuel Sutphen of Somerset County, joined the Patriot cause as a substitute for his owner, Casper Berger. His original owner, Barbardus LaGrange, had declared his loyalty to Britain and fled to New York, leaving Sutphen to be confiscated as part of a forfeited Loyalist estate. Berger bought Sutphen from the state and offered him freedom if he served as his master's substitute for the war's duration. Sutphen agreed and joined the Somerset County militia and later served in a Cumberland County unit as well. In his 1832 federal pension application, Sutphen claimed that he fought at the Battle of Long Island and served on garrison duty at several locations in New Jersey during the winter of 1776. In January 1777, he fought at Princeton with Washington, engaged in several skirmishes in the summer and fall of 1777 around the Millstone River, and, by 1778, marched to Monmouth, where he narrowly missed the battle with the British. Sutphen then joined the expedition to Fort Stanwix, New York, where he and his unit pursued Britain's Indian allies as far north as Buffalo. On his return south, Hessians and British Highlanders ambushed his company in Westchester County, where a bullet drove his pants button into his right leg just above the ankle. Waylaid for almost three months because of his injury, Sutphen returned to Readington, New Jersey, and served until 1780. Upon Sutphen's discharge, however, Berger reneged on his promise of freedom and sold him to Peter Ten Eyck. Ten Eyck sold him to John Duryea, who then sold him to Peter Sutphen. Samuel Sutphen finally achieved legal freedom in 1805 only by purchasing himself.[39]

Aged eighty-five when he applied for a federal pension, Sutphen secured numerous letters of support from prominent Somerset whites who believed, as William Gaston claimed, that Sutphen was "highly meritorious of a pension" because he "ably and nobly performed" his duties as a soldier. The federal government, however, rejected his claim. Because he was "a slave originally," the rejection letter explained, Sutphen "was not bound to serve in the militia and the circumstances of each tour of actual service [were] not . . . stated as was required." As debate on his claim continued, the Pension Office in 1834 and 1835 maintained that his service against the Indians remained "very doubtful" and that Sutphen most likely had not served a full six months, as required by the pension law. In an unlikely show of support for a black veteran, the Frelinghuysen family, a powerful New Jersey political dynasty, petitioned the state legislature to support Sutphen. In response, the state granted Sutphen a pension for the last five years of his life.[40]

Aside from the detailed records about Sutphen, only the most basic information can be found about other Jersey blacks who fought for the

Patriots. Sketchy military service records indicate that at least twenty-nine blacks served in New Jersey, including Negro Stephen, who joined the Second Regiment of Continental Dragoons in December 1781 as a private. Negro Pomp, a teamster in charge of a four-horse wagon, served in Trenton in 1780. Negro Jack, Negro Cezar, Negro Dick, and Negro Will all did the same, but no information survives to reveal more than their names and occupations within the army. Because New Jersey, like most other states, never actively recruited black soldiers or promised freedom in exchange for military service, it stands likely that most of these enslaved men returned, like Samuel Sutphen, to their masters as slaves.[41]

IN CONCLUSION, the emergence of a strong post-Revolutionary slavery system able to survive abolitionism into the nineteenth century owed much to New Jersey's unique position as a borderland between Patriot and Loyalist America. Before and during the war, abolitionists had championed the idea of black freedom; but with no organized state-level abolition society and the reality of British forces nearby, legislative action stalled. The ravages of total war combined with the fears created by the actions of Colonel Tye and other ex-slaves who joined the British army convinced many whites that wartime abolition would result in further dislocation and disorder. Of course, Jersey blacks used the Revolution to seek freedom on their own terms; yet these methods proved largely ineffective in overturning entrenched proslavery thought and practice for more than a small minority of slaves. Their exploits actually reinforced the state's racial boundaries, strengthened anti-abolition sentiment, and limited abolition's reach because absconding slaves helped exacerbate white anxieties of revolt.

In the end, the state's limited use of slaves in its own battle for freedom and the lack of recognition and reward even for those who fought for the Patriots meant that Revolutionary freedom would not extend to African Americans in New Jersey. The Revolution therefore reinforced the colonial slave system in the short run instead of convincing New Jerseyans to support gradual abolition laws, as had occurred in Pennsylvania, Connecticut, and Rhode Island. New Jersey did not even begin gradual abolition until twenty-one years after the Revolution's end in 1804, allowing slavery's slow death to linger well into the 1830s and 1840s.

NOTES

1. Gary B. Nash and Jean R. Soderlund, *Freedom by Degrees: Emancipation in Pennsylvania and Its Aftermath* (New York: Oxford University Press, 1991), 81–82, 89–90; Jean R. Soderlund, *Quakers and Slaves: A Divided Spirit* (Princeton, NJ: Princeton University Press, 1985), 8–14, 169–172; Gary B. Nash, *Forging Freedom: The Formation of Philadelphia's Black Community, 1720–1840* (Cambridge, MA: Harvard University Press, 1988), 42; Arthur Zilversmit, *The First Emancipation: The Abolition of Slavery in the North* (Chicago: University of Chicago Press, 1967), 78–83.

2. Thomas Slaughter, *The Beautiful Soul of John Woolman, Apostle of Abolition* (New York: Hill and Wang, 2008), 103, 132–134, 163; *An Epistle of Caution and Advice Concerning the Buying and Keeping of Slaves* (Philadelphia: Printed and sold by James Chattin, 1754); Maurice Jackson, *Let This Voice Be Heard: Anthony Benezet, Father of Atlantic Abolitionism* (Philadelphia: University of Pennsylvania Press, 2009), 52–55, quote on page 53.

3. *Friends' Intelligencer*, May 9, 1874.

4. Granville Sharp to Samuel Allinson, July 28, 1774, and Samuel Allinson to Patrick Henry, October 17, 1774, Allinson Family Papers (MC 796), Special Collection and University Archives, Rutgers University Libraries (hereafter cited as RUSC); David Brion Davis, *Inhuman Bondage: The Rise and Fall of Slavery in the New World* (New York: Oxford University Press, 2006), 144–145; David Brion Davis, *The Problem of Slavery in Western Culture* (New York: Oxford University Press, 1965), 291–493.

5. Nash and Soderlund, *Freedom by Degrees*, 81–82, 89–90; Soderlund, *Quakers and Slaves*, 8–14, 169–172; Nash, *Forging Freedom*, 42; Zilversmit, *First Emancipation*, 78–83; Jackson, *Let This Voice Be Heard*, 248–249.

6. Zilversmit, *First Emancipation*, 91–93; Petition of Inhabitants of Chester Township, Burlington County to the General Assembly Advocating the Gradual Abolition of Slavery, November 9, 1775, Legislative Records, 1770–1781, box 1-14, Bureau of Archives and History, New Jersey State Archives (hereafter cited as BAH-NJSA); Petition of Inhabitants of Burlington County to the New Jersey State Legislature Advocating the Manumission of Slaves and Petition of Inhabitants of Cumberland County to the New Jersey State Legislature Advocating the Manumission of Slaves, Legislative Records, no date, box 1-19, BAH-NJSA.

7. Petition of the Citizens of Perth Amboy to the General Assembly Opposing Slave Manumissions, January 12, 1774, Legislative Records 1770–1781, box 1-14, BAH-NJSA.

8. *Votes and Proceedings of the General Assembly of the State of New-Jersey . . .* (Burlington, NJ: Printed by Isaac Collins, 1777), October 5, 1776, 36–38; Davis, *Inhuman Bondage*, 144–145; F. Nwabueze Okoye, "Chattel Slavery as the Nightmare of the American Revolutionaries," *William and Mary Quarterly*, 3rd ser., 37, no. 1 (1980): 5–28; Ari Helo and Peter Onuf, "Jefferson, Morality, and the Problem of Slavery," *William and Mary Quarterly*, 3rd ser., 60, no. 3 (2003): 583–614.

9. Jacob Green to the Synod of New York and Philadelphia, October 18, 1779, Minutes of the Presbyteries of New York, Morris County, and Newark (MG 839), New Jersey Historical Society (hereafter cited as NJHS); Jacob Green, *A Sermon Delivered at Hanover, April 22, 1778, Being the Day of Public Fasting and Prayer throughout the United States of America* (Chatham, 1779), as printed in David Mitros, *Jacob Green and the Slavery Debate in Revolutionary Morris County, New Jersey* (Morristown: Morris County Heritage Commission, 1993), 35–44; also see 7–14.

10. Giles R. Wright, "Moving Toward Breaking the Chains: Black New Jerseyans and the American Revolution," in *New Jersey in the American Revolution*, ed. Barbara Mitnick (New Brunswick, NJ: Rutgers University Press, 2005), 130.

11. *New Jersey Journal* (Chatham, NJ), November 29, 1780; Nash, *Forging Freedom*, 39.

12. *New Jersey Journal*, December 27, 1780.

13. *New Jersey Journal*, January 17 and January 24, 1781. For other debates about Green, see *New Jersey Journal*, January 10, January 24, and January 31, 1781.

14. Ira Berlin, *Many Thousands Gone: The First Two Centuries of Slavery in North America* (Cambridge, MA: Harvard University Press, 1998), 193.

15. For violence, see Simon Schama, *Rough Crossings: Britain, the Slaves, and the American Revolution* (New York: HarperCollins, 2006), 111–112; Graham Russell Hodges, *Root and Branch: African Americans in New York and East Jersey* (Chapel Hill: University of North Carolina Press, 1999), 143; *New Jersey Gazette* (Burlington, NJ), October 4, 1780. For other newspaper debates, see *New Jersey Gazette*, November 8, 1780, January 10, 1781, February 14, 1781, March 21, 1781, April 1, 1781, and June 27, 1781; Zilversmit, *First Emancipation*, 141–142; William Livingston to Samuel Allinson, July 25, 1778, in *The Papers of William Livingston*, ed. Carl Prince et al., 5 vols. (Trenton: New Jersey Historical Commission; New Brunswick, NJ: Rutgers University Press, 1979–1988), 2:399–404.

16. Schama, *Rough Crossings*, 113–114; Graham Russell Hodges, *Slavery, Freedom, and Culture among Early American Workers* (Armonk, NY: M. E. Sharpe, 1998), 67.

17. Robert Middlekauff, *The Glorious Cause: The American Revolution, 1763–1789*, rev. ed. (New York: Oxford University Press, 2005), 360–369.

18. Papers and Affidavits Relating to the Plunderings, Burnings, and Ravages Committed by the British, 1775–1784, in National Archives and Records Administration microfilm publication M247, *Papers of the Continental Congress, 1774–1789*, RG 360, pp. 29–39.

19. Richard Varick to Philip Van Renssalaer, October 30, 1778, as cited in Hodges, *Slavery, Freedom, and Culture*, 43–44; Gary B. Nash, *The Forgotten Fifth: African Americans in the Age of Revolution* (Cambridge, MA: Harvard University Press, 2006), 67; Woody Holton, *Forced Founders: Indians, Debtors, Slaves, and the Making of the American Revolution in Virginia* (Chapel Hill: University of North Carolina Press, 1999), 156–157.

20. For the David Jones quote, see Douglas R. Egerton, *Death or Liberty: African Americans and Revolutionary America* (New York: Oxford University Press, 2009), 84.

For Henry Clinton's proclamation, see "Proclamation of Sir Henry Clinton," *Royal Gazette* (New York), July 3, 1779. For Dunmore's proclamation, see Nash, *Forgotten Fifth*, 26–27; David N. Gellman, *Emancipating New York: The Politics of Slavery and Freedom, 1777–1827* (Baton Rouge: Louisiana State University Press, 2006), 38; Nash, *Forging Freedom*, 45; Berlin, *Many Thousands Gone*, 257–258; Wright, "Moving Toward Breaking the Chains," 127; Holton, *Forced Founders*, 156–163.

21. *The Journals of Henry Melchior Muhlenberg*, trans. Theodore G. Tappert and John W. Doberstein, 3 vols. (Philadelphia: Evangelical Lutheran Ministerium of Pennsylvania and Adjacent States, 1942–1958), 3:78, as cited in Nash, *The Forgotten Fifth*, 30.

22. Erica Armstrong Dunbar, *A Fragile Freedom: African American Women and Emancipation in the Antebellum City* (New Haven, CT: Yale University Press, 2008), 22; Egerton, *Death or Liberty*, 89; Graham Russell Hodges and Alan Edward Brown, eds., *"Pretends to Be Free": Runaway Slave Advertisements from Colonial and Revolutionary New York and New Jersey* (New York: Garland, 1994); Billy Smith, "Runaway Slaves in the Mid-Atlantic Region during the Revolutionary Era," in *The Transforming Hand of Revolution: Reconsidering the American Revolution as a Social Movement*, ed. Ronald Hoffman and Peter J. Albert (Charlottesville: University Press of Virginia, 1995), 199–230.

23. Earl of Dunmore to Sir Henry Clinton, February 2, 1782, and "Scheme for Raising Black Troops in South Carolina," January 5, 1782, Colonial Office Correspondence, CO 5/175/67–68 and 264–266.

24. Dunbar, *Fragile Freedom*, 21.

25. Inventories of Damages by the British and Americans in New Jersey, 1776–1782, Legislative Records, NJSA, microfilm. For specific claims mentioned, see Middlesex County claims 1 and 214. For the battleground between slavery and freedom, see Schama, *Rough Crossings*, 111–118.

26. Schama, *Rough Crossings*, 114; Michael Adelberg, "An Evenly Balanced County: The Scope and Severity of Civil Warfare in Revolutionary Monmouth County, New Jersey," *Journal of Military History* 73, no. 1 (January 2009): 9–48; Abraham Clark to James Caldwell, February 4, 1777, Louis Bamberger Autograph Collection (MG 11), NJHS; Zilversmit, *First Emancipation*, 242; Hodges, *Root and Branch*, 143.

27. Hodges, *Slavery, Freedom, and Culture*, 72; Dorothy Stratford, "Docket of Jacob Van Noorstrand," *Genealogical Magazine of New Jersey* 43 (1968): 58–67.

28. Graham Russell Hodges, *Slavery and Freedom in the Rural North: African Americans in Monmouth County, New Jersey 1665–1865* (Madison, WI: Madison House, 1997), 94–95.

29. *Claypoole's American Daily Advertiser* (Philadelphia), December 19, 1776, as cited in *The Papers of Alexander Hamilton*, ed. Harold C. Syrett et al., vol. 20 (New York: Columbia University Press, 1974), 471–473.

30. Jonathan Dickinson Sergeant to John Adams, August 13, 1776, in *Papers of John Adams*, ed. Robert Taylor et al., vol. 4 (Cambridge, MA: Harvard University Press,

1979), 453–455; newspaper extract from the *New York Packet and the American Advertisers*, July 1, 1779, in *Documents Relating to the Revolutionary History of the State of New Jersey*, 2nd ser., 5 vols. (Trenton, 1901–1917), 3:490; Edwin Hatfield, *History of Elizabeth, New Jersey* (New York: Carlton and Lanahan, 1868), 476; Nash, *Forging Freedom*, 45; Wright, "Moving Toward Breaking the Chains," 126.

31. Proclamation of Sir Henry Clinton, June 30, 1779, Henry Clinton Papers, vol. 62, Clements Library, University of Michigan, Ann Arbor (hereafter cited as CL); Alexander Innes to Lord Dartmouth, May 16, 1775, in *The American Papers of the Second Earl of Dartmouth in the Staffordshire Record Office* (East Ardsley, UK: Microform Academic Publishers, 1993); Robert Pigot to Sir William Howe, April 10, 1778, in *British Headquarters (Sir Guy Carleton) Papers* (Washington, DC: Microfilming Service, 1957), item 2094; Thomas Gage to Lord Barrington, June 12, 1775, in Thomas Gage Papers, English Series, vol. 29, CL; Nathanael Greene to George Washington, July 21, 1776, in *The Papers of General Nathanael Greene*, ed. Robert E. McCarthy (Wilmington, DE: Scholarly Resources, 1989), microfilm; Earl of Dunmore to Sir Henry Clinton, February 2, 1782, Colonial Office Correspondence, CO 5/175/67–68 and 264–266. These microfilm sources are available at the David Library of the American Revolution, Washington Crossing, PA.

32. Reverend Alexander MacWhorter's letter in *Documents Relating to the Revolutionary History of the State of New Jersey*, 2nd ser., 1:350–353.

33. Patrick Ferguson, "Proposed Plan for Bringing the Army Under Strict Discipline with Regard to Marauding," November 1779, Clinton Papers, vol. 78, CL.

34. Schama, *Rough Crossings*, 114–115; Egerton, *Death or Liberty*, 65–67; extract of a letter from Monmouth County, June 12, 1780, in *Documents Relating to the Revolutionary History of the State of New Jersey*, 2nd ser., 4:434–435; *New Jersey Gazette*, April 12, 1780; *Old Times in Old Monmouth: Historical Reminiscences of Old Monmouth County, New Jersey* (Freehold: Monmouth Democrat, 1887), 70–115, esp. 72–75.

35. John Fell to Robert Morris, July 10, 1779, in *Letters of Delegates to Congress, 1774–1789*, 26 vols. (Washington, DC: Library of Congress, 1976–2000), http://web.archive.org/web/20110114033744/http://etext.lib.virginia.edu/etcbin/toccer-new2?id=DelVol13.xml&images=images/modeng&data=/texts/english/modeng/parsed&tag=public&part=200&division=div1.

36. A letter from Freehold, April 15, 1782, in *Documents Relating to the Revolutionary History of the State of New Jersey*, 2nd ser., 5:424; Hodges, *Slavery and Freedom in the Rural North*, 102–106; Schama, *Rough Crossings*, 115–116; William Livingston to Asher Holmes, March 21, 1780, in *Papers of William Livingston*, 3:343–344.

37. Nash, *Forging Freedom*, 51–52; Nash, *Forgotten Fifth*, 10–11; Dunbar, *A Fragile Freedom*, 22; Gary B. Nash, *The Unknown Revolution: The Unruly Birth of Democracy and the Struggle to Create America* (New York: Viking, 2005), 329; Henry Wiencek, *An Imperfect God: George Washington, His Slaves, and the Creation of America* (New York: Farrar, Straus, and Giroux, 2003), 227; "An Act for the better regulating the Militia," March 15, 1777, *Acts of the General Assembly of the State of New-Jersey*,

1st sess., ch. XX, 26; "An Act for the Regulating, Training and Arraying of the Militia," April 14, 1778, *Acts*, 2nd sess., 2nd sitting, ch. XXII, 44–45; Robert Gough, "Black Men and the Early New Jersey Militia," *New Jersey History* 88, no. 4 (December 1970), 227–238.

38. Nash, *Forgotten Fifth*, 10–13; Nash, *Unknown Revolution*, 327–339; William Livingston to George Washington, February 22, 1777, in *Papers of William Livingston*, 1:250–251. For more on slaves serving in the military, see Egerton, *Death or Liberty*, 74–81; Philip S. Foner, *Blacks in the American Revolution* (Wesport, CT: Greenwood Press, 1975); Robert Ewell Greene, *Black Courage, 1775–1783: Documentation of Black Participation in the American Revolution* (Washington, DC: National DAR, 1984); and Glenn A. Knoblock, *Strong and Brave Fellows: New Hampshire's Black Soldiers and Sailors of the American Revolution, 1775–1784* (Jefferson, NC: McFarland, 2003).

39. Revolutionary War Index Files, NJSA; Samuel Sutphen federal pension application, August 15, 1832, NARA M805, roll 783, file R10321; A. Van Doren Honeyman, ed., "The Revolutionary War Record of Samuel Sutphen, Slave," *Somerset County Historical Quarterly* 3 (1914): 186–190, as reprinted in *New Jersey in the American Revolution, 1763–1783: A Documentary History*, ed. Larry Gerlach (Trenton: New Jersey Historical Commission, 1975), 354–360. For more on Sutphen, also see William Schleicher and Susan Winter, "Patriot and Slave: The Samuel Sutphen Story," *New Jersey Heritage* 1, no. 1 (Winter 2002): 30–43. Casper Berger died in 1815; see Bergun Brokaw Account Book, 1812–1851 (MC 362), RUSC, for his coffin purchase. For other cases of slaves who did not gain their freedom from service in the Revolution, see Benjamin Quarles, *The Negro in the American Revolution* (Chapel Hill: University of North Carolina Press, 1961), 183–184.

40. Samuel Sutphen federal pension application, August 15, 1832. For another example of a rejected pension from a black soldier, see Margot Minardi, "Freedom in the Archives: The Pension Case of Primus Hall," in *Slavery/Antislavery in New England*, ed. Peter Benes (Boston: Boston University, 2005), 128–140.

41. New Jersey Revolutionary War Numbered Manuscripts, 5970–5975, NJSA.

9

A Loyalist Homestead in a World Turned Upside Down

DONALD SHERBLOM

The sun was setting and eighteen-year-old Mary Grandin Vought was about to give birth. She had reason to be apprehensive. Her sister-in-law Christiana had died in childbed six months earlier. Mary and her husband, John, had taken Christiana's infant son into their household. As darkness enveloped their farmstead, Mary's contractions grew stronger and more frequent until nine o'clock, when the cries of a newborn pierced the night. John and Mary named her Christiana. As Mary lay with her newborn daughter on this mid-September 1773 night, a decade of controversy over Parliamentary authority was coming to a head. In Philadelphia, men were organizing to stop the import of East India Company tea. When the *Polly* sailed up the Delaware in October with a tea shipment, activists persuaded the captain to return his cargo to England. Inspired by their resistance, in December a crowd in Boston boarded ships and dumped cases of East India Company tea into the harbor. The dispute roiling Atlantic seaports would soon spread and develop into rebellion, disrupting the peaceful lives of New Jersey farmers like John and Mary in Hunterdon County's Lebanon Township.

Parliament responded to the destruction of the tea in Boston with the Coercive Acts, which closed that port to shipping, revoked the province's charter of 1691, and prohibited town meetings, thereby punishing the entire Massachusetts population for the actions of a crowd. Revoking the charter set a dangerous precedent: if Parliament could cancel one colony's fundamental law, no province was safe, no rights were protected from the overreach of distant legislators. Rural New Jersey was drawn into this mounting crisis as local committees sent aid to the people of Boston. The American crisis divided communities, especially in the Middle Colonies of Pennsylvania, New York, and New Jersey. Here the controversy and the push for independence entailed a civil war. The Voughts' friend and neighbor Thomas Jones represented Hunterdon County in the Provincial Congress, which endorsed the Continental Congress in Philadelphia. Christiana was but three when her father John and grandfather Christopher Vought rode off with seventy-five Hunterdon Loyalists to join the Loyalist New Jersey Volunteers as the British army swept through New Jersey in December 1776. Washington's retreating Continental troops barely escaped across the Delaware River in boats collected by Daniel Bray and Thomas Jones of the Hunterdon militia. Christopher and John became local leaders of those who remained loyal; Thomas Jones joined the rebel cause. Formerly close neighbors faced one another on opposing sides at war.

Tradition holds that when the British surrendered at Yorktown in 1781, their band played "A World Turned Upside Down." In New Jersey, loyal British Americans experienced that reversal of fortunes much earlier, when Washington re-crossed the Delaware in the winter of 1776. His unexpected victories at Trenton and Princeton revived the failing rebellion and prompted British troops to withdraw from most of New Jersey. Patriots resumed control of a province with widespread Loyalist sympathies and overwhelming British forces at its borders. With so many farmers serving in the Patriot militia or royal Provincial troops, the role of managing their farms fell to their wives. Christopher Vought's wife, Cornelia, and her daughter-in-law Mary managed the 488-acre Vought farm as the wives of loyal British Americans under the increasing dominion of a Patriot government, in a world turned upside down.

During the American Revolution's early and most vulnerable years, from the decision to declare independence to the victory at Saratoga that prompted the 1778 French alliance, New Jersey was the primary theater of war. In this contested territory—with a restive Loyalist minority and internecine warfare, the scene of major Continental battles and frequent enemy incursions, "under the shadow of the British Army's mighty garrison in New York City"—the new state struggled to assert its authority, raise taxes, and organize the militia.[1] The experiences of the Vought family

reveal how a newly independent state emerged and established its authority in these first crucial years of upheaval. Their story also provides an
unusual example of the widespread practice of colonial wives managing
their husbands' farms during the war, a necessity that, combined with
revolutionary ideals, gave impetus to greater social and political equality
in the new republic.

CHRISTIANA VOUGHT WAS born that September 1773 night in the stone
house her grandfather Christopher built in 1759. It was an impressive two-
and-a-half-story colonial facing south toward the Brunswick Pike, set well
back from the road. A brick chimney rose from each end of its cedar shake
roof. Next door to the east, Thomas Jones kept a tavern, the site of township
meetings, where travelers along the great road from New Brunswick to
Easton stopped for refreshment, sharing news from distant towns. Behind
the house was a good barn, outbuildings, and a newly purchased 203-acre
wooded parcel. The now 488-acre Vought farmstead "was under good cultivation, 165 acres were in tillage, 25 acres of meadow, and the rest timber."[2]

From the fields around the house, where dozens of sheep, hogs, and
cows grazed, the Vought farm stretched west across the Raritan River,
above the union of the Raritan and Spruce Run, where David McKinney
built a stone mill dam. The boundary ran north along the river to Allen's
Union Iron Works, where river water powered the bellows at the furnaces
and worked the slitting mill. By 1773, John Allen owned the ironworks. He
was the son of William Allen, an ally of the Penn proprietors and one of
the wealthiest men in Philadelphia, who had started the iron plantation
with his partner Joseph Turner in 1742. At the height of its production, the
Union Iron Works shipped tons of pig iron, wrought iron, and refined
anchonies from two furnaces and a forge, plus finished products such as
rods and nails from the slitting mill, by wagon to the Delaware and down-
river to Philadelphia. This rural enclave of woodcutters, charcoal colliers,
ore miners, furnace workers, and teamsters—a mix of wage earners, indentured immigrants, and enslaved workers—provided a ready market for
local farm produce. The Vought farm sold wheat and butter at the company store. Transportation links to Philadelphia and to New York (via
sloops from New Brunswick) allowed farmers to send wheat and other
farm produce to those port cities and to international markets.

John Allen's ties to the Philadelphia merchant firm of Allen and Turner meant that farmers in rural Lebanon Township had access at the company store to a variety of imported goods from across the empire, including fine textiles that competed with homespun fabrics. Christopher and John Vought bought silks, molasses, rum, tea, and sugar. They also purchased flints, gunpowder, shot, clay pipes, snuff, and cards for making woolens. John bought a pair of silver buckles.[3] As T. H. Breen notes, colonists were drawn into the Atlantic trade and participated in a consumer revolution decades before the War for Independence: "they celebrated the comforts of a new and expanded material culture."[4] Their importance as consumers also gave colonists leverage to force the repeal of Parliamentary laws through boycotts as early as the 1765 Stamp Act and to resist their colonial status over the next decade. Boycotts also created a political environment in which "private decisions about mundane purchases became matters of public judgment." Consumer sacrifice united strangers across the colonies in a common cause and divided them from the perceived enemies of American liberty.[5]

Both the cultural heritage of the Vought family and the influence of the British Atlantic world are evident in the house Christopher built, with its blend of Germanic and British architecture. The chimneys at the gable ends and the center hall floor plan are typically British, while the "wattle and daub" decorative plaster ceilings (built on a lattice of woven twigs, not lathe) and geometric patterns scribed into the ceilings of four rooms reflect the Vought's Palatine German heritage. Other Palatine homes had ceilings with symmetrical patterns, but this home's center hall called forth a uniquely linear design. A plaster serpent slithers down the hall ceiling to the foyer and part way back, its head turned to face the front door. Ornamental plaster ceilings, chair rails, and moldings set off the Vought family's fine furniture, which included a dining table and chairs, a chest of drawers, a valuable great clock, and, of course, a tea table.

The Vought family's assimilation into British Atlantic culture crossed religious lines. Christopher Vought was a Palatine Lutheran; his wife, Cornelia, was Dutch. Their daughter Christiana married a Lutheran minister; their son John wed Mary Grandin, whose parents were Quakers, at a local Anglican church. At about the time of John and Mary's ceremony, in November 1772, Christopher Vought was feeling his age; he retired and made over his property to John, who became the head of their household. As the new patriarch, John Vought held the property and made decisions for the family.

John and Christopher were both prominent farmers and leaders in Lebanon Township. Christopher had been a road commissioner. John Vought was elected town clerk at the annual township meeting held at Thomas Jones's tavern in March 1774, a year of controversy in British America over the Coercive Acts, which led to the First Continental Congress in Philadelphia that fall. The New Jersey General Assembly chose five delegates to this extralegal body, which approved a boycott of British imports until Parliament repealed the Coercive Acts. This non-importation agreement would rely on county and township committees to enforce compliance by pressuring reluctant citizens to join boycott associations. John Vought did not support this boycott of British goods but "signed an Association and attended the training of the Militia" because he "durst not declare his sentiments."[6] He remained active in township politics and was reelected "town clark" in March 1775, a month before the outbreak of war at Lexington and Concord.[7]

Local committees also elected men to attend New Jersey's extralegal Provincial Congress. In January 1775, the Voughts' neighbor Thomas Jones was among those chosen. These committees included previously uninvolved men and every member of the legal colonial assembly, except the speaker, Cortland Skinner, and Richard Lawrence, a Quaker from Monmouth County, a near unanimity that gave the Provincial Congress an aura of legitimacy.[8] However, the formation of local committees also "altered the political chemistry in the cities, towns, and counties of America. It was on this level that ordinary men and women declared their independence."[9] As prospects for reconciling differences with the mother country receded over the next year, the Provincial Congress displaced New Jersey's legal government. The boycott of British goods, obligatory militia drills, and taxation by the Provincial Congress brought the imperial crisis home to New Jersey's farmers. The sale or consumption of British imports in violation of the boycott invited action by local committees and men like Thomas Jones. Turning out for militia drills also became a political act, especially when the outbreak of war heightened tensions within communities.

The war began at Lexington and Concord just before the Second Continental Congress convened in Philadelphia in May 1775. In June, the Battle of Bunker Hill proved a costly victory for the British. The Continental Congress authorized the invasion of Canada to bring that province into the resistance. Montreal was taken, but the Patriot army failed at Quebec. Cannon from Fort Ticonderoga, which fell to Patriot forces, were sledded to heights above Boston. This action forced the British to evacuate that city for Halifax, Nova Scotia. By the end of this first year of warfare, New Jersey's William Franklin was the only one of seven royal governors not to have gained the protection of a British warship.

A rural colony with no major ports, New Jersey had been peripheral to the agitation churning port cities and the battles fought in New England and Canada. That isolation was about to evaporate as John and Mary Vought hosted the wedding of Mary's sister Jane Grandin to Jonathan Furman at their impressive stone farmhouse in April 1776. Once reinforced, General William Howe's troops were poised to descend on the inhabitants of New York and New Jersey. Lebanon Township was drawn inexorably into the crisis being debated in Philadelphia when the Continental Congress resolved that royal authority in each colony be "totally suppressed, and all the powers of government exerted, under the authority of the people."[10] May elections to New Jersey's Provincial Congress effectively became a referendum on independence. Although "a decided majority of New Jerseyans favored the curtailment of Parliamentary authority over the North American colonies, most also strongly opposed the establishment of an independent nation."[11] Hunterdon moderates and Loyalists succeeded in electing Union Iron Works owner John Allen to the Provincial Congress. John's sister Anne was married to Governor John Penn of Pennsylvania. His brother Andrew Allen was Pennsylvania's attorney general and served in the Continental Congress as a strong advocate for reconciliation with Great Britain, a role John Allen would play during his brief tenure as a deputy for Hunterdon in New Jersey's Provincial Congress.

When the Provincial Congress met in June, it considered a petition from Hunterdon County inhabitants protesting John Allen's election and asking that it be overturned.[12] Patriots held a large majority in the new congress, which considered the petition but upheld the legitimacy of Allen's election. To prepare the defense of New York City and coastal

New Jersey, the Provincial Congress summoned men to attend militia drills. In Lebanon Township, Joseph Lee, a manager at the Union Iron Works, and John Vought were among those who refused to serve in the Patriot militia. According to Lee, they were "repeatedly summoned to attend the trainings and other publick meetings of the Militia which they from principles of Loyalty as often refused, and in consequence thereof were subject to fines and amercements to a great amount." Determined "not to take up arms against their Lawful sovereign they openly opposed the officers of the Militia and for sometime avoided their usurpation."[13] The congress learned of the disturbances in Hunterdon County and ordered John Vought and three others to appear before it.[14] Years later, John testified that he had "attended the training of the militia," but when his company was drafted to serve in the militia, "to a man they refused to turn out. After this he was ill-used as they blamed him and Captain Lee for the company not serving. He resisted and raised men, and returned the ill usage."[15]

A visitor to Lebanon Township reported in June that the militia companies were "Not above half full although Some of the Companies have Augmented the Bounty to Eight pounds." Such practical concerns as the seasonal needs of farm work motivated some of the resistance. Because their families could not survive without them during planting season, "there are Numbers of Tennants that Say if they are take[n] away at this Season of Year they may as Well knock their famalys in the head for that they will be Ruined."[16] Some resistance also derived from the perceived illegitimacy of the extralegal Provincial Congress and took a form of protest familiar to the previous generation, which had witnessed New Jersey's land riots.

Starting in 1742, the West Jersey Society leased and then sold land to Allen and Turner for the Union Iron Works. Some of that land had been cleared by families who claimed title to the farms they had cultivated. Eviction suits led to riots, especially in the "3,100 acres leased to Allen and Turner in the vicinity of Spruce Run. The wood lots which were being cut over to provide fuel for the iron furnace built by Allen and Turner were claimed by squatters who had previously settled on the tract."[17] The manager of the ironworks, Colonel John Hackett, and his men arrested several squatters. While they were jailed in Trenton, a club-wielding mob gathered, attempted to break them out, but failed. The "club men" then attacked and pulled down a structure at the Union Iron Works.[18]

New Jersey's larger land disputes began in East Jersey, occasionally drawing crowds of more than two hundred people. According to historian Brendan McConville, "acts of collective violence quickly spread from the New York border south to Trenton. Hundreds of yeomen engaged in violence against the colony's gentry, their clients and tenants, and royal officials."[19] The term "club men" came to illustrate "how self-imposed limits on collective action operated. Land claimants refused to carry guns or swords, even when they knew their opponents were armed."[20] Club men acted as loyal subjects protecting their communities from the illegitimate actions of local authorities. Pauline Maier notes that these "instances of popular disorder became prima facie indictments not of the people, but of authority. In 1747, for example, New Jersey land rioters argued that 'from their numbers, Violences and unlawful Actions' it was 'to be inferred that . . . they are wronged & oppressed, or else they would never rebell agt. the Laws.'"[21]

During the turmoil of the land riots, Christopher Vought had paid rent to and later purchased land from a proprietor of the West Jersey Society, which had prevailed in the disputes. A generation later, John Vought led local farmers and ironworkers who protested the Provincial Congress's usurpation of royal authority by employing the self-limited violence of club men. On Friday, June 21, 1776, the congress addressed the question of what to do with the former royal governor, since Franklin had "refused to answer the questions put to him, denying the authority of this body, which he alleged had usurped the king's government in this Province." It determined that "William Franklin be confined in such place and manner as the Honourable Continental Congress shall direct." The Provincial Congress then resolved to form a new government "pursuant to the recommendation of the Continental Congress."[22] As the push for independence gained momentum, those who held to the goal of reconciliation with Britain had little recourse. John Allen was one of only three delegates who voted against the motion for a new government. He stopped attending the Provincial Congress after Friday's vote and left for home.

He returned to a Lebanon Township already in turmoil. Instead of bringing their muskets to a militia muster held "to Recruit men, one half of Two Companies Came with Clubs, Colonel Johnson was knocked down by them & was Afterwards Obliged to Retreat, the Same day one of the Capts. Was much beat by them."[23] Monday, June 24, 1776, was the high point of local resistance to independence. Around midnight, John Vought and Joseph Lee led two dozen club-wielding men to the tavern of former congressional delegate and militia captain Thomas Jones, where they came upon and beat John Shurts. Captain Jones heard Shurts's cries for help, grabbed his gun, and ran up from the basement. Outnumbered, Jones trained his gun on the club men and ordered them to leave or he would "blow their Brains out. They answered Gd Dam him he presents his Gun at us, & twisted it out of his hands & beat him on the head & sundry parts of his body w' their Clubs." He broke away and ran into the house, but John Vought and the other club men "broke open the outside door and several inside doors . . . and threatened to kick his wife if she did not tell them where he was." After they left, Jones staggered down the stairs with his wife's help to find they had also stolen £20 from the bar.[24] The Provincial Congress ordered the arrest of Christopher and John Vought, Joseph Lee, and the others. They were held in jail until the end of July, then faced a trial before the same delegates, now sitting as the state legislature, who had ordered their arrest. The legislature heard charges against these "disaffected and dangerous persons . . . considered the several matters alleged and proved relative to the said charges" and levied fines of £100 each on Christopher Vought, John Vought, and Joseph Lee, along with smaller fines on the other men.[25]

A similar club man uprising took place at a militia muster in Upper Freehold, Monmouth County, where Anthony Woodward "exhorted the crowd, claiming that the rebel merchants 'oppressed them by Raising [prices] upon their Goods more than England would do,' and that those who refused to sign the Continental Association were disenfranchised." The genuine complaints from these farmers about "harassment, disenfranchisement, fines, and compulsory oath taking were intermingled with more questionable ones such as a plot by Whig merchants to inflate prices and outrageous rumors regarding rebel leaders."[26] The Provincial Congress ordered these Monmouth County club men to appear before it and bond themselves to ensure good behavior. Not surprisingly, that bond proved insufficient to curb their behavior, just as it ultimately failed to reform the Loyalist affinity of Christopher and John Vought.

In August 1776, William Livingston was inaugurated governor under the new state constitution. British and Hessian troops arrived in New York Harbor and debarked on Staten Island. By November, they had captured

Long Island and New York City and crossed the Hudson, scaling the Palisades to capture Fort Lee. The retreat of Washington's disintegrating army across New Jersey, the nadir of the Revolution so eloquently lamented in Thomas Paine's "The American Crisis," interrupted Patriot rule. New Jersey's legislature quickly relocated from Princeton to Burlington, then Pittstown, and finally Haddonfield, where it dissolved. In early December, Thomas Jones, Daniel Bray, and Jacob Gearhart, all captains in the Hunterdon militia, rounded up every boat along the Delaware to speed Washington's escape and slow the British.[27] Christopher and John Vought and Joseph Lee led seventy-five Loyalists to join the British. After a brief skirmish with a band of militia turned out to intercept them, these Loyalists made their way to New Brunswick and joined Cortland Skinner's New Jersey Volunteers, which, according to Robert M. Calhoon, "ultimately enlisted at least 2,450 men," making it one of the largest provincial corps in the colonies. Based on enlistment figures, roughly 35 percent of New Jersey's population became active Loyalists.[28] Another 3,000 New Jersey people sought protection from General Howe by signing an oath of allegiance.

This Loyalist resurgence ended with Washington's surprise re-crossing of the Delaware on Christmas night. After the American victories at Trenton and Princeton, Howe relinquished all of New Jersey except Perth Amboy and New Brunswick, leaving the families of Loyalists to their fate as Patriot authorities reasserted control. Although the legislature had dissolved in early December, "courts, law enforcement, local markets, and public records—including the land titles so vital to an agricultural economy—all remained in Patriot hands."[29] New Jersey's constitution of July 1776 had continued English common law and "Statute-Law, as heretofore practiced in this colony," but extended the right to vote to "all Inhabitants of this Colony of full Age, who are worth Fifty Pounds."[30] New Jersey legislators thereby "enfranchised property-owning single women, or, at the very least, made no efforts to disenfranchise them, settling on gender-neutral language" in a break with the past.[31] State government was also designed to be very responsive to the electors; the annually elected legislature would choose the governor after each election. As the fledgling state struggled to reestablish its control in 1777, its most pressing problems were its own institutional ineffectiveness and disorder among local militia units, which led to instances of looting.

In the chaotic early months of 1777, General Washington wrote to Governor Livingston to urge that the legislature regulate the militia, both to ensure that more men turned out for duty and to stop officers from leading men into "plundering the inhabitants, under pretence of their being tories."[32] Patriots plundered the home of sixty-six-year-old Cornelia and twenty-two-year-old Mary Grandin Vought, whose husbands were in fact "tories" serving with the British army. When Mary went to John on Staten Island later that year, she "told him that the rebels had carried off everything they had."[33] In fact, many of their possessions and household furnishings were not taken and later appeared in the accounts of commissioners for the confiscation of Loyalist property. Although exaggerated, Mary's statement reflected looting by local militia, that is, the neighboring farmers and ironworkers who had turned out for the militia and sought revenge on families of the disaffected. Under Patriot rule, Cornelia and Mary Grandin Vought would have to deal with hostile neighbors, the Patriot Council of Safety, and property confiscation laws passed by the new state, but their immediate concern was managing their large productive farm.

Mary and Cornelia effectively became "deputy husbands," running the family's 488-acre farm while also maintaining domestic production for themselves, three young children, and two slaves. The Vought farmstead had a typical Palatine separation of areas that revolved around the house and domestic activities and the barns and fields that produced largely for the market, roughly reflecting the division of responsibilities on rural colonial farms.[34] Christopher, then John had organized the cultivation and harvesting of acres of wheat and corn, the tending of two dozen cows, two dozen pigs, fifty sheep, and other livestock, and the negotiations with markets and mills. Both men had accounts at the Lebanon store, exchanged farm produce at local and distant markets, and left homespun woolens for processing at the fulling mill. Cornelia and Mary largely filled their days with domestic production and raising children. Their female slave may have helped Cornelia and Mary grow food in the kitchen gardens near the house, cook in the fireplace in the kitchen cellar, and preserve food for the winter. She may have helped with other domestic work (carding, spinning, and weaving cloth from the sheep's wool) and may have worked in the fields in the spring and autumn.

Farm wives in this part of rural Hunterdon County, which included a
mix of Dutch, German, English, and a few Africans among the free inhabitants, generally did not engage in the sale of farm products. Few went to
market, as recorded in account books kept at the Lebanon store from
1770 to 1772. With a handful of exceptions like the Widow Little, women
did not have store accounts, and wives drew on their husbands' accounts
in fewer than 5 percent of the entries. Cornelia Vought and Thomas
Jones's wife were among the few farmers' wives who retrieved consumer
items—indigo, textiles, tea, ribbon, and rice—at the store on their husbands' accounts. Christopher and John made more trips to the store, and
Christopher would occasionally send his male slave to pick up items. The
Lebanon store bought local farm produce, including buckwheat, rye, and
corn, crediting farmers' accounts or making payment. As far as we know,
few if any wives sold produce at the store, although the Voughts' neighbor, the miller David McKinney's wife, was paid for fish sold to the store
on his account.[35] The Union Iron Works account book for 1773 and 1774
registers payments—often in iron bars due to the shortage of currency—
for a range of tasks performed at the works. It also records the sale of
imported fabrics, rum, and household goods, but rarely lists a female
name.[36] The daybook kept at the Grandin fulling mill lists hundreds of
men who brought fabric for processing over the course of nine years,
from 1774 to 1785. Some of the few women who left cloth are specifically
identified as widows.[37] In what was overwhelmingly a man's domain,
Cornelia and Mary would manage the farmstead and deal directly with
local markets and mills.

In managing farm production, Cornelia and Mary could hire men for
seasonal work as their husbands had done, although even hired workers
were required to turn out for militia duty or be subject to fines.[38] Heavy
enlistment in Loyalist provincial troops or the Patriot militia and
Continental army meant there were fewer laborers available for farm
work. In 1773, William Allen and Joseph Turner had begun to wind down
the once-bustling Union Iron Works plantation, dividing the 3,100 acres
into salable parcels over the next six years and transferring some to their
heirs.[39] John Allen's furnace plantation had an account with Allen and
Turner as early as August 1772, and the furnace on Spruce Run evidently
continued making pig iron. The slitting mill on the Raritan also continued

to operate. Ironworks manager Robert Taylor later bought the mill when Allen and Turner's properties were confiscated.[40] In October 1777, Allen and Turner hired out several of their enslaved ironworkers to John Patton, initially for a period of a year. When former Pennsylvania governor John Penn and his chief justice, Benjamin Chew, an heir to Joseph Turner, resided at the Union estate in the winter of 1777–1778, Turner encouraged Chew to have Robert Taylor reconcile the Allen and Turner accounts.[41] Had the ironworks remained viable and the forge, furnaces, smith shop, and mill fully active, the labor force required to meet the wartime need for iron wares and ammunition would have increased demand for farm produce, but the diminished ironworks generated little stimulus in the local farm economy.

New Jersey's Council of Safety presented new political uncertainties for the Vought family and the disaffected throughout New Jersey. The state's governing institutions had proven inadequate to the threats posed by British forces at its borders and Loyalist partisans within. In March 1777, Governor Livingston persuaded the General Assembly to grant him and twelve legislators extraordinary powers to act against the enemy as a Council of Safety during the legislature's recess. This body combined legislative, executive, and judicial functions. The Council of Safety could visit places where local justices were perceived to be unreliable in punishing the disaffected and "order arrests, hear witnesses, jail suspects, and even transport them to safer prisons elsewhere in the state. In a single day of such emergency procedures in Morristown, in July 1777, the Council ordered the arrest of forty-eight persons."[42] In October, the Council of Safety turned its attention to Hunterdon County.

In early October, as General Howe began his campaign to occupy Philadelphia, Governor Livingston learned that Pennsylvania's former royal governor and former chief justice, John Penn and Benjamin Chew, had been removed from the city but granted the parole they requested at Allen's Union Iron Works. He protested to the Continental Congress: "We are extremely sorry that persons of their political caste and rank in life should be sent into this state, which is nearly encircled by the enemy, to say nothing of our domestic foes. . . . Of all Jersey, the spot in which they are at present is the very spot in which they ought not to be. It has always been considerably disaffected, and still continues despite all our efforts, owning we imagine, in part to the interests, connection, and influence of Mr. John Allen, brother-in-law of Mr. Penn, who is now with the enemy."[43] Penn and Chew employed their connections to prominent Patriots and status as gentlemen to blunt the governor's attempts to have them removed, and by December, Congress decided Penn and Chew could remain on parole at the Union Iron Works. They returned to Philadelphia after the British evacuated that city in 1778.[44]

Later in October, the Council of Safety acted on the testimony of Timothy Lake of Hunterdon County, who had been arrested as a suspected Loyalist and called before Governor Livingston and the Council of Safety in April 1777. He testified against John and Christopher Vought, took an oath of abjuration and allegiance, and was discharged. Lake's deposition recounted his experience behind General Howe's lines near New Brunswick in early December 1776, when he "did see both John and Christopher Vought of the County of Hunterdon afors. and divers others afors. at a certain meeting held . . . for the purpose of enlisting men for the British Service" and that John Vought "did ask this deponent to enlist in such company for the Service aforesaid."[45]

On October 22, 1777, Governor Livingston and the Council of Safety ordered ten wives of Hunterdon Loyalists to appear before them "to shew cause why they should not be removed with their children. into the Enemies lines according to Law, and on default of their appearance that they be removed accordingly." The next day the council interrogated eight of them: "The wives of Christopher Vooght, George Casner, Peter Young, Conradt Eikler, Michael Dennis, Philip Cyphers, John Mills, Joseph Lee, & Jacob Foust; And the Council having enquired into their respective Circumstances & Situation, were unanimously of opinion, That it would not be expedient to remove them for the present."[46]

The fact John Vought's wife did not appear suggests that Mary was behind enemy lines with her husband by October. The Vought family's two slaves probably crossed to Staten Island with Mary Vought and her three toddlers. It is unlikely they were with Christopher and John Vought when they joined the New Jersey Volunteers during the British invasion. Most Loyalists expected the rebellion to end quickly, and their slaves would have been essential farm labor during the absence of Christopher and John. Yet they were not living on the farm in 1778: they were not among the movable property sold at auction that year. The two slaves who sailed to Nova Scotia with the Vought family after the war were almost certainly part of John's household after his wife and children joined him on Staten Island in 1777, leaving Cornelia to cope as best she could.

Mary's father, Philip Grandin, owned a large tract of land along the Raritan, downstream from the Vought farm, with a store and a fulling mill, where woolen material pounded in water was made smoother and, as the fibers interlock, thicker and durable as felt. Grandin's mill would have used "heavy—a hundred pounds or more—wooden hammers lifted by water power and allowed to fall on bundles of cloth."[47] Christopher and especially John Vought brought fabric to the mill. When their farm was thriving in 1775, John brought more than twelve yards of worsted wool in March, and in November he brought thirty-one yards of all-wool fabric to be processed and dyed, including eight yards to be "dyed red and made flannel for under petticoats" and marked with a "V."[48] In stark contrast, when Cornelia Vought visited Grandin's mill for the first time in March 1778, she brought two pale blue pieces of linsey-woolsey, one for blankets, and a white piece.[49] The difference in both the quantity and the quality of fabric reflected the reduced production of the farmstead that Cornelia, well past the age at which her husband had retired, managed alone after 1777. The juxtaposition of a Loyalist wife and Patriot neighbors is highlighted by the fact that Continental army commissary Colonel Charles Stewart and his deputy Captain Thomas Jones patronized Grandin's fulling mill three or four times a year, occasionally ordering material for great coats and flannel.[50]

In April 1778, the New Jersey legislature passed an act allowing county commissioners to sell the belongings of confirmed Loyalists and to lease their real estate. Although ownership of the Vought farm was not yet at issue, the forced sale of livestock and farm tools would impede Cornelia's means of support, and the loss of personal belongings and household furnishings would only compound the precariousness of her situation. Juries of inquisition regarding Christopher Vought and John Vought were held at the house of Captain Thomas Jones on June 2, 1778. At the auction of the farm's livestock on June 11, 1778, Cornelia Vought bought back ten hogs and fifteen "Piggs," plus two cows, one with a calf, providing her with milk and pork. Cornelia's son from a prior marriage, Henry Traphagen, bought a cow and four calves. Henry also rented the farm, not for himself, since he was already married and settled elsewhere, but for his mother's use. The Vought family lost fifty-one sheep, twenty-five cows, and six horses to their neighbors, but the purchases by Henry and Cornelia allowed her to remain on the farm. Philip Grandin bought a red calf that day, possibly for Cornelia.[51]

Sympathetic local men of means also came to the aid of Loyalist wives. James Parker was a prominent Loyalist from Perth Amboy who was jailed, then paroled in Morristown for refusing to take the oath of abjuration and allegiance required of those the Council of Safety thought disaffected. He was exchanged in 1778 for a Patriot held in New York and allowed to return to Shipley, his 650-acre estate three miles from the Vought farm, along the road to Pittstown. On December 18, 1778, the Vought family's farm equipment and household furniture were sold; among the tables, chests, and beds, the great clock fetched the highest price, £40. That same day, James Parker wrote in his diary, "Docr Smith solicited my contribution to the relief of some women, the wives of some persons that had gone in to the British lines and had all their effects sold, by purchasing for them a cow apiece and their beds."[52] Dr. Issac Smith had purchased two heifers and a milch cow at the June auction and arranged the repurchase of personal possessions in December, perhaps out of chivalry and perhaps, like Parker, sympathy with the Loyalist cause.

By the fall of 1778, Mary Grandin Vought was living with John on Staten Island; she gave birth to a baby girl in June 1779. This daughter, named for her long-suffering mother-in-law, unfortunately died in September. Back in Hunterdon, Cornelia was losing her hold on the family real estate. The New Jersey legislature declared Loyalist men guilty of treason by passing bills of attainer, bypassing judicial protections and obscuring the separation of powers, contrary to British-American norms. This declaration of treason allowed confiscation of Loyalists' real estate. The auction of the 488-acre Vought farm, with its excellent barn and impressive stone house, in April 1779, three years after John led the attack on Thomas Jones's tavern, completed the transfer of the family's personal property and real estate under the authority of the new state John had protested that night. The sale of the original 285-acre farmstead for the large sum of £8,550 reflected "the extensive improvements to and the overall desirability of the farm." The Vought's relatively unimproved 203-acre parcel brought £3,451, just over half as much per acre.[53]

After their farm was sold, Cornelia may have lived with her son Henry or with her daughter-in-law's parents, Philip and Eleanor Grandin, but she also spent time across enemy lines, on Staten Island, visiting her husband and John's family. Both Cornelia and Mary crossed enemy lines at least once. It is unlikely these women slipped secretly across New Jersey's border, risking the danger of approaching the front lines from enemy territory. Cornelia, traveling alone, and Mary with three toddlers and two servants probably received passes to cross the lines to visit family. Even low-level officers, such as captains, could issue passes, something that concerned both Washington and Livingston. Yet it was relatively easy for women to get a pass to cross into enemy territory and back; they were considered "nonentities in the political sphere," their lives defined by familial relations.[54] The wives of John Penn and Benjamin Chew obtained passes to leave British-occupied Philadelphia, visit their husbands at the Union Iron Works, and return to Philadelphia. The vigilant Governor Livingston vehemently objected in October 1777 to the presence of Penn and Chew and their potential influence in Hunterdon County; yet later that month he and the Council of Safety unanimously decided that eight Loyalists' wives living near the Union posed no significant threat. Cornelia remained on the farm until the sale of the Vought's stone house, great barn, and 488 acres finally dislodged her in April 1779. Cornelia visited Staten Island in November 1781, when her grandson Philip Grandin was almost ten months old. She evidently intended to return to Hunterdon, where she may have resided for the duration of the war.[55]

After the British defeat, approximately 60,000 Loyalist refugees left the colonies.[56] In September 1783, John's family left New York as part of the exodus of almost 30,000 Loyalists to Nova Scotia and New Brunswick. Also in New York, more than 2,000 Africans recorded in the "Book of Negroes," to assuage Patriots seeking the return of their "property," received passes to leave for Nova Scotia as free men and women, a fraction of the approximately 9,000 runaways who answered the emancipation proclamations issued by British commanders and left America after the war as free people.[57] Ironically, those men and women enslaved by Loyalists had no such opportunity. In September 1783, Christopher, John and Mary, their four children, nephew George, and two slaves left New York Harbor aboard the *Ranger* for life as expatriates in Nova Scotia. Cornelia was not listed on the ship's return and may have joined them later.[58] They lived on the outskirts of Parrsboro, Nova Scotia, for the next eight years.

Loyalty to the British had cost the Vought family everything they owned in New Jersey. In a claim filed with the British government's Loyalist Claims Commission, John Vought produced a valuation sworn "at New York City, by William Rutherford and Philip Grandn [Grandin], at 5 pounds 10 shillings per acre." He also had "a certificate of sale sworn to before Henry Traphagen made by Peter Brunner, one of the Commissioners to dispose of the Real and Personal Estate of Refugees."[59] John's father-in-law and his stepbrother remained on the Patriot side of the great divide. Nonetheless, the Vought family retained relatives and friends in Hunterdon. Over time, the intense hatred of Loyalists faded in New Jersey and New York, two provinces where the civil strife had been greatest. By the time Bev Robinson, son of the prominent New York Loyalist Beverly Robinson, returned in the 1790s, "legal sanctions had largely been repealed or suspended. He like many relatives of attained Loyalists, fought for years in state courts for the restitution of confiscated property and unpaid debts, with some success."[60] John Vought's claim for lost property before the British commissioners included 2,000 acres near Albany, New York, that Christopher had purchased in 1772 as an inheritance for his son and daughter. John was able to recover title to this land, and in 1792 the family migrated from Nova Scotia to this larger, more fertile property.

CHRISTIANA VOUGHT HAD barely known her birthplace in Lebanon Township. She and her cousin George were only four years old when they left the fine stone house near the Union Iron Works with her younger sister and mother in 1777. She was ten when they sailed to Nova Scotia in September 1783. Eight years later, in May 1792, Christiana began a travel journal: "My father with his family Embarked on board of the Scooner Alice, Comanded by John Osburn." They sailed from Parrsboro, Nova Scotia, past Partridge Island and down the Bay of Fundy, along the Atlantic coast to New York City, where a river sloop would take them up the Hudson.[61]

At New York, they dined on board Captain John Bogart's sloop and spent a few days in the city before embarking "for Albany at 9 o'clock in the morning with a fine breeze," which continued the next day with a "good wind and everything agreeable, our Capt. is very Polite and obliging."

On Friday, they lay "at anchor before Mr. Timbrooks house; here Capt. Bogart leaves us as he is obliged to be in Albany at an appointed time. In the afternoon we were invited ashore to tea by Capt. B's. Sister in law, A young Lady where we were treated with Politeness—they are Dutch People and apear to be very Neat and Clean." Captain John Bogart had been drafted into the New York militia at age fifteen. As captain of the sloop *Magdeline*, he transported Patriot troops and supplies up and down the Hudson. After the war, John continued working the river and married Catherine Ten Broeck ("Timbrooks" above), who died in February 1792. The Voughts anchored at the Ten Broeck house until Sunday, when Christiana reported our "Captain is Come down from Albany in a scooner, you are Welcome Sir on Board, again is Echo,d through the Ship. This is about 2 o'clock in the afternoon. We find him more agreeable as we are more acquainted with him."[62]

Christiana lived in a different world than her parents and grandparents; the upheaval of war had produced a cultural shift. New Jersey's 1776 constitution allowed "inhabitants" worth £50 to vote. The gender-neutral language encompassed the same widows and other single women of property who had accounts at stores and mills. New Jersey was the only colony to extend the vote to women, and although the legislature reverted to the perhaps universal pronoun "he" to reference voters in 1777 and 1783, it explicitly defined voters as "he or she" in 1790.[63] As Jan Ellen Lewis notes, "the problem—or the possibility—of Revolutionary thought was that it could not easily be contained. Once revolutionary principles were articulated, there was no controlling them." When colonists turned one of the "most hallowed principles of British constitutional thought, no taxation without representation, against Parliament, it sparked a constitutional crisis which resulted in a war for independence. So too, New Jersey "carried Revolutionary doctrine to its furthest—but logical—extreme." If property ownership provided the independence of thought necessary for citizens of a republic, then why should women with property not be allowed to vote?[64] The rise of Federalist and Democratic-Republican political parties brought increasing numbers of women to the polls. The impact of a significant number of women voting, intense partisanship, and transparently corrupt voting practices provided the impetus for a post-Revolutionary backlash and disenfranchisement in the early nineteenth century, but in the early republic, more egalitarian notions prevailed.[65]

During the recent conflict, women had been encouraged to participate in political actions, to forgo tea and imported luxuries. They engaged
in "gender-appropriate" activities like making homespun to aid non-
importation and collecting blankets or donations for the troops. By the
war's end, the prospect of women being involved in politics had become
less exceptional. Their explicitly continued political franchise in New
Jersey shows that the Revolution's radical impulses were not without
effect. Even within the bounds of a *femme covert* legality, overt political
actions, Revolutionary ideals, and wives' widespread experience of managing farms for absent husbands all served to undermine patriarchal family
relations. A new model of the affectionate family was gaining favor, especially among genteel young women, whose ideals of romantic love and
physical attraction could be more significant in selecting a life partner.[66]
"Dependent on the ability of young people to choose for themselves, the
struggle was not easily won, particularly where the economic function of
the family was paramount."[67] In choosing a husband, Christiana Vought
may have been responsive to parental advice; but unlike her grandmother
Cornelia, who even as a widow had secured a written license from her
father before marrying Christopher in 1749, she would have found it odd
for a minister to require parental consent prior to a marriage.[68] Her attraction to the "very polite and obliging" John Bogart, whom she found "more
agreeable as we are more acquainted with him," led to their marriage at
the Albany Dutch Reformed church four years after the Loyalist Vought
family sailed up the Hudson.

With the Voughts' arrival in Albany, Christiana's journal provides a
glimpse of the society she was about to enter. Her family went

> to the house of Captain Bogart's parents we met the old lady (his
> Mother) on the Porch Who Conducted us in a well furnished room
> then turn.d about "your welcom here" said she—Now Comes in Miss
> Bogart (Sister to Capt. B.) "Miss Vought you are welcome here I hope
> you will make this as your home." "I thank you Madam," said I; "you
> have had a long Passage"; "Yes, but A very agreeable one, Miss Bog-
> art." So the Conversation turn,d—Now in Comes Garet B. "I am hapy
> to see you here Ladys I wish you not to Make Strange." Mamah
> returned the Compliment; When diner was ready we were bid in,

Garet and Miss B. did the honours of the table; their Parents is old People wich I expect is the reason they take this on themselves— After Tea Miss Bogart Took My sister & I thro the Most Capital Streets of the City. When we returned Mr. Garet asked us if we would not walk up to the Springs (this is a Spring about 3 quarters of Mile out of Town where many walks about Sun set and after). "I have no objection" was the General answere; accordingly we went and saw A Number of People there Drinking of this Very Cold Water—We all sup.d at Mr. Bogarts and then returned to the Sloop where we Lodged.[69]

The next day, "At Eleven o'clock we left Albany, at 2 o'clock din,d 7 mile from Albany and at 9 in the evening arrived at Voughts Patton our Place of residence. C.V." Christiana's journal ends at their new home, where John divided the 2,000-acre parcel: half for George, the nephew he and Mary raised from infancy; and half for his household, which included his aging parents, Christopher and Cornelia, his wife, Mary, his daughters Christiana and Eleanor, two sons named for their grandfathers Philip and Christopher, and two slaves.

Christopher Vought's grandson and namesake was born on Staten Island four months before the Treaty of Paris and grew to manhood on the Vought patent in New York. He fought with the New York militia in the War of 1812, a war that finally forced Great Britain to respect the full sovereignty of a now federated United States of America. Just as the balance between states and the Union would be a major point of contention before the Civil War and even today, so too were the Revolutionary principles cited to resist Parliamentary authority and articulated in the Declaration of Independence. Struggles to achieve "unalienable rights" to freedom and equality for all men and women would become a central theme in American history over the next two centuries. As Captain Christopher Vought returned home from the War of 1812, that American Revolution had barely begun.

NOTES

1. Robert M. Calhoon, "The Suppression of the Loyalists in Pennsylvania, Delaware, and New Jersey," in Calhoon, *The Loyalists in Revolutionary America 1760–1781* (New York: Harcourt Brace Jovanovich, 1973), 402.

2. William Gordon Ver Planck, *The Vought Family: Being an Account of the Descendants of Simon and Christina Vought* (New York: Press of Tobias A. Wright, 1907), 9.

3. Daybook, Lebanon Store, December 1770–May 1772, Hunterdon County Historical Society, Hiram E. Deats Memorial Library, Flemington, NJ (hereafter cited as HCHS).

4. T. H. Breen, *The Marketplace of Revolution: How Consumer Politics Shaped American Independence* (New York: Oxford University Press, 2004), 199.

5. Ibid., 200.

6. Ver Planck, *Vought Family*, 9.

7. Hunterdon County elections, box 7, items 21 and 23, New Jersey State Archives, Trenton.

8. Larry R. Gerlach, *Prologue to Independence: New Jersey in the Coming of the American Revolution* (New Brunswick, NJ: Rutgers University Press, 1976), 212.

9. Breen, *Marketplace of Revolution*, 326.

10. "Resolutions and Recommendations of the Continental Congress," May 15, 1776, http://www.founding.com/founders_library/pageID.2349/default.asp (accessed May 15, 2014).

11. Gerlach, *Prologue to Independence*, 320.

12. *Minutes of the Provincial Congress and the Council of Safety of the State of New Jersey* (Trenton: Naar, Day, & Naar, 1879), 452.

13. W. Bruce Antliff, *Loyalist Settlements 1783–1789: New Evidence on Canadian Loyalist Claims* (Toronto: Ministry of Citizenship and Culture, 1985), 44–45.

14. *Minutes of the Provincial Congress and the Council of Safety*, 465.

15. Ver Planck, *Vought Family*, 9.

16. Edward Thomas, "From Edward Thomas Lebanon Township about 40 miles W . . . June 30: 1776 Hunterdon County," in *The Papers of William Livingston*, ed. Carl E. Prince et al., vol. 1, *June 1774–June 1777* (Trenton: New Jersey Historical Commission, 1979), 59.

17. Peter O. Wacker, *Land and People: A Cultural Geography of Preindustrial New Jersey Origins and Settlement Patterns* (New Brunswick, NJ: Rutgers University Press, 1975), 361.

18. Charles S. Boyer, *Early Forges and Furnaces in New Jersey* (Philadelphia: University of Pennsylvania Press, 1963), 236.

19. Brendan McConville, *These Daring Disturbers of the Public Peace: The Struggle for Property and Power in Early New Jersey* (1999; Philadelphia: University of Pennsylvania Press, 2003), 454.

20. Thomas L. Purvis, "Origins and Patterns of Agrarian Unrest in New Jersey, 1735–1776," *William and Mary Quarterly*, 3d ser., 39, no. 4 (1982): 623.

21. Pauline Maier, *From Resistance to Revolution: Colonial Radicals and the Development of American Opposition to Britain, 1765–1776* (New York: Norton, 1991), 22.

22. *Minutes of the Provincial Congress and the Council of Safety*, 470–471.

23. Thomas, "From Edward Thomas Lebanon Township," in *Papers of William Livingston*, 1:59.

24. Hunterdon County, New Jersey, miscellaneous court record number 5716.

25. *Minutes of the Provincial Congress and the Council of Safety*, 527.

26. David J. Fowler, "'Loyalty Is Now Bleeding in New Jersey': Motivations and Mentalities of the Disaffected," in *The Other Loyalists: Ordinary People, Royalism, and the Revolution in the Middle Colonies, 1763–1787*, ed. Joseph S. Tiedemann, Eugene R. Fingerhut, and Robert W. Venables (Albany: State University Press of New York, 2009), 52–53.

27. David Hackett Fischer, *Washington's Crossing* (New York: Oxford University Press, 2004), 134.

28. Calhoon, *Loyalists in Revolutionary America*, 362.

29. Mark Edward Lender, "The 'Cockpit' Reconsidered: Revolutionary New Jersey as a Military Theater," in *New Jersey in the American Revolution*, ed. Barbara Mitnick (New Brunswick, NJ: Rutgers University Press, 2005), 50.

30. Larry R. Gerlach, ed., *New Jersey in the American Revolution, 1763–1783: A Documentary History* (Trenton: New Jersey Historical Commission, 1975), 214.

31. Jan Ellen Lewis, "Rethinking Women's Suffrage in New Jersey, 1776–1807," *Rutgers Law Review* 63, no. 3 (Spring 2011): 1019.

32. Washington's letter quoted by Livingston in *Papers of William Livingston*, 1:209.

33. Ver Planck, *Vought Family*, 10.

34. Damon Tvaryanas et al., *Phase I and II Cultural Resource Investigation, Christoffel Vought Farm Site (28HU550), Proposed Clinton Township Middle School, Clinton Township, Hunterdon County, New Jersey* (Trenton, NJ: Hunter Research Inc., 2005), 4-65.

35. Daybook, Lebanon Store, December 1770–May 1772, HCHS. For the role of markets in providing opportunities for women to gain greater independence, see Joan M. Jensen, *Loosening the Bonds: Mid-Atlantic Farm Women, 1750–1850* (New Haven, CT: Yale University Press, 1986).

36. Union Iron Works daybook, Taylor-Wharton Iron & Steel Company Records, 1742–1950 (MS 1292), Hagley Museum and Library, Wilmington, DE.

37. Walter J. Young, "Grandin Fulling Mill Book, 1774–1785," *Genealogical Magazine of New Jersey* 52, no. 1 (January 1977): 1–10; 52, no. 2 (May 1977): 89–94; 53, no. 3 (September 1978): 136–144. Grandin Fulling Mill Day Book, manuscript 003, HCHS.

38. Charles W. Parker, "Shipley: The Country Seat of a Jersey Loyalist," *Proceedings of the New Jersey Historical Society* 16, no. 2 (April 1932): 132.

39. Taylor-Wharton Iron & Steel Company Records, 1742–1950, box 7, blueprint maps 1–10. Chew Family Papers, series 21, New Jersey Land Papers, Miscellaneous: Surveys—draft of division made between William Allen and Joseph Turner, 1779,

box 764, folder 10, Historical Society of Pennsylvania (hereafter cited as Chew-HSP).

40. New Jersey Land Papers, Hunterdon County: Accounts—William Allen and Joseph Turner, 1765–1779, box 765, folder 2, Chew-HSP.

41. Correspondence: Joseph Turner to Benjamin Chew, 1761–1780, box 12, folder 5, Chew-HSP.

42. Calhoon, *Loyalists in Revolutionary America*, 403.

43. Governor William Livingston to John Hancock, Princeton, October 4, 1777, in Gerlach, ed., *New Jersey in the American Revolution*, 374–375. Contrary to Gerlach's head note, Penn and Chew remained at the Union through the winter.

44. Joseph Nourse to John Penn and Benjamin Chew (War Office, December 29, 1777), Benjamin Chew to Robert Morris (Union Iron Works, Jerseys, March 31, 1778), Chew-HSP.

45. Deposition of Timothy Lake against John and Christopher Vaught, sworn in Council of Safety April 22, 1777, Burlington, NJ, Council of Safety Manuscripts, folder 58, New Jersey State Archives.

46. *Minutes of the Council of Safety of the State of New Jersey* (Jersey City: Printed by John H. Lyon, 1872), 155–157.

47. Young, "Grandin Fulling Mill Book," 1.

48. Grandin Fulling Mill Day Book, November 11, 1775, HCHS.

49. Linsey-woolsey was a coarse fabric with a linen warp and a woolen weft common in the American colonies. The daybook entry of lincey no doubt referred to linsey-woolsey. Other entries note when the fabric is all wool.

50. Young, "Grandin Fulling Mill Book."

51. Tvaryanas et al., *Christoffel Vought Farm Site*, 3-54.

52. Parker, "Shipley," 132.

53. Tvaryanas et al., *Christoffel Vought Farm Site*, 3-54.

54. Judith L. Van Buskirk, *Generous Enemies: Patriots and Loyalists in Revolutionary New York* (Philadelphia: University of Pennsylvania Press, 2002), 63.

55. Tvaryanas et al., *Christoffel Vought Farm Site*, 3-55.

56. Maya Jasanoff, *Liberty's Exiles: American Loyalists in the Revolutionary World* (New York: Alfred A. Knopf, 2011), 353.

57. Cassandra Pybus, *Epic Journeys to Freedom: Runaway Slaves of the American Revolution and Their Global Quest for Liberty* (Boston: Beacon Press, 2006), 71; Jasanoff, *Liberty's Exiles*, 89–90.

58. "Return of Officers and Men of the Second Battalion New Jersey Volunteers going to Annapolis Royal in Nova Scotia in the Brig *Ranger*," Great Britain, Public Record Office, War Office, class 60, vol. 32, pt. 1 (available at http://www.royalprovincial.com/military/rhist/njv/njvretn2.htm; accessed May 4, 2014).

59. Ver Planck, *Vought Family*, 10.

60. Jasanoff, *Liberty's Exiles*, 319.

61. C. V., "Diary of Christiana Vought," in Ver Planck, *Vought Family*, 21.

62. Ibid., 23.

63. Lewis, "Rethinking Women's Suffrage in New Jersey," 1020. See also Judith Apter Klinghoffer and Lois Elkis, "'The Petticoat Electors': Women's Suffrage in New Jersey, 1776–1807," *Journal of the Early Republic* 12, no. 2 (Summer 1992): 159–193.

64. Lewis, "Rethinking Women's Suffrage in New Jersey," 1022.

65. Ibid., 1030. See also Rosemarie Zagarri, *Revolutionary Backlash: Women and Politics in the Early American Republic* (Philadelphia: University of Pennsylvania Press, 2007).

66. Mary Beth Norton, *Liberty's Daughters: The Revolutionary Experience of American Women, 1750–1800* (Boston: Little, Brown, 1980), 45–46.

67. Stephanie Grauman Wolf, *As Various as Their Land: The Everyday Lives of Eighteenth-Century Americans* (New York: HarperCollins, 1993), 72.

68. Ibid., 74.

69. C. V., "Diary of Christiana Vought," 24.

NOTES ON CONTRIBUTORS

MICHAEL S. ADELBERG has been researching the American Revolution in New Jersey for twenty-five years. He has published the award-winning *The American Revolution in Monmouth County*, the well-reviewed historical fiction book *The Razing of Tinton Falls*, two reference books, and essays in leading scholarly journals like the *Journal of Military History* and the *Journal of the Early Republic*. He has earned distinctions from the New Jersey Historical Commission (101 Great New Jersey Books), the Monmouth County government (Jane Clayton Award), and the Woodrow Wilson International Center for Scholars (recognition in *The Wilson Quarterly*). A New Jersey native, Adelberg now lives in Virginia with his wife and sons.

BRUCE A. BENDLER earned his Ph.D. at the University of Delaware in 2000. His dissertation examined political culture in Delaware during the Revolutionary era, focusing on the emergence of the Federalists as the state's dominant party during the First Party System in the 1790s. Bendler is a frequent contributor to *Delaware History*, the journal of the Delaware Historical Society, and has also been published in *New Jersey History*. He has written articles for the Salem County (New Jersey) Historical Society, the Historical Society of Cecil County (Maryland), and two chapters for a history of Newark, Delaware. He teaches courses on colonial, revolutionary, and Civil War history at the University of Delaware.

TODD W. BRAISTED has authored numerous journal articles and books on the American Revolution. He is a fellow of the Company of Military Historians, honorary vice president of the United Empire Loyalist Association of Canada, and a past president of the Bergen County Historical Society. He has appeared as a guest historian on such programs as *History*

Detectives and *Who Do You Think You Are.* A lifelong resident of Bergen County, he currently lives in Mahwah with his wife, Susan.

JAMES J. GIGANTINO II earned his Ph.D. from the University of Georgia in 2010. He is currently an assistant professor of history at the University of Arkansas. In 2010, he received the Alfred E. Driscoll Prize from the New Jersey Historical Commission for his dissertation on slavery in New Jersey. His first book, *The Ragged Road to Abolition: Slavery and Freedom in New Jersey, 1775–1865*, was published by the University of Pennsylvania Press in 2014.

WILLIAM L. KIDDER is a retired history teacher who taught for thirty-nine years in Ewing Township and at the Hun School of Princeton. A veteran of the US Navy, in the 1980s he was the lead researcher and writer for the Admiral Arleigh Burke National Destroyermen's Museum aboard the USS *Joseph P. Kennedy, Jr.* For the past twenty-five years he has been a volunteer interpreter and historian for the Howell Living History Farm (part of the Mercer County Park System), located in the Pleasant Valley section of Hopewell Township. He has published *The Pleasant Valley School Story: A Story of Education and Community in Rural New Jersey*, which won the 2013 scholarship and artistry award of the Country School Association of America, and *A People Harassed and Exhausted*, which retells the experiences of the militiamen of the First Hunterdon Regiment in the American Revolution.

ELEANOR H. McCONNELL teaches American history at Frostburg State University in western Maryland, where she studies the economic, legal, and social history of the colonial and early national periods. She received her Ph.D. from the University of Iowa in 2008.

ROBERT A. SELIG is an independent historian with a Ph.D. in history from the Universität Würzburg in Germany. His area of expertise is the role of French troops under the comte de Rochambeau in the American war between 1780 and 1782. He serves as historical consultant and project historian to the National Park Service for the Washington-Rochambeau Revolutionary Route National Historic Trail (W3R-NHT) project. In August 2011, the French government honored his research on the contributions and role of France in the American War of Independence by awarding him the *Ordre des Palmes Académiques.*

DONALD SHERBLOM, a resident of Annandale, New Jersey, earned a Ph.D. in political science from the New School for Social Research in New York City. He has taught at the City University of New York, Seton Hall University, and Cedar Crest College in Allentown, Pennsylvania. Dr. Sherblom is president of the 1759 Vought House, A Revolutionary War Loyalist Homestead, a nonprofit organized to acquire and preserve what will be New Jersey's only Loyalist museum and educational center. In 2011, he published *Neighbors at War: The Vought Family and the Revolution* to increase public awareness of the rich history of the Vought house and has given a series of lectures on the Revolution and divided loyalties in New Jersey.

GREGORY F. WALSH received his Ph.D. in American history from Boston College in 2011. His research on the American Revolution challenges the simple dichotomy that divides the Revolutionary War population into either Patriots or Loyalists and examines fluctuations in popular commitment to both Whig ideology and the war effort. He is the recipient of the 2012 Alfred E. Driscoll Prize from the New Jersey Historical Commission and currently serves as the chair of the Liberal Arts Department at Marian Court College in Swampscott, Massachusetts.

INDEX

The letter *t* following a page number denotes a table. Page numbers in boldface refer to authors of chapters. All places are in New Jersey unless otherwise noted.

OCT 0 6 2015

CPSIA information can be obtained at www.ICGtesting.com
Printed in the USA
LVOW06s0059150815

450257LV00002B/172/P

9 780813 571911